Psychotic Disorders in Children and Adolescents

Developmental Clinical Psychology and Psychiatry Series

Series Editor: Alan E. Kazdin, Yale University

Recent volumes in this series . . .

Psychotic Disorders in Children and Adolescents

Robert L. Findling
S. Charles Schulz
Javad H. Kashani
Elena Harlan

Volume 44
Developmental Clinical Psychology and Psychiatry

Sage Publications, Inc.
International Educational and Professional Publisher
Thousand Oaks ▪ London ▪ New Delhi

For information:

SAGE Publications, Inc.
2455 Teller Road
Thousand Oaks, California 91320
E-mail: order@sagepub.com

SAGE Publications Ltd.
6 Bonhill Street
London EC2A 4PU
United Kingdom

SAGE Publications India Pvt. Ltd.
M-32 Market
Greater Kailash I
New Delhi 110 048 India

Printed in the United States of America

Library of Congress Cataloging-in-Publication Data

Main entry under title:
    Psychotic disorders in children and adolescents / Robert L. Findling ... [et al.].
        p.   cm.—(Developmental clinical psychology and psychiatry; v. 44)
    Includes bibliographical references and index.
    ISBN 0-7619-2019-6 (alk. paper) — ISBN 0-7619-2237-7 (pbk.: alk. paper)
    1. Psychoses in children.   2. Psychoses in adolescence.   I. Findling, Robert L.
II. Title.   III. Series.
RJ506 .P69 P793   2000
618.92′89—dc21   00-009512

01 02 03 04 05 06 7 6 5 4 3 2 1

Acquiring Editor:	Jim Brace-Thomson
Editorial Assistant:	Anna Howland
Production Editor:	Diane S. Foster
Production Assistant:	Candice Crosetti
Designer/Typesetter:	Siva Math Setters, Chennai, India
Indexer:	Janet Perlman

CONTENTS

SERIES EDITOR'S INTRODUCTION

Interest in child development and adjustment is by no means new. Yet, only recently has the study of children benefited from advances in both clinical and scientific research. Advances in the social and biological sciences, the emergence of disciplines and subdisciplines that focus exclusively on childhood and adolescence, and greater appreciation of the impact of such influences as the family, peers, and school have helped accelerate research on developmental psychopathology. Apart from interest in the study of child development and adjustment for its own sake, the need to address clinical problems of adulthood naturally draws one to investigate precursors in childhood and adolescence.

Within a relatively brief period, the study of psychopathology among children and adolescents has proliferated considerably. Several different professional journals, annual book series, and handbooks devoted entirely to the study of children and adolescents and their adjustment document the proliferation of work in the field. Nevertheless, there is a paucity of resource material that presents information in an authoritative, systematic, and disseminable fashion. There is a need within the field to convey the latest developments and to represent different disciplines, approaches, and conceptual views on the topics of childhood and adolescent adjustment and maladjustment.

The Sage Series on the Developmental Clinical Psychology and Psychiatry uniquely serves several needs of the field. The Series encompasses individual monographs prepared by experts in the fields of clinical child psychology, child psychiatry, child development, and related disciplines. The primary focus is on developmental psychopathology, which refers broadly here to the diagnosis, assessment, treatment, and prevention of problems that arise in the period from infancy through adolescence.

A working assumption of the Series is that understanding, identifying, and treating problems of youth must draw on multiple disciplines and diverse views within a given discipline.

The task for individual contributors is to present the latest theory and research on various topics including specific types of dysfunction, diagnostic and treatment approaches, and special problem areas that affect adjustment. The Series addresses core topics within clinical work. Authors are asked to bridge potential theory, research and clinical practice, and to outline the current status and future directions. The goals of the Series and the tasks presented to individual contributors are demanding. We have been extremely fortunate in recruiting leaders in the fields who have been able to translate their recognized scholarship and expertise into highly readable works on contemporary topics.

The present monograph, *Psychotic Disorders in Children and Adolescents*, is by Robert L. Findling, S. Charles Schultz, Javad H. Kashani, and Elena Harlan. This is an extraordinary book and without peer in elaborating the diverse ways in which psychotic symptoms and disorders are manifested among children and adolescents. Multiple disorders in which psychotic symptoms may be evident are presented, each with comments regarding etiology, age of onset, differential diagnosis, course, and prognosis. Case vignettes and research are carefully woven to convey the scope of symptoms and impairment of the children and lines of work that shed light on the disorders. Assessment is covered as well; several measures are described and evaluated for assessing clinical dysfunction in children and adolescents. Finally, the book ends with directions for research. Overall, the authors bring to bear remarkable experience and expertise on child and adolescent dysfunction. This book will be extremely useful to those who wish to understand child and adolescent psychoses and the clinical and research challenges these disorders raise.

ALAN E. KAZDIN, PHD

ACKNOWLEDGMENTS

The authors would like to express sincere gratitude to the Stanley Foundation for supporting the research done under the auspices of the Stanley Bipolar Disorder Research Center. The authors would also like to express thanks to the Prentiss Foundation. These foundations have generously supported intervention and neuroimaging research for children and teenagers with bipolar spectrum and psychotic disorders at University Hospitals of Cleveland/Case Western Reserve University. The authors would also like to thank Alan Kazdin, PhD, for his encouragement and guidance in the preparation of this book. The authors are grateful to Barbra DePasquale and Toni Deutschlander for their assistance in manuscript preparation.

1

AN OVERVIEW OF PSYCHOTIC DISORDERS

When considering the significant psychological problems and psychiatric conditions that often adversely effect children and adolescents, people generally do not think about psychosis. However, when psychosis does occur in a youth, the symptoms can be extremely distressing to the young person experiencing them. In addition, parents, caretakers, and even professionals often find it quite disturbing to watch a child or teenager actively hallucinate or experience other symptoms of psychosis. For these reasons, when youths do experience psychotic symptoms, it is essential that these patients receive prompt, thorough, and careful assessment and treatment.

However, accurate assessment and intervention early in the course of a psychotic illness often does not occur in young patients. Unfortunately, in many instances, youths with psychotic illnesses often suffer for months or for even years before they receive an accurate diagnosis and are provided with appropriate care. Sometimes only when the untreated symptoms of the condition become so severe and impairing that they are almost impossible not to recognize does the young patient receive appropriate assessment and treatment.

It is likely that one of the other reasons that many youths with psychotic disorders go undiagnosed for months or years is because the evaluation of young patients with psychotic disorders or psychotic symptomatology is often not a simple process. For example, it is often not appreciated that psychosis may present in a variety of fashions. As will soon be seen, psychosis is a syndrome characterized by a variety of disturbances in thought, affect, and behavior. The diagnostic process for psychotic disorders is further complicated by the fact that there is no single symptom that is pathognomonic for psychosis and because there is no laboratory test that can be used to diagnose these conditions.

For example, when one thinks about the symptoms most characteristic of psychosis, one generally thinks of hallucinations. However, not all youths who are experiencing a psychotic episode present with hallucinations as an integral symptom. Because it is sometimes believed that hallucinations are pathognomonic for psychosis, psychotic youths who do not describe hallucinations to others may suffer for a substantial period of time without ever having their condition properly assessed, accurately diagnosed, or effectively treated.

The following case vignette highlights the importance of recognizing that a youth with psychosis may not always present for clinical care suffering from overt hallucinations.

CASE VIGNETTE

The patient is a 15-year-old young man who was brought to the emergency room due to a 2-day history of "acting strangely." Although he generally attended high school regularly, the patient refused both to leave his home and to attend school for the two days prior to assessment. In addition, during the days prior to presentation, the patient began speaking in brief phrases that at times were unintelligible. He also began speaking to himself. During the prior 48 hours, the patient began speaking less and less and by the time his parents brought him into the emergency room, he was no longer speaking at all. Furthermore, at home, the patient was noted by his family to be making purposeless gestures and would grimace without provocation. By the time he arrived in the emergency room, he was motionless. Toxicology screen, CT scan, and electroencephalogram (EEG) were all unremarkable.

Further history from the patient's family revealed the fact that although the patient's precipitous onset of gross impairment occurred during a 2-day period, he had, in fact, been having difficulties for several months. The patient was generally a "loner" as a child and had had few friends. However, in the months prior to his presentation, he began associating with a new group of older males who were often in trouble with the police. The patient's mother felt that these peers easily manipulated her son. In fact, the patient had recently been arrested because these older boys left the patient sitting in a stolen vehicle.

The patient's mother also noted that although the patient generally seemed to enjoy school, he had become reticent to attend classes. According to the patient's mother, the patient had become concerned that people at school were trying to "mess with him." The patient had become increasingly fearful about attending classes and had become suspicious of most of his peers. The only peers the patient seemed to trust were the group of older youths who had gotten the patient in trouble.

Discussion with the patient's family practitioner revealed that the patient had no significant past medical history. However, the family practitioner did note that the patient had come to his office several months prior to his emergency room presentation concerned that he might have contracted a sexually transmitted disease. Although he was not sexually active, had never dated, and was asymptomatic, the patient was concerned about sexually transmitted disease exposure from brief, superficial classroom interactions with girls from his high school whom he considered promiscuous. The family practitioner attempted to alleviate the patient's concerns by informing him that this was not the way sexually transmitted diseases were acquired. However, no amount of reassurances from this physician reduced the patient's fears that he had contracted a sexually transmitted disease. In hopes of proving to the youth that he did not have a sexually transmitted disease, the pediatrician tested the patient for this disease. Not surprisingly, the test was negative. This, however, did not reduce the patient's anxiety. In the intervening months he had called the family practitioner's office regularly to ensure that either his test results had not changed or to request another laboratory test.

In the emergency room, the patient was lying motionless on a stretcher with his eyes open. He had one arm resting on top of his head with another on his side. He did not respond to questions, but would follow people in and out of the room with his eyes. When offered liquids, he clamped his lips shut.

When the patient's mother was then asked if anyone in the family had ever suffered from a psychiatric condition, she acknowledged that there was an uncle who was diagnosed with schizophrenia. He lived a solitary and reclusive life. Because she feared that her son might also be suffering from the same condition as his uncle, she was reticent to seek help for her child.

Based on the presenting symptoms of catatonia and disorganization, coupled with a history of paranoia, a working diagnosis of schizophrenia was made. Further evidence to support this diagnosis came from a history of childhood asociality, a history of a prodromal phase prior to the development of gross disorganization and catatonia, and family history of schizophrenia. Successful treatment for catatonia and psychosis was then initiated.

This vignette highlights some key heuristic points. First, although this youth suffered from schizophrenia, the diagnosis was not made for quite some time. However, once a careful inspection for the presence of psychotic symptomatology was undertaken, a history of ever-increasing paranoia and disorganization was able to be elicited. With this information, an accurate diagnosis was made. By obtaining a careful developmental, longitudinal, and family history, further evidence to confirm that schizophrenia was indeed the correct diagnosis was supported.

The purpose of this book is to provide for the beginning practitioner or clinician-in-training an introductory review of the psychotic disorders in children and adolescents. To do this, the symptoms that characterize psychosis will be reviewed. As will be discussed later in this work, not all patients with psychotic symptomatology suffer from schizophrenia. Mood, substance abuse, and personality disorders may all present with symptoms of psychosis.

Psychotic disorders are relatively common in children and adolescents. In addition, other psychiatric disorders in which psychotic symptomatology may be present are in fact quite prevalent. Therefore, it is essential that practitioners who work with young people are familiar with the assessment and management of these conditions.

HISTORICAL PERSPECTIVE

In the psychological and psychiatric literature, the word *psychosis* is frequently encountered. One might naturally assume, therefore, that a concise description or definition would be easily accessible. However, this does not prove to be the case. In fact, the symptoms and disorders that are considered psychotic have varied significantly over time. Even now, a definitive consensus on the definition of what psychosis is has still not been reached.

The word psychosis has been broadly defined in the past as being either an impairment in the ability to process information in a conventional manner or as a condition associated with problems with reality testing. Other early conceptualizations of psychosis were equally global and overly inclusive.

However, accurate and insightful clinical descriptions of the psychotic disorders have been available for decades. For example, Emil Kraepelin first coined the phrase *dementia praecox*, a syndrome that is now known to us as schizophrenia. Schizophrenia is the prototypic psychotic disorder. Kraepelin's description of dementia praecox focused on the chronic course and poor outcome of an illness characterized by impairments of perception, cognition, emotion, and behavior. Eugen Bleuler, who later invented the term schizophrenia, noted that what we now call schizophrenia consisted of key symptoms that included impaired associations, affective disturbances, ambivalence, and autism (removing oneself from reality).

Yet, even centuries before Kraepelin had coined a term for the presence of psychotic symptomatology, societies had created their own methods for understanding and describing disorders of this nature. Methods by which societies conceptualized psychiatric illnesses date back to ancient times. Many individuals during these earlier epochs attributed psychotic illnesses to supernatural forces. Considering the amount of scientific information that was available during these times, attributing these conditions to the supernatural was the only way for a society to make sense of these kinds of disorders.

For example, during the seventh century BC, the Chinese culture attributed the presence of a mental illness to an imbalance in certain essential natural forces. Likewise, the ancient Greek philosophers Hippocrates and Galen believed that emotional disorders were due to a disequilibrium in the body's four humors. This theory asserted that the body consisted of four different humors, each of which was associated with a certain type of temperament. Blood, black bile, yellow bile, and phlegm were associated with sanguine, melancholic, choleric, and phlegmatic temperaments, respectively. Depressive symptoms were thought to be caused by an excess of black bile. Likewise, an excess of yellow bile was thought to be associated with anxiety and irritability. In addition, those who suffered from fatigue or great mood changes were believed to have an excess of phlegm or blood, respectively.

Although the model of the four humors was a means by which mental illnesses could be conceptualized by the ancients, more important is that this model is a medical model. It recognizes that a biological disturbance is responsible for emotional and mental illness. This medical model appreciated that those who were suffering from emotional or mental conditions were experiencing disorders worthy of treatment and should not be the targets of derision. Furthermore, this model asserted that treatment for these individuals was best provided and monitored by physicians. Because the Hippocratic model considered mental disturbances to be due to an internal bodily condition, these conditions were, therefore, not deserving of stigma, blame, or shame.

Along with Hippocrates, other ancient Greek philosophers such as Plato and Aristotle promoted humane and civil treatment for individuals who were mentally disturbed. For example, they believed that those who were mentally ill should not be held responsible for their own actions. During ancient times, other psychiatric disorders, such as substance abuse and pathological behaviors associated with aging, were also recognized. Yet, despite the influence of Hippocrates and other Greek philosophers, most ancient Greeks believed that psychiatric disorders were the result of supernatural forces such as possession by either the gods or by demons.

During the early medieval era, pathological or aberrant behaviors were primarily understood in a religious context. During this epoch, societies often believed that individuals who suffered from psychiatric illnesses were being punished for their sins. There were others whose mental illnesses were believed to be the result of a religious curse. For these people, exorcisms were routinely performed in hopes of ridding the individual of the evil spirits that were possessing him or her.

There were rare occasions during the early Middle Ages when a disturbed person was actually thought to be afflicted with an illness. In these cases, the individual was usually cared for in a humane and compassionate manner. However, it was much more common during the early medieval era for persons with mental illnesses to be treated in an extremely cruel manner. These unfortunate individuals were often both verbally and physically abused. Some of the abuses that were inflicted on them included food deprivation, flogging, and other forms of torture.

In the latter part of the Middle Ages, a sense of fear and of helplessness was generated by both the social upheaval of the times and the bubonic plague. This led to further solidification of the beliefs that misfortune and suffering were the result of evil forces. In addition, mental illnesses were sometimes seen as the result of being cursed due to a person's sexual practices or criminal activities. Belief in witchcraft as a cause for psychosis, most notably espoused in the *Malleus Maleficarum* (Hammer of Witches), justified the practice of witch-hunts and established procedures by which they should be conducted. As a result of these witch-hunts, many mentally ill individuals who were believed to be involved in various types of rituals, were either tortured or executed.

The practice of torturing and executing the mentally ill continued into the Renaissance period. Witch-hunting was also common during this time. However, this particular period marked the beginning of more humane treatment for mentally disturbed individuals. One famous physician and philosopher, Paracelsus, doubted the idea that evil spirits possessed mentally ill individuals. He asserted that mental illnesses were caused by disturbances from within the body and that they were not the result of external forces. Because of the notion that volitional transgressions and evil spirits were not always the cause of some people's disturbances, the number of mentally ill individuals who were executed or tortured began to decline.

Paracelsus was not the only prominent Renaissance physician who conceptualized mental disturbances outside of a religious context. A German physician by the name of Johann Weyer noted in his book *De Praestigiis Daemonum* that those considered to be either possessed or witches were in fact mentally ill and, therefore, should be treated by a physician and not tended to by the clergy. However, his ideas and the ideas of the few others that thought like him were not generally well accepted and were often frowned on by religious authorities.

As beliefs slowly changed regarding the causes of mental illness, some reforms on how to deal with these disturbed individuals were instituted. Beginning in the middle of the 16th century, early institutions or asylums were built to house the mentally ill. Before these establishments were created, many disturbed individuals were sheltered inside monasteries. However, the creation of institutions for the mentally ill did not necessarily lead to humane treatment. Rather, mentally ill people were often chained to the walls in these asylums. They were put on display for the general public who would pay to tour the facilities. During these times, institutions for the mentally ill were often described as chaotic and disorganized and were believed to be more like prisons than hospitals.

However, further reformations in the treatment of the mentally ill were implemented during the turn of the 19th century. A French physician by the name of Philippe Pinel took action to improve conditions at the Salpêtrière, a large hospital in Paris. He ensured more humane treatment of the patients by allowing them exercise and clean living quarters. He also prohibited physical abuse by the institution's staff. Pinel's work led to the implementation of similar practices in other mental institutions. During this period, many other asylums both in Europe and the United States began to provide improved conditions and more compassionate treatment for the mentally ill.

Other reformers, such as William Tuke, Benjamin Rush, and Dorothea Dix, also played a large role in ensuring the humane treatment of the mentally ill. Tuke established a rest home for disturbed individuals in England where they were encouraged to engage in work and prayer. In addition, patients were encouraged to take walks and obtain adequate amounts of rest. Rush, an American, was one of the first physicians to establish a medical course in psychiatry. He also insisted that disturbed people be treated humanely. Likewise, another American, Dorothea Dix, advocated that mental institutions around the United States establish compassionate treatment for mentally ill individuals.

The establishment of these asylums eventually fostered attempts at further understanding the mental disorders from which their patients suffered. Thus, more scientifically based explanations for psychiatric illnesses emerged. Although unsophisticated when compared with current standards, these explanations included the establishment of diagnostic categories for persons with mental illnesses.

The conceptualization that severe mental disturbances were indeed medical conditions that deserved compassionate, scientifically based care has only recently received relatively wide acceptance. However, it should be noted that most of the available history on psychiatric illnesses has focused on these conditions in adults and not young people. In fact, the scientific study of behavioral or emotional disturbances among children and adolescents was almost unheard of until recently. This is likely due to the fact that childhood onset of severe mental illness was generally thought to be uncommon. For example, Kraepelin noted that only about 6% of patients with dementia praecox developed the condition prior to 15 years of age.

Besides trying to develop an understanding about the etiology, nature, and treatment of these conditions, it was a challenge to gain an understanding of how best to describe the more severe symptomatology characteristic of the psychotic disorders. Emil Kraeplin's diagnostic category of dementia praecox appeared to be the widely accepted definition of psychosis during the latter part of the 19th century. In recent years, however, efforts have been made to more clearly define the meaning of psychosis. Characteristics of the disorders, such as age at onset, degrees of functional impairment, and effects of normal developmental processes on symptom expression have all been taken into consideration in regard to its definition.

Despite recent progress in refining the definition of psychosis, *Stedman's Medical Dictionary* still rather imprecisely describes psychosis as "a mental disorder causing gross distortion or disorganization of a person's mental capacity, affective response, and capacity to recognize reality, communicate, and relate to others," thus, interfering with one's "capacity to cope with the ordinary demands of everyday life." Although this definition does capture some characteristics of psychosis, the most essential characteristics are believed to be hallucinations, delusions, and formal thought disorder.

However, it is important to note that the presence of any one of these symptoms in an individual does not mean that the person experiencing the symptoms is necessarily psychotic. For example, it is important to recognize that perceptual distortions may occur in a variety of settings. They may not be the result of a psychosis. Sensory impairments, head trauma, toxic conditions, and altered states of consciousness all have the capacity to lead to psychotic-like symptoms (such as hallucinations or disorganized thinking) in individuals. In addition, language disorders, low intellectual functioning, other developmental disorders, and personality disorders have been known to make it difficult for individuals to communicate thoughts in a logical and coherent manner. As far as delusions are concerned, some individuals may hold beliefs that are unconventional or defy scientific proof even though they are not suffering from any type of trauma or disorder. Therefore, these beliefs alone do not warrant that a diagnosis of a psychotic disorder be made.

As can be seen, the definition of psychosis has been continually transformed and refined throughout history, which makes it difficult to come up with a single, concise definition for it. For simplicity's sake, and for the purpose of this book, the following definition of psychosis will be used: "the impaired ability to process and respond to stimuli in a conventional manner as evidenced by peculiarities in speech, behavior, cognition and/or emotion." Descriptions of the symptoms that characterize psychosis follow.

PSYCHOTIC SYMPTOMS

Hallucinations

For patients with psychotic disorders, hallucinations are probably the most commonly observed manifestations of the psychosis. According to current nosology, a hallucination is defined as "a sensory perception that has a compelling sense of reality of a true perception, but occurs without external stimulation of the relevant sensory organ." *Diagnostic and Statistical Manual of Mental Disorders*, Fourth Edition (*DSM-IV*) notes that hallucinations can lead to distortions in sensory perception in any or all of the five human senses. By far, the most common hallucinations are auditory (hearing) and visual (seeing), but olfactory (smelling), gustatory (tasting), and tactile (touching) hallucinations are also frequently reported phenomena.

Hearing voices, either inside or from outside of the head, is the most typical for patients with psychotic illnesses; hearing sounds, noises, or even unintelligible mumbling can also occur. There is no limit to the variety of visual images, distinct shapes, or amorphous perceptions that have been reported by patients with visual hallucinations. For those experiencing olfactory hallucinations, odors are frequently described as either being unwanted or noxious. The tastes experienced by those with gustatory hallucinations are generally described as being unpleasant. *Formication* is a specific type of tactile hallucination in which the sufferer feels that bugs are crawling on or under the skin. A related, yet rare, category, called a somatic hallucination, involves feeling a sensation within the body.

However, not all phenomena such as these would necessarily be considered manifestations of a psychotic state or illness. The misperception or misinterpretation of an actual stimulus is well-known to occur in circumstances such as when one drifts off to sleep or awakens from sleep (hypnagogic or hypnopompic hallucinations, respectively), under conditions of stress or exhaustion (as in a mirage), or in everyday illusions. In addition, numerous drugs and several general medical and neurological conditions may lead a young person to have unusual perceptual experiences that are not necessarily a part of a psychotic state.

Delusions

Currently, a delusion is defined by the *DSM-IV* as "a false belief based on incorrect inference about external reality that is firmly sustained despite what almost everyone else believes and despite what constitutes incontrovertible and obvious proof or evidence to the contrary." Delusions must be distinguished from their less strongly held counterparts, *overvalued ideas*, which are illogical or unusual beliefs that the individual may admit to be false. Culturally supported beliefs, such as witchcraft or the ability to communicate with the dead, are not considered to be delusions. Some delusions are so patently outside the realm of culturally sanctioned thought that they are referred to as bizarre, whereas a large number of delusions have at least an air of plausibility.

Delusions are categorized on the basis of their content. They may include beliefs that one's private thoughts are being projected outward so that others have access to them. This is known as *thought broadcasting*. Conversely, *thought insertion* involves the belief that thoughts are being placed in a person's mind against his or her will by someone or something. A youth with a psychotic disorder may also have delusions that an external force is directing or controlling his or her cognitive, emotional, or behavioral experiences. *Erotomania* is a specific form of delusion in which the afflicted person believes that another individual, usually from a higher social or economic level, is in love with him or her. The unshakable conviction that one's significant other is engaging in additional sexual liaisons is known as *delusional jealousy*. Individuals who insist that "events, objects, or other persons in one's immediate environment have a particular and unusual significance" are referred to by the *DSM-IV* as having *delusions of reference*. The focus of a *persecutory delusion* is on being pursued, threatened, assaulted, denigrated, swindled, or plotted against. Delusions may also be of a grandiose nature. A person with a *grandiose delusion* may claim to have extraordinary importance, abilities, influence, intelligence, powers, or relationships. An individual may suffer from *somatic delusions* which involve a preoccupation with bodily appearance, bodily functioning, or both.

Hallucinations and delusions often can be broadly classified into two mutually exclusive categories based on whether or not they are consistent with the prominent emotional state being experienced by the psychotic person. Examples of *mood-congruent* psychotic symptoms include depressed individuals who hear voices telling them to kill themselves, see coffins, smell rotting flesh, or believe that their internal organs are no longer working. Mood-congruent delusions also can occur in patients suffering from mania. Youths with abnormally elevated mood may believe that they are people of great importance or that they are endowed with special powers (such as being able to predict the future). Conversely, *mood-incongruent* psychotic features occur when there is a discrepancy between the mood state of the youth and the content of the hallucinatory phenomena or delusional thinking the youth is experiencing. An example of a mood-incongruent delusion is when a young male patient with bipolar disorder, currently in an elevated or manic state with no general medical conditions, believes that he is dying from cancer because he states he can feel his internal organs rotting away.

Formal Thought Disorder

Distortions in thinking frequently occur in patients with psychosis. Some of the other cognitive difficulties that can be present in young patients with psychosis are referred to as *formal thought disorder*. The form or manner in which the patient presents his or her thoughts to the listener can be described by a number of clinically observable characteristics. Rambling, illogical, overly vague, elaborate, or repetitive speech or reasoning can occur in patients with psychosis and thought disorder. In addition, patients suffering from psychosis and a formal thought disorder may use novel or unusual word choices and have inappropriate breaks in their flow of speech. However, the current diagnostic manual notes that disorganized speech and disorganized behavior may be manifestations of either gross disorganization or catatonia, both of which are symptoms of psychosis.

Although the cognitive functions of children and adolescents certainly differ from those of adults, it should be noted that after 7 years of age, normally developing children do not generally exhibit loose associations or illogical thinking. Therefore, youths older than 7 who manifest these disturbances in cognition may have a formal thought disorder. Moreover, there is evidence to suggest that the symptoms of thought disorder are similar in both adult and adolescent patients with schizophrenia.

ETIOLOGY

As seen in the preceding sections, psychosis and psychotic symptoms have been conceptualized and defined in a variety of different ways. Consequently, it is not surprising that numerous theories have existed on the origins of the psychotic processes. Early theories of the origins of hallucinations are now largely relegated to discussions of historical interest. For example, one theory of the etiology of hallucinations focused on Freudian concepts. Hallucinations were believed to serve as mechanisms of wish fulfillment and served to gratify the cravings of the id. Therefore, hallucinations occurred when the ability to satisfy the desires of the id could not be met in the real world.

As psychiatry became more empirically oriented and the ability to examine neurological processes became more advanced, efforts turned to locating the source of psychotic symptoms and disorders in neural substrates. Some of the earlier research that investigated how the biological functions of the brain might play a role in the existence of psychotic symptoms focused on the relationship between psychosis and dreams. For example, individuals with disorders in rapid eye movement were noted to experience an increased frequency of hypnagogic and hypnopompic hallucinations. Based on the available evidence, it was hypothesized that there was a "dream state generator" in the pons. It was also suggested that disordered firing of the reticular activating system could result in the inclusion of novel information in dreams and might lead to overt hallucinations in awake individuals.

Most recently, with the development of advanced neuroimaging technology, the biological underpinnings of hallucinations have been further explored. Two groups of investigators have used positron emission tomography (PET) to examine which regions of the brain may be involved in hallucinatory experiences. PET is a means in which regional cerebral blood flow (CBF) can be measured. Increases in CBF to a particular brain region are indicative of activation of those brain areas. Conversely, decreases in CBF to different regions of the brain reflect reductions of brain activity in those areas.

In one study, adult volunteers who were not suffering from psychiatric disorders were given intravenous procaine. It had been previously noted that procaine administration can lead to euphoria or fear and hallucinations. When compared to those who did not experience procaine-induced hallucinations, subjects who did experience procaine-induced visual hallucinations had both greater global and occipital lobe CBF increases. In another report, investigators assessed changes in CBF using PET in persons who readily hallucinate under hypnosis as well as in persons who do not hallucinate when hypnotized. Increases in the right anterior cingulate area of the cortex were found only in the people who experienced auditory hallucinations. The results of these studies suggest that improper brain activity may underlie hallucinatory experiences.

In terms of the origins of delusions, much less research is available. It is generally accepted, however, that delusions, like hallucinations, are the result of dysfunction within the central nervous system. It is clearly established that in adults, neurological disorders often precede the development of delusional symptomatology. For example, approximately half of Alzheimer's disease patients suffer from delusions. In addition, delusions often occur in disorders associated with metabolic dysregulation, drug-induced states, and nutritional deficiency syndromes. Hypothesized areas of dysfunction include various regions of the cortex as well as the hippocampus.

Research into formal thought disorder implicates attentional and information processing abnormalities (i.e., distractibility) as contributing to the expression of psychotic symptomatology. In addition, linguistic and semantic aberrations also seem to play a key role. Communication errors, such as vague references and omission of conjunctions (the latter to link ideas), have been described as reasons that the speech patterns of psychotic individuals appear to be disorganized and difficult to follow. Recent evidence suggests that abnormalities in the frontal lobes, temporal lobes, and the limbic system all may play a role in the thought disorder seen in patients with schizophrenia.

EPIDEMIOLOGY

Although there have been numerous studies on the prevalence of psychotic disorders and the prevalence of their component symptoms in adults, there is a relative lack of sound research that has investigated how often these same kinds of syndromes and symptoms are present in children and adolescents. However, although specific prevalence rates for psychotic disorders in young people is not known, it is clear that psychotic disorders are less prevalent in adolescents than they are in adults. Similarly, psychotic disorders appear to be even less common in children when compared to adolescents.

As previously noted, an isolated psychotic symptom is not enough to warrant diagnosing a person with a psychotic disorder. Because many youths who have symptoms of psychosis do not suffer from schizophrenia or a schizophrenia-spectrum disorder, the frequency with which young people experience psychotic symptoms is considerably higher than the prevalence of psychotic disorders in children and adolescents. The precise rates at which children and adolescents suffer from psychotic symptoms are not known yet.

SUMMARY

As shown in this overview, the presentation of psychosis can be quite varied. Moreover, the differential diagnosis of psychosis is rather extensive. For these reasons, evaluating and accurately diagnosing a youth in whom psychotic symptomatology is present is not an easy task. This text will provide the reader with current information regarding the epidemiology, clinical phenomenology, etiology, and treatment for the psychotic disorders that occur in children and adolescents. Although this book will focus on recent scientific advances, it also will provide the reader with knowledge on incorporating this information into state-of-the art care for children and adolescents.

When the presence of psychotic symptoms is elicited by a clinician, it is often difficult for the practitioner to establish from which particular psychiatric disorder the youth in question suffers. This is due, in part, to the multiple ways in which psychotic symptomatology may be expressed by children and adolescents. This is also a result of the fact that psychotic symptomatology may be present in numerous psychiatric conditions and nonpathological states.

The following chapters describe the diagnostic symptom criteria for many of the psychotic disorders that occur in either children or adolescents. First, the adult presentation of the psychotic condition being considered will be reviewed. A discussion of the clinical features and the psychotic symptomatology of the illness as they pertain to children and adolescents will follow. A review of adult symptomatology is important because, although the clinical presentation of a certain disorder may be different in children and adolescents when compared to adults, diagnostic symptom criteria are often similar across the life cycle. In this book, differences in the clinical presentations that these conditions may have in adults, children, and adolescent-aged patients will be emphasized.

2

SCHIZOPHRENIA

Schizophrenia is considered to be the archetypal psychotic disorder. It is arguably the most severe of the psychotic illnesses. Schizophrenia is not a rare disorder. It is present in approximately 1% of the population worldwide. There have been international epidemiological studies that have revealed that the rates of schizophrenia vary little from country to country or continent to continent. Males and females are affected at equal rates.

SYMPTOMS

Schizophrenia is characterized by significant disorders of perception such as auditory hallucinations, visual hallucinations or visions, and can even include tactile, gustatory, or olfactory hallucinations. For many patients suffering from schizophrenia, delusions—fixed false beliefs—of a strikingly unusual or bizarre nature are often present. These two types of symptoms have been considered the hallmarks of schizophrenia.

During the last two decades, however, difficulties in cognition as well as in volition have received significant examination as symptoms of schizophrenia. Along with the symptoms of hearing voices and having unusual beliefs, many patients who suffer from schizophrenia have substantially disorganized thinking, difficulties with judgement, problems with sustained attention, and deficits in a number of cognitive functions. In addition, a lack of volition is one of the more frequent problems seen in schizophrenia and is part of the collection of problems termed *negative symptoms*. Whereas most of the literature on schizophrenia has focused on hallucinations and delusions, it is the negative symptoms—lack of motivation and decreased spontaneous speech—that are often most troublesome to patients. Like hallucinations and delusions, these negative symptoms are also associated with poor social and functional outcome.

Finally, there are two other key symptoms associated with schizophrenia. These are affective and psychomotor disturbances. The most typical affective disturbances include blunted affect, inappropriate affect, or anhedonia (the inability to feel pleasure). Although many individuals with schizophrenia suffer from blunted affect, this symptom is characteristic of many other psychiatric disorders. For example, it is not uncommon for a youth with schizophrenia to be misdiagnosed as suffering from depression due to the presence of a blunted affect.

An individual with inappropriate affect does not react to situations in a way that is expected. Individuals with inappropriate affect may laugh at a sad incident or may cry at a happy or humorous event. Anhedonia, another affective disturbance, is usually characterized by an individual's inability to find pleasure in social contact or activities. The presence of anhedonia is another reason that adolescents with schizophrenia are occasionally erroneously diagnosed as having a depressive disorder.

In addition to affective disturbances, some psychomotor disturbances that may occur in patients with schizophrenia include abnormal mannerisms, grimacing, catatonia, and posturing. Some patients develop catalepsy in which they assume a position (which may appear uncomfortable to maintain) and become immobile.

Another important aspect of schizophrenia as it relates to children and adolescents is the phenomena of the prodrome. For most patients suffering from schizophrenia, there is a period of time preceding the onset of the psychotic symptoms in which a person may develop social avoidance, difficulties with attention, sleep disturbance, and anxiety. These nonspecific symptoms are confusing for family members and clinicians alike because of their lack of specificity. After treatment has been initiated in a patient with schizophrenia similar nonspecific symptoms may persist after other psychotic symptoms of schizophrenia have resolved. These symptoms are referred to as residual symptoms.

Due to the variability of symptoms that may be present in individuals who suffer from schizophrenia, different subtypes of the illness have also been described. According to current nosology, there are five subtypes of schizophrenia. The most prominent symptom of the paranoid subtype is preoccupation with one or more delusions. The person may also have auditory hallucinations consistent with a theme related to his or her delusion(s). Patients with the paranoid subtype of schizophrenia do not generally have prominent inappropriate affect or disorganized behavior, but they may become angry or violent or experience significant anxiety as a result of their delusional beliefs. In adults, the prognosis for this subtype tends to be better than the other subtypes of schizophrenia.

In adults, the disorganized subtype of schizophrenia has generally been reported to be associated with a poorer prognosis. The prominent symptoms that occur in patients with this subtype of the illness consist of verbal incoherence, extremely disorganized behavior, loosening of associations, and inappropriate affect. A wide variety of delusions or fragmented delusions and hallucinations that are not related to any particular central theme are usually present. An individual afflicted with this subtype of schizophrenia may also have extreme psychosocial dysfunction.

The catatonic subtype is marked primarily by psychomotor disturbances such as rigid posture and unresponsiveness. A person with this subtype of schizophrenia may seem to be in a stupor or trance-like state. The existence of mutism or the refusal to speak is also a common feature of this subtype. However, it should be noted that an individual with the catatonic subtype of schizophrenia might fluctuate between states of stupor and periods of excitement.

The undifferentiated subtype of schizophrenia is less precise in terms of its characteristic symptomatology. Usually, an individual is most aptly described as suffering from this subtype if he or she has prominent symptoms of psychosis but does not have a single cluster of predominant symptoms that would make the diagnosis of another of the subtypes more appropriate.

Finally, the residual subtype of schizophrenia is usually diagnosed in individuals without prominent positive symptoms, but who have previously experienced a psychotic episode and still manifest negative symptoms. Usually, people with the residual subtype of schizophrenia remain socially withdrawn, inactive, and may possess bizarre thoughts. They also may suffer from other impairing negative symptoms such as flat affect and poverty of speech.

Considering the numerous manifestations of schizophrenia, it is understandable that the diagnosis of this disorder in children and adolescents is challenging. In addition to taking into consideration the presence or absence of the symptom criteria themselves, to diagnose this condition accurately in the young, one must also look at the affects that development has on the expression of the symptomatology. Research has demonstrated that the symptoms that characterize schizophrenia in adults also characterize the condition in both children and teenagers with this illness. As in adults, a child or adolescent must exhibit social dysfunction, poor academic achievement, and continuous signs of disturbance for at least 6 months to meet diagnostic symptom criteria for schizophrenia. However, given the fact that schizophrenia can manifest in a wide variety of ways, careful consideration of other disorders must be given before giving a child or adolescent a diagnosis of schizophrenia. Many of these disorders will be considered in more detail later in this book.

Often a young person who develops schizophrenia has a history of being a "loner" or has a history of being socially isolated and rejected. Many of these young people have had poor social skills even before onset of the prodrome. In addition, a child may have other significant premorbid symptoms that are present before the development of the prodromal phase of the illness. These include a history of delayed motor and verbal development, poor social skills, disruptive behaviors, and poor academic performance despite normal intelligence.

Prodromal symptoms may be manifested by a youth's inability to achieve a developmentally expected level of functioning as opposed to experiencing a decline in psychosocial functioning. However, after exhibiting the first symptoms of a prodrome, months or years may pass before a child or adolescent meets full diagnostic symptom criteria for schizophrenia.

Due to the fact that a wide variety of difficulties can occur both premorbidly and during the prodrome that antecedes full symptom development, youths may meet symptom criteria for a wide variety of conditions prior to manifesting a more complete expression of schizophrenia. For this reason many youths with schizophrenia may receive prior diagnoses of one or more of the following: disruptive behavior disorders, mood disorders, learning and communication disorders, pervasive developmental disorders.

Developmental issues are important to consider when evaluating a youth in which a psychotic disorder is suspected. For example, when investigating whether or not a youth is suffering from hallucinations or delusions, one must take into account that between the ages of 5 and 7, normally developing children often combine fantasy with reality. Therefore, an appreciation that childhood onset schizophrenia is very uncommon and that this developmentally expected process may occur should both be considered before one makes a diagnosis of schizophrenia in a very young child. However, if a diagnosis of schizophrenia is established in a young person, it is important to realize that a youth's hallucinations and delusions may seemingly be more age appropriate due to the influence of the patient's developmental level.

As in adults, the most common form of hallucination in young people with schizophrenia is auditory rather than visual hallucinations. It should be noted that visual hallucinations do occur in young people with schizophrenia and may be quite frightening. Along with hallucinations, delusions seem to occur in approximately half of all young people with schizophrenia. These delusions often increase in frequency and complexity as a youth gets older. Usually, hallucinations and delusions reflect a child's experiences, which may be centered on a theme that involves toys, video games, and school concerns. Other symptoms that may be present include blunted or inappropriate affect. Thought disorder that may be characterized by loosening of associations, thought blocking, illogical thinking, and poverty of thought also occurs quite frequently. Unlike adults, a child with schizophrenia generally does not exhibit poverty of speech content, but rather often fails to speak at the level of other youths of equal intelligence. In addition, the speech of a young person with schizophrenia may seem ambiguous when referring to people or objects. Other features, such as poor motor functioning and attention deficits, may also appear during the course of the illness.

AGE OF ONSET AND ETIOLOGY

Overall, males have an earlier age of onset than females and males are more commonly affected with schizophrenia during the preadult years than females. It has been noted that nearly 40% of males who are being treated for schizophrenia for the first time experienced their psychotic symptoms before the age of 19 years. Therefore, schizophrenia is not a rare disorder in adolescents.

Schizophrenia rarely develops during the first decade of life. It has been estimated that only 1 in 10,000 children under the age of 12 years suffers from schizophrenia. However, schizophrenia has been reported to occur in children as young as 5 years of age.

The etiology of schizophrenia is not fully understood, although there are important clues to why this disease develops in some people. The adult-onset form of schizophrenia is the most widely investigated, and little is known about what factors lead to the development of this condition in childhood or adolescence.

Genetics appears to be one risk factor that may be associated with the development of schizophrenia. For many decades now, schizophrenia has been known to run in families or to be associated with familial aggregation. For example, it is more likely for a relative of a person who suffers from schizophrenia to develop the illness than it would be for a member of a control group. Also, the rates of schizophrenia increase dramatically with the closeness of the genetic relationship. For example, the son or daughter of a person with schizophrenia has a chance of developing the illness at rates of approximately 10%. This is substantially higher than among the general population (1%), but substantially lower than the rates of concordance for identical twins—a rate which approaches 50%. Further evidence to suggest that genetic factors contribute to the development of schizophrenia come from twin studies that have demonstrated that the concordance rate for schizophrenia is higher in monozygotic twins than in dizygotic twins.

However, familial aggregation studies do not address issues of shared environment. Interestingly, over the last three decades, adoption studies that have examined environmental effects and the development of schizophrenia have found that growing up away from the biological family with schizophrenia does not reduce the risk of developing the disease.

There are now sophisticated genetic technologies that have allowed researchers to link or associate specific genes or small portions of the chromosome to illness states. Many laboratories from around the world are hoping to find the genes that may predispose a person to develop schizophrenia. To date, there has not been a single gene or part of a chromosome which has been substantially linked or associated with schizophrenia. The future may lead to the identification of a group of genes that convey an increased risk for developing the illness.

Another avenue of research has suggested that abnormalities in neurodevelopment may contribute to the etiology of schizophrenia. This theory is not independent of the genetic hypothesis of schizophrenia, but it does not depend on it either. The neurodevelopmental hypothesis states that there is a yet-to-be-identified "lesion" which interacts with the developing brain to ultimately lead to illness development. This "lesion" is not a mass or malformation but a brain abnormality that disrupts function. There are several avenues of evidence that support the neurodevelopmental hypothesis of schizophrenia. For example, significant differences in brain structure have been identified between people with schizophrenia and control groups. In addition neuropathological studies have noted that brains of patients with schizophrenia lack signs of infection or brain injury. Interestingly, people who develop schizophrenia have histories of more obstetrical complications and maternal difficulties, such as viral infection, during their gestation. The role, if any, these early stressors play in aberrant neurodevelopment has yet to be determined.

Etiology addresses the ultimate cause of an illness, whereas pathophysiology addresses the problems underlying the condition. For schizophrenia, there are theories that suggest that abnormalities in neurotransmitter functioning contribute to the pathophysiology of the disease. The predominant neurotransmitter theory of schizophrenia during the last four decades is the dopamine hypothesis. Dopamine is a neurotransmitter found in many parts of the brain and perhaps is most well-known for its function in the basal ganglia associated with smooth, coordinated movements. Deficiencies in dopamine in these parts of the brain lead to the illness Parkinsonism. Because efficacious antipsychotic medications avidly bind to dopamine receptors and because stimulation of dopamine in patients suffering from schizophrenia can lead to an exacerbation of their symptoms, many investigators have reasoned that high levels of dopamine are an important part of the pathophysiology of the illness. However, this theory is not completely proven or it may be only a part of the overall pathophysiology.

Stimulation of one of the serotonin receptors can also lead to psychotic symptoms. Perhaps the most famous serotonin stimulator that can lead to psychotic symptoms is lysergic acid diethylamide (LSD). Recently introduced medications for schizophrenia have been found to block serotonin receptors. Therefore, researchers are avidly exploring the role that serotonin may have in the pathophysiology of this illness.

Third, a complex neurotransmitter system—the glutamate system—has received attention as being a putative pathophysiological contributor to schizophrenia. Modulation of the glutamate system, which can be accomplished by the anesthetic agent ketamine or with the dangerous recreational drug phencyclidine (PCP), can lead to many psychotic symptoms similar to those seen in patients with schizophrenia.

In the past, there were numerous theories that family environment might contribute to the development of schizophrenia. Some focused on the behavior of a patient's mother leading to the phrase *schizophrenogenic mother*. Other theories describe deviant communication patterns that were hypothesized to be etiologic for the disorder. These communication and family theories are not supported by empiric research as risk factors for the development of schizophrenia. However, over the last 25 years, a substantial number of investigators have noticed that certain environmental factors are associated with a greater frequency of relapse of psychosis in patients suffering from schizophrenia. High familial *expressed emotion* (EE) is associated with relapse and rehospitalization in stabilized patients with schizophrenia when compared to the relapse rates of patients living with families characterized by low expressed emotion. A high level of critical communication was one of the prominent factors noticed to predict relapse in high EE families.

Therefore, in addition to the biologic pathophysiological theories discussed above, it does appear that the specific stressful environment of high expressed emotion is part of the pathophysiology puzzle but not a etiological risk factor.

DIFFERENTIAL DIAGNOSIS

At the earliest stages of schizophrenia, the most important part of developing a differential diagnosis is the consideration of general medical conditions that may lead to the psychotic symptoms associated with schizophrenia. Evaluation for substances of abuse, which may serve as psychotomimetic agents, is also quite important. Drugs of abuse such as LSD, cocaine, amphetamines, inhalants, and PCP should all be considered. The use of these agents can be assessed by a combination of history taking and toxicology screens. Certain rarer metabolic disorders such as Wilson's disease should be considered and can be assessed by physical examination and laboratory tests. Psychosis secondary to temporal lobe epilepsy is not rare; however, a seizure history often can be elicited. An electroencephalogram can be an important part of the medical diagnostic evaluation for individuals in whom a seizure disorder is considered a possibility. People suffering from schizophrenia can occasionally have structural brain abnormalities. When a neuroanotomical abnormality is suspected, a brain imaging evaluation (such as with magnetic resonance imaging, MRI) may be very appropriate.

It should be emphasized that comorbidity is a real possibility for young patients with schizophrenia. Youths with psychotic illnesses may also be afflicted by general medical conditions. In addition, teenagers with substance abuse disorders may also suffer from mood or psychotic disorders. Therefore, it is vital for the clinician to remember that identification of a substance abuse disorder or a general medical condition in a young person with psychotic symptoms does not exclude the possibility of a coexisting psychotic illness.

The psychiatric differential diagnosis for schizophrenia is extensive, but a clinician should initially consider other severe psychotic disorders. Bipolar disorder and major depression with psychotic features need to be considered. The major difference between schizophrenia and these two disorders is the presence of prominent mood symptoms and generally a mood congruent delusional pattern. Some patients may meet full symptom criteria for a mood disorder as well as meet symptom criteria for schizophrenia. In these patients, the diagnosis of schizoaffective disorder may be appropriate. Brief psychotic episodes may occur in patients with borderline personality disorder, a brief psychotic episode, or schizotypal personality disorder. Therefore, these diagnoses should also be considered.

Other symptoms that are common for patients with schizophrenia can be seen in other psychiatric disorders. Youths with Asperger's disorder and other pervasive developmental disorders may be misdiagnosed as suffering from schizophrenia. This is likely due to the fact that both conditions are associated with poor social relatedness, asociality, or both. However, there are several key factors to consider when differentiating a pervasive developmental disorder from a psychotic-spectrum disorder. First, it should be remembered that hallucinations and delusions do not characterize pervasive developmental disorders. In addition, symptoms of pervasive developmental disorders such as autism usually emerge prior to 5 years of age, whereas it is rare for the "positive" symptoms of schizophrenia to develop before this age. Because pervasive developmental disorders differ from psychotic disorders in terms of treatment and prognosis, being able to distinguish from the two groups of conditions is essential. However, it should be noted that patients can meet diagnostic criteria for both autistic disorder and schizophrenia.

Also of special concern for the clinician focusing on the child and adolescent patient is that of making the diagnosis of schizophrenia prematurely. Recent studies indicate that the diagnosis of schizophrenia can be made accurately in teenagers. On the other hand, not every psychotic adolescent or child can be readily assigned a diagnosis with confidence. In such cases, the concerns about reaching a diagnosis too rapidly are important. For example, some youngsters have symptoms of psychosis within the context of euthymic mood and normal relatedness. In such cases, careful longitudinal assessment is vital.

Considering the multiple disorders that may be misdiagnosed as schizophrenia, it is important that a thorough assessment is obtained prior to diagnosis being made. Because patients with schizophrenia may have problems with premorbid development and experience a prodrome that antecedes the development of active symptoms, a thorough longitudinal history is essential. In summary, the differential diagnosis or evaluation of a severely psychotic patient presumed to be suffering from schizophrenia includes a thoughtful evaluation of possible medical illnesses, an assessment of mood disturbances, investigation of possible substance abuse, a careful family history, and a longitudinal assessment of the development of psychotic symptoms.

TREATMENT

Due to the significant impact schizophrenia can have on emotions, perceptions, and cognition, the approaches to treatment of this condition are multimodal. However, during the course of treatment, the first and foremost concern is for the safety and comfort of the patient. An assessment of the appropriate placement—hospital, day treatment, or ambulatory care—must be carefully considered. A patient may pose a risk to either him- or herself or others during psychotic episodes.

Medications are the mainstays of treatment for patients with schizophrenia and are prescribed to reduce symptoms of psychosis. For schizophrenic adults, the antipsychotic medications have demonstrated significant amelioration of psychotic symptoms. Recently, newer agents termed *atypical* antipsychotic medications have been introduced. These newer medications are considered to be atypical because they have a reduced propensity to cause extrapyramidal neurological side effects such as acute dystonic reactions, akathisia, Parkinsonism, and tardive dyskinesia.

In adults, the atypical antipsychotics have been shown to be superior to placebo treatment and, in some instances, superior to the older "typical" agents. Besides "positive" symptom reduction, the newer antipsychotic medications may also have the ability to reduce disorders of cognition and to improve negative symptoms in ways the older medicines did not. It appears that the cognitive and negative symptoms of schizophrenia can have pronounced effects on social and occupational function. Therefore, it may be of substantial importance to reduce these symptoms.

The treatment of schizophrenia in teenagers has many parallels to that of adult patients. The traditional antipsychotic medications were found to be helpful for patients under 18 years of age, however, the actual number of studies that were performed in this population was quite low. Unfortunately, the older or traditional "typical" antipsychotic medications were found to cause extrapyramidal side effects and other adverse events at high rates. Such agents' side effect profiles often limited their full usefulness and at times adversely effected the therapeutic alliance between patients and their families and the prescribing physician. It is our impression that because the older medications often led to troubling extrapyramidal side effects, clinicians frequently delayed initiation of treatment.

Besides their suboptimal side effect profile, another shortcoming of the typical antipsychotics was that not all youths who were prescribed these agents were noted to have an adequate response to treatment. In fact, there is evidence to suggest that younger patients may be at particularly high risk for treatment resistance to these typical antipsychotics.

Clozapine (Clozaril®) was the first atypical antipsychotic tested in young patients with schizophrenia. Clozapine carries with it the risk of potentially fatal agranulocytosis and has not been extensively tested in young people. For both these reasons, it is currently indicated only for treatment-resistant adult patients with psychosis. Moreover, due to its potential for hematological side effects, ongoing monitoring with regularly scheduled blood draws is necessary during the course of clozapine therapy. Because clozapine has had robust salutary effects in many treatment-resistant adult patients with schizophrenia, physicians began to examine the role clozapine might have in the treatment of neuroleptic unresponsive younger patients. Numerous open label and one double-blind study suggested that clozapine may provide significant clinical benefit to treatment resistant youths with schizophrenia. Despite these promising reports, clozapine does not appear to be commonly prescribed to young people. This is most likely due to the recent availability of newer "first line" atypical antipsychotics that do not carry the risk of agranulocytosis and that do not require ongoing hematological monitoring. It should be noted that despite its potential for adverse events, clozapine remains the only antipsychotic medication that has demonstrated substantial impact on treatment resistant adult patients. Due to its side effect profile, we generally recommend clozapine be used only after treatment with at least two front line atypical antipsychotics and treatment with a typical antipsychotic have failed.

As noted above, within the past few years there have been several first line atypical antipsychotics released in the United States. They are risperidone (Risperdal®), olanzapine (Zyprexa®), and quetiapine (Seroquel®). All three successfully reduce symptoms of psychosis in adult patients with schizophrenia and they all have distinct receptor binding profiles. There is a growing body of evidence that these three medications may hold substantial promise for the treatment of younger patients with schizophrenia. Some case series involving each of the agents have shown substantial diminishment of symptoms with good rates of acceptability. These new medicines are helpful; however, they should be used with care because they all have the potential for adverse events, including tardive dyskinesia. The most commonly observed side effects during short-term treatment with these agents are sedation and increased appetite and weight gain.

Currently, however, there is not a single medication that is the best choice for pharmacological treatment of schizophrenia in children and adolescents. Based on the available literature, we generally recommend treatment be initiated with one of the front line atypical antipsychotics. Because it appears that rapid increases in antipsychotic dosing may increase the risk of side effects, a rational approach to treating young patients with these agents is to start at a low dose and gradually increase the dose as needed. It should also be remembered that antipsychotics should be used to treat psychosis and that responses to these medications are not immediate. However, early in the course of treatment, difficulties with agitation may be problematic. In these instances we recommend temporary use of an adjunctive medication to target this symptom until the salutary effects of the antipsychotic are manifested rather than a rapid increase in the dose of the antipsychotic.

As treatment with medications helps with the reduction of psychotic symptoms, there is clearly a role for psychosocial treatments when caring for an adolescent with schizophrenia. During the initial stages of treatment, psychoeducational meetings with patients as well as their families are very important. It is important to ensure that both the youngster and his or her family are educated extensively about the disorder. Individual and group therapies that focus on social skills training and cognitive rehabilitation have shown substantial promise in adults. Such interventions should also be considered in young people with schizophrenia.

Especially for children and adolescents, a family-based approach to the treatment of schizophrenia is crucial. Clinicians need to be aware of the tremendous impact that the diagnosis of schizophrenia in a child or adolescent has on the entire family. In our work, we have noted that many families react to the news that their child has schizophrenia in a fashion similar to that seen in families who are informed that their child is suffering from a severe general medical illness. This, of course, should not be surprising. Unfortunately, it may not always be recognized. Besides family therapy, parents and youths may benefit greatly from involvement groups that have active roles in both patient advocacy and family support, such as the National Alliance for the Mentally Ill (NAMI).

Lastly, recent studies have demonstrated that even adolescents suffering from schizophrenia have substantial cognitive difficulties. These problems in attention and memory should not be ignored in planning for school or vocation. We have noted that neuropsychological testing may be of use if formal testing of attention and memory can assist in the appropriate school rehabilitation for adolescents with psychosis.

COURSE AND PROGNOSIS

In the earlier years of the 20th century, schizophrenia was felt to be an illness that was uniformly associated with a poor prognosis. The introduction of the traditional antipsychotic medications in the 1950s led to symptom reduction in many but not all patients suffering from this disorder. Newer treatments—the atypical antipsychotics—have lead to improved outcomes in adult patients over the last decade. However, many persons suffering from schizophrenia still have substantial cognitive problems and negative symptoms, which limit their full recovery.

The course of illness in young people with schizophrenia is variable. Risk factors associated with poor outcome include earlier age at onset, more pronounced premorbid dysfunction, and an insidious onset of psychotic symptomatology. In addition to these factors, one other element that obviously impacts on the eventual prognosis of a youth is the accuracy of the initial diagnosis. Many youths who are initially diagnosed with schizophrenia eventually receive another diagnosis.

For clinicians treating children and adolescents it is important to note that schizophrenia may be most responsive to treatment in the early stages of the illness. Studies conducted on first episode patients indicate that as many as 85% of adults suffering from schizophrenia may achieve a remission of symptoms. For younger people, the course of illness is less clear as there are very few follow-up studies.

Although prior studies that have examined the course of schizophrenia in young people did not often present an optimistic future for these patients, changes in the approach to the treatment of schizophrenia provide the possibility of a better prognosis. With the introduction of newer atypical antipsychotic medications, some clinicians feel that earlier identification and more assertive pharmacological intervention are possible. Early, effective interventions may be associated with better long-term course and clinical researchers will be examining this possibility in the future. It has also been suggested that these newer medications reduce cognitive dysfunction and negative symptoms, thereby leading to better social and functional outcomes. In our opinion, these approaches, combined with appropriate family and cognitive rehabilitation, offer the possibility of brighter futures for young patients with schizophrenia.

3

MOOD AND MOOD-RELATED DISORDERS

MAJOR DEPRESSIVE DISORDER

Major depressive disorder (MDD) occurs more frequently in children and adolescents than schizophrenia does. Among preadolescents, the prevalence of MDD is reported to be about 2%, and among adolescents it is reported to be about 4%. These rates appear to be unrelated to ethnicity, education, or socioeconomic status. In prepubertal children, boys appear to be affected more by the disorder than girls, however MDD is believed to be two to three times more common in adolescent females than in adolescent males. Because MDD affects many more children and adolescents than are affected by schizophrenia, far more is known about juvenile MDD than is known about child and adolescent schizophrenia.

Symptoms and Psychotic Features

According to current nosology, to meet diagnostic symptom criteria for a major depressive episode, a person must have either a depressed mood or lose interest or pleasure in almost all activities for a distinct period that lasts at least 2 weeks. Furthermore, to meet diagnostic symptom criteria for a major depressive episode, these symptoms must be accompanied by at least four other symptoms that are characteristic of this syndrome. These symptoms include significant changes in appetite that is associated with either weight loss or weight gain; insomnia or hypersomnia; psychomotor agitation or retardation; fatigue or loss of energy; feelings of worthlessness or extreme guilt; a diminished ability to think or concentrate; and recurrent thoughts of death or suicidal ideation.

Individuals who are afflicted with a major depressive episode often experience difficulties with intrafamilial and other interpersonal relationships.

In addition, depressed people often have difficulties maintaining premorbid levels of functioning in either occupational or educational domains. The level of dysfunction associated with MDD is often associated with the magnitude of symptom severity. During episodes of milder intensity, some individuals may be able to maintain their premorbid levels of functioning. In these instances, the person with MDD may need to exert a significant amount of extra effort to maintain the level of premorbid functioning that existed prior to the onset of the mood episode. However, in individuals who are afflicted with episodes of greater symptom severity, the ability to attend to the most basic of tasks (such as maintaining personal hygiene) may be profoundly affected.

Making a diagnosis of MDD is not always an easy task to undertake. This is because patients with MDD can manifest the symptoms of their illness in a variety of ways. Most adult patients with MDD state that they feel sad, depressed, hopeless, or discouraged. However, some patients may simply complain that they feel empty, are devoid of feelings, or may simply state that they feel as if they have no motivation. Due to the subjective experience of these mood states, depressed persons often lose interest or pleasure in activities they typically would enjoy, such as athletics or hobbies. In addition, adult patients with MDD may also report decreased sexual interest or desire.

A common symptom of MDD is insomnia. Just as there are a variety of different ways that patients with MDD subjectively experience and express the mood states associated with this condition, the symptom of insomnia may manifest in several different ways. Some patients experience initial insomnia. Initial insomnia is characterized by difficulty falling asleep. Other patients wake up in the middle of the night and have difficulty falling back to sleep. This is called middle insomnia. Some persons experience early morning awakening and the inability to return to sleep. This phenomenon is known as terminal insomnia. Patients with MDD may experience one or more types of insomnia during the course of their illness. Conversely, some depressed patients do not suffer from insomnia at all but may experience hypersomnia, or the tendency to sleep excessively.

In a similar fashion, the changes in appetite and behavior seen in people who are afflicted with depression can be quite varied. Some patients with MDD experience pronounced anorexia and feel as if they have to force themselves to eat. In contrast, some depressed persons develop increases in their appetite and may develop cravings for certain foods (frequently sweets). When changes in dietary intake are pronounced, significant weight gain or weight loss is possible. Most patients with MDD suffer from a subjective experience of feeling as if they have reduced amounts of energy. These patients may complain of being easily fatigued. Others may even develop slowing of speech. If a patient becomes noticeably more sedentary, this reduction in psychomotor activity is often readily observed by others. On the other hand, some patients with MDD can become quite restless and agitated.

The diagnostic criteria of increased feelings of worthlessness and guilt can be expressed as lowering of self-esteem or unrealistic negative feelings about oneself. Depressed people may become preoccupied with minor past failings or they may erroneously assume that unfortunate prior events are the result of personal mistakes, shortcomings, or transgressions. People who experience difficulties with concentration may develop difficulties with organization or complain of difficulties with their memory. They may also become quite indecisive.

Probably of greatest importance is the fact that individuals with MDD may develop recurrent thoughts of death or suicidal ideation. These patients may even act on these thoughts by committing deliberate self-injurious acts. Unfortunately, approximately 15% of individuals who suffer from MDD ultimately commit suicide.

Although the clinical presentation of MDD may be somewhat different in children and adolescents from that of adults, the diagnostic criteria for the disorder are the same across the life cycle. Most noteworthy is the fact that many depressed young people will not appear to be sad or depressed. Youths who suffer from MDD often manifest an irritable mood state that is frequently accompanied by increased defiance towards authority figures. Unfortunately, these major depressive episodes are often erroneously dismissed by adults as being "just a phase" that the youth is experiencing. Youths who suffer from MDD may also be afflicted with other distressing symptoms. These include increases in levels of anxiety, the development of panic attacks, or both. Young people with MDD may also develop excessive somatic complaints (such as headaches or stomachaches).

MDD can be associated with pronounced dysfunction in a young person suffering from this condition, as in adults. For example, significant conflicts within the family may occur during the course of a major depressive episode. Both depressed children and adolescents may suffer from poor academic performance, social withdrawal, poor peer relationships, substance abuse, and peer rejection.

Suicide is probably the most catastrophic outcome of a major depressive episode. Suicide attempts in adolescents with MDD are far more common than in children. This is because adolescents have greater capabilities of following through with thoughts of suicide than children do. In fact, there is evidence to suggest that 75% to 85% of inpatient samples of adolescents suffering with MDD report thoughts of suicide, and approximately 60% have attempted to commit suicide. Suicide during adolescence is a major public health concern in the United States. In fact, suicide is the third leading cause of death in adolescents.

Occasionally, depressed young people may experience symptoms of psychosis. However, psychotic features are present in only the most severely affected youths with MDD. A review of the phenomenology of MDD in youths suggested that the psychotic features in children and adolescents with MDD are similar to the psychotic features that are present in adults with MDD. For example, during these episodes of MDD with psychotic features, a youth may experience delusions or hallucinations that are consistent with their subjective feelings of profound depression. These delusions and hallucinations are considered to be *mood congruent.*

It appears as if delusions occur more frequently in adolescents than in children. Delusions that occur during a major depressive episode are often characterized by themes of guilt, disease, nihilism, death, and personal inadequacy. For example, a youth may believe that he or she deserved to be punished. Hallucinations occur in both depressed children and adolescents. They are typically auditory and are most commonly characterized by a single voice (as opposed to multiple conversing voices). These auditory hallucinations are often either critical of the patient or derogatory in nature. The voice may blame the youth for certain character flaws or past mistakes.

Individuals may also have persecutory delusions (the belief that one is being conspired against), delusions of thought broadcasting (the belief that one's thoughts are being transmitted to others), or delusions of thought insertion (the belief that another is inserting ideas or thoughts into one's head). It should be noted that in adults, the presence of psychotic symptoms during a major depressive episode is associated with an increased risk of attempted suicide.

The following is a case report by Kashani and Ray (1987) that depicts the presence of psychotic features in a 5-year-old boy named Bobby who was diagnosed with MDD:

> Prior to his referral he was convinced that his mother was poisoning his food "to get rid" of him. He then became suspicious that all meals had been poisoned, smelling and tasting all food carefully before eating … When asked if he thought he was smart, he characteristically would say, "No, I am dumb." At times, he stated he was "crazy" and punished himself by standing in the

corner of the room ... Bizarre responses to some tests items (on the Wechsler Preschool and Primary Scale of Intelligence) were noted. For example, his response to the item, "Why do we go to the toilet before we go to bed?" was "Because you have to try to go to the bathroom, then Santa's going to come; you have to try to go to the bathroom and make feces, but not when he's not here." ... The Children's Apperception Test protocol yielded further evidence of bizarre thought patterns. For example, on card 3, which pictures a lion as a king sitting on a throne, Bobby's response was, "The tiger is sitting down smoking his pipe and the mouse is in the hole. Did I say it very crazy? Rah, rah, like that?" ... On card 10, a card displaying two dogs in a bathroom, Bobby's story commenced in the following way: "Once upon a time this doggy went to get in the tub, then there was a pincher bug and it got in his skin. He went all the way up to the floor and then he got pinched, and the dad was spanking him. See the dog crying. He went to the bathroom. He defecated out claws, then the dad looked in the commode and said, 'Why did you peel your claws and put them in there?' And then he tasted it and said, 'Agh,' and then threw the claws back in the commode." Such bizarre thoughts are encapsulated in an otherwise fairly normal flow of thought.

Age of Onset and Etiology

The average age of onset for MDD is in the third decade of life. However, as noted above, the disorder can even be diagnosed during the preschool years. A noticeable increase in the number of cases of MDD occurs during late adolescence. During this epoch, more females develop the condition than males.

To date, the precise cause of MDD in children and adolescents remains unknown. However, there are several hypotheses as to what may contribute to the development of the disorder. The most commonly accepted conceptualization for the etiology of MDD in children and adolescents is a biopsychosocial model. This hypothesis asserts that MDD may be precipitated by a combination of genetic, biological, psychological, and environmental factors.

Evidence that genetic factors may have a role in the development of MDD has come from a variety of different types of studies. One avenue of research has investigated the prevalence of MDD in the offspring of depressed individuals. These studies have found that children who have one depressed parent have two to three times the probability of developing the condition, when compared to the general population. When compared to the population as a whole, people who have two depressed parents have four times the probability of developing the disorder. Similarly youths with MDD have higher rates of depression in family members than normal controls.

Further evidence that genetic factors contribute to the development of MDD comes from research involving twins. In these twin studies, the concordance rate for depression among monozygotic twins has been found to be double the concordance rate seen in dizygotic twins. There is also evidence to suggest that genetic factors may affect the age at onset of MDD. This comes from research that has shown that individuals with early onset depression are more likely to have relatives who are afflicted with the disorder than those patients who develop this condition later in life. Other studies that have examined the influence that genetic factors may have on the expression of MDD have demonstrated that children who have severe episodes of MDD usually have a rich family history of the disorder.

There are also data to suggest that a dysfunctional family environment, stressful life events, or both may contribute to the development of MDD in children and adolescents. In fact, the onset of a major depressive episode oftentimes follows a major psychosocial stressor.

Differential Diagnosis and Treatment

As with other conditions that have psychotic features, it is important to consider whether or not the clinical picture of the patient in question is more consistent with the presentation of another psychiatric disorders prior to diagnosing a youth with MDD. There are several disorder that share a variety of the symptoms of MDD. For example, attention-deficit hyperactivity disorder (ADHD) may present with symptoms of agitation, inattention, and poor school performance. All these symptoms can also occur in children and adolescents with MDD. Moreover, ADHD may also occur as a comorbid condition in some patients with MDD. In these patients, a comorbid diagnosis of ADHD may be considered to be present if, after the remission of mood-related symptoms, the child or adolescent still meets diagnostic symptom criteria for ADHD.

In addition, youths who suffer from anxiety disorders or eating disorders may also present with a depressed mood. Patients who have experienced physical or sexual abuse or those youths who are suffering from an adjustment disorder with depressed mood all could potentially manifest depressive symptoms. If the individual has recently experienced a loss of a loved one, bereavement should also be considered as a possible diagnosis.

Individuals who are suffering from a general medical condition or are abusing substances also may exhibit depressive symptomatology. Depressive symptoms often are present when a person is under the influence of or withdrawing from an abused substance such as alcohol or illicit drugs.

Several psychotropic medications that may be prescribed to youths with neuropsychiatric disorders can also induce depressive symptomatology. In addition, numerous general medical conditions including neurological, endocrine, or infectious diseases may lead to the expression of symptoms of depression.

Considering the fact that there are many disorders that may be characterized by depressive symptoms, and there are different ways in which MDD can be manifested, it is important to conduct a comprehensive evaluation prior to concluding that a young person is suffering from MDD. This evaluation should include obtaining information from parents, teachers, and other relevant sources (such as clergy or peers). As with other disorders in young people, an appreciation of the longitudinal development and expression of the difficulties manifested by a young person, for whom the diagnosis of MDD is considered, is helpful to confirm or refute this diagnosis. To do this, the clinician should obtain accurate information about the onset and pervasiveness of symptoms. Finally, the clinician should obtain a thorough psychosocial and family history.

Compared to what is known about the treatment of MDD in adults, there is very little known about the treatment of MDD in young people. It is important to remember that treatments that are effective for adults may not be useful for youths and treatments that are not useful for adults may eventually be shown to be useful for children, adolescents, or both. Currently, there are several psychological and biological intervention modalities that may be employed either singly or in combination in the treatment of MDD in children and adolescents.

There are several forms of psychotherapy that appear to be useful in the treatment of adolescent depression. Cognitive-behavioral therapy, which is a combination of behavior therapy and cognitive psychology, has been shown to be effective in the treatment of MDD in adolescents. This type of therapy addresses cognitive processes and perceptions. It also addresses problem solving strategies. There are other preliminary data to suggest that interpersonal psychotherapy (which focuses on a patient's relationships with others) may also have utility in depressed adolescents. In addition, systemic family therapy and psychoeducation may also be helpful for young people who are suffering from depression.

In addition to psychotherapy, the use of medications to help treat MDD is quite common. The most widely prescribed medications for the treatment of MDD are antidepressants. Specifically, the use of serotonin selective reuptake inhibitors (SSRIs) appears to be the most favored because they seem to be relatively safe and reasonably well tolerated. Despite the fact that these medications are frequently prescribed to young people, and that open-label treatment is often associated with significant reductions in depressive symptomatology, there are very few data to suggest that treatment with these agents is superior to placebo. At present, fluoxetine (Prozac®) has been described as being superior to placebo in only one study of children and adolescents. Other SSRIs used to treat MDD in children and adolescents may include sertraline (Zoloft®), paroxetine (Paxil®), fluvoxamine (Luvox®), and citalopram (Celexa®). Other relatively new antidepressants that may be prescribed to youths with MDD include buproprion (Wellbutrin®), nefazodone (Serzone®), mirtazapine (Remeron®) and venlafaxine (Effexor®). Although it seems that these newer antidepressant agents are reasonably well tolerated in young people, what remains to be seen is whether or not these agents are truly safe and superior to treatment with placebo in pediatric MDD.

The tricyclic antidepressants (such as amitriptyline, desipramine, and imipramine) were previously the mainstays of pharmacological treatment for childhood and adolescent MDD, however, these medications are now prescribed far less frequently for MDD than they were in the past. This is for two reasons. First, a body of evidence has accumulated over the years to indicate that these agents are not superior to placebo in the treatment of pediatric depression. In addition, treatment with these agents sometimes was associated with potentially catastrophic life-threatening side effects when prescribed to young people, even at therapeutic doses. The monoamine oxidase inhibitors are drugs from an older class of agents, some of which have been shown to have efficacy in the treatment of depression in adults. However, due to the difficulties associated with the dietary restrictions with which a patient must comply to safely take these agents, the monoamine oxidase inhibitors have only been minimally investigated in depressed pediatric patients. It should also be noted that when psychotic features are present in young patients with MDD, combination pharmacotherapy with an antidepressant and antipsychotic is often employed. This occurs despite the fact that this form of combination treatment has not been extensively studied in children or adolescents.

There has been minimal investigation on the use of electroconvulsive therapy (ECT) for the treatment of MDD in children and adolescents. However, some reports suggest that this method may be useful and safe for the treatment of symptoms in adolescents suffering from MDD who are resistant to all traditional psychotherapy and pharmacotherapy approaches. Some examples of resistant symptoms may include psychosis, catatonia, and pronounced suicidal ideation.

Course and Prognosis

The prognosis for MDD in children and adolescents is influenced by several factors, some of which include the age of onset, the severity of the episode, and whether or not other comorbid disorders, such as disruptive behavior, anxiety, or substance abuse, are present. Because MDD is in most cases an episodic disorder, full remission usually occurs and the individual returns to his or her former state that existed prior to the onset of MDD. However, in approximately 20% to 30% of individuals who suffer from MDD, mild symptoms may persist for many months or even years. Individuals who are afflicted with more severe symptoms of MDD at a younger age are at risk for a poorer prognosis.

However, it is important to remember that symptoms of major depression may recur throughout a person's lifetime, with depressive episodes appearing between periods of remission. The mean length of a depressive episode in children and adolescents is approximately 6 to 9 months. Suicidal ideation, suicide attempts, and earlier age at onset of MDD are associated with briefer time to MDD recurrence.

It should be noted that children and adolescents who suffer from MDD appear to subsequently develop bipolar disorder at higher rates than adults that suffer from MDD. In fact, as many as one third of children with MDD may eventually develop bipolar disorder. Certain clinical characteristics such as the presence of psychotic features and having a family history of bipolar illness appear to increase this likelihood.

BIPOLAR DISORDER

As is MDD, bipolar disorder is considered a mood disorder. The prevalence of bipolar disorder is lower than that of MDD, with approximately 1% of the general population afflicted with the condition during their lifetime. Bipolar disorder, which is characterized by having both major depressive symptomatology and mania, is equally common in both women and men. The disorder generally develops during adolescence in both males and females. In fact, bipolar disorder appears to be as prevalent during adolescence as it is in adulthood. Although bipolar disorder was generally considered to be rare during the first decade of life, there is a growing appreciation that bipolar disorder can be a severe, disabling condition even in young children. It should be appreciated that a significant number of children who are initially diagnosed with MDD will subsequently develop symptoms of mania, thereby meeting diagnostic criteria for bipolar disorder.

A description of the syndrome follows, beginning with adult symptomatology and followed by a review of ways in which symptoms may be expressed in adolescents and children.

Symptoms and Psychotic Features

According to the *DSM-IV*, there are two major forms of bipolar affective illness: bipolar disorder type I and bipolar disorder type II. The feature of bipolar I disorder that distinguishes it from other psychiatric conditions is the occurrence of one or more manic or mixed episodes during the course of the illness. In addition, individuals with bipolar disorder type I often experience one or more major depressive episodes during their lives.

A manic episode is defined as a specific and distinct period of time during which an individual has an elevated, expansive, or irritable mood. To meet diagnostic criteria for a manic episode, the episode must have duration of at least one week. However, if psychiatric hospitalization is required due to the effects of the mood state, the episode can last less than one week and still meet symptom criteria for a manic episode.

Other than the characteristic mood state, to meet full diagnostic criteria for a manic episode an individual must manifest other symptoms associated with mania. These include inflated self-esteem or grandiosity, decreased need for sleep, pressure of speech, flight of ideas, distractibility, and excessive involvement in pleasurable and goal-oriented activities. The disturbance usually is enough to cause considerable impairment in the individual's life, especially within the social and occupational areas. As noted above, sometimes the disturbance may be severe enough to lead to hospitalization.

It should be noted that the quality of the mood that is experienced during a manic episode may be quite varied. An individual who is suffering from a manic episode can have an elevated mood that is associated with feelings of euphoria. During such times, the afflicted person may report feeling exceptionally good, cheerful, or even "high." During these elevated states, an individual's excessive behaviors may be characterized by an increased enthusiasm for interpersonal, sexual, or occupational interactions. These acts are generally considered atypical or "out of character" for the individual. Alternatively, a manic episode can be characterized by dysphoric, intense irritability. As stated above, the presence of a mixed episode is also characteristic of bipolar I disorder. A mixed episode is considered to be present when an individual is suffering from symptoms that meet diagnostic symptom criteria for both a major depressive episode and a manic episode for at least one week.

During periods of abnormally elevated mood, a patient can develop an inappropriately increased sense of self-regard that can range in severity from an increased level of self-confidence to haughtiness. For this reason, a patient with mania may attempt to give advice or express knowledge or expertise about matters about which he or she knows little. In addition, a person who is experiencing a manic episode may also attempt to create new inventions or initiate and conduct large-scale, difficult to accomplish projects. Patients with mania may even develop delusions of grandeur. For example, the afflicted individual may believe that he or she has a special relationship with a higher being, or in fact is deified. A person with mania may also change his or her physical appearance, possibly to be more sexually suggestive, or start to become a "show off."

Along with these symptoms, when a person is suffering from a manic episode, a change in sleep patterns often occurs. A patient with mania often has a decreased need for sleep. During the manic phase of a bipolar illness, a person may wake up full of energy despite the fact that they had slept only for a few hours. In more severe cases, some individuals may not sleep for several days.

Changes in speech may also occur during a manic episode. The presence of pressured speech is also a common symptom of mania. Patients with pressured speech often talk in a very loud and rapid manner. They may disregard others' desire to talk as well. To observers it may appear as though the afflicted individuals' thoughts are racing and that they cannot communicate their ideas fast enough. In more severe instances, a person's speech may become extremely disorganized and even incoherent. The person may tell jokes or amusing anecdotes and act in a theatrical or dramatic way. In addition, the individual's speech may be characterized by clanging (the use of words for their sound and not for their relevancy). Those individuals who have a manic episode associated with an irritable mood state may complain or make hostile comments.

Distractibility is also common during a manic episode. The patient is often unable to screen out irrelevant stimuli, making it difficult to concentrate on a particular conversation or task. People with mania-induced increases in goal-directed activity may unrealistically attempt to engage or participate in a large number of activities. In addition, the person may engage in very hasty decisions and take extreme risks without thinking about their consequences.

Engaging in antisocial or rebellious behaviors may be characteristic of an individual with mania, and he or she may disregard previous morals or concerns. Occasionally, a person may become violent or aggressive toward others or may possibly become suicidal. Hasty and extreme behavior may often result in financial debt or getting in trouble with the law. Other symptoms such as psychomotor agitation, restlessness and pacing may also be present during a manic episode. In addition, patients suffering from mania or mixed states can develop symptoms of psychosis.

Several difficulties may occur when trying to obtain treatment for adult patients with mania. Because the patient's mood state may be pleasurable, some people with mania deny that there is anything wrong with them. For this reason, they may resist seeking treatment. In addition, patients with mania may travel impulsively and subsequently lose contact with loved ones.

The other major form of bipolar disorder is bipolar II disorder. Individuals who suffer from this form of bipolar illness have symptoms similar to those who are afflicted with bipolar I disorder. Bipolar I disorder is primarily differentiated from bipolar II disorder by the briefer episode duration and the reduced severity of symptomatology that are present during manic-like mood states. These less extreme manic-like mood episodes are referred to as *hypomania*. Hypomania is defined as a distinct period that, like mania, is characterized by an abnormally elevated, expansive, or irritable mood. However, unlike mania, this episode needs to last only 4 days to meet diagnostic criteria for a hypomanic episode. Although psychotic features are not present during hypomanic episodes, symptoms seen during hypomania may be identical to those that occur during a manic episode. An episode of hypomania may lead to clinically significant changes from an individual's previous level of functioning, however, these changes are not as severe as those seen during manic episodes.

Despite the difference in the severity of mania between mania and hypomania, individuals with bipolar II disorder and bipolar I disorder may experience similar degrees of symptom severity during a major depressive episode. In addition, although the history of a major depressive episode is not necessary for a person to meet diagnostic criteria for bipolar I disorder, a history of a major depressive episode is necessary for a patient to meet full diagnostic symptom criteria for bipolar II disorder.

A subset of individuals may develop psychotic symptomatology during the course of a manic or mixed episode. Mood-congruent features usually characterize the psychotic symptoms experienced during a manic episode. The individual may have delusions that he or she has special or divine powers, or that he or she is deified. Similarly, the person with mania may have delusions of persecution that are related to grandiose themes. However, an individual suffering from a manic episode may experience mood-incongruent psychotic features. These may be characterized by persecutory delusions, thought insertion, thought broadcasting, delusions of control, or catatonia.

For those individuals who are suffering from a mixed episode, mood-congruent psychotic features can also be present. Usually, the afflicted individual suffers from psychotic features that are consistent with whichever mood state he or she is experiencing at the time. However, mood-incongruent symptoms can be present during a mixed state. The symptoms of psychosis may seriously impair the individual's functioning in occupational or social areas. In fact, the symptoms of psychosis may be severe enough to warrant psychiatric hospitalization.

The symptoms of bipolar affective disorder in children and adolescents appear to be similar to those in adults. However, the degree of severity for certain symptoms typically vary with age. For example, a study of the phenomenology of youths with bipolar disorder found that children younger than 9 years of age, who were suffering from mania, possessed symptoms of irritability, aggressiveness, and emotional lability. However, children older than 9 possessed symptoms of euphoria, grandiosity, and flight of ideas. Both age groups suffered from hyperactivity, pressure of speech, and distractibility.

Unlike children, adolescents seem to have a clinical presentation during manic episodes that is similar to that seen in adults. However, there is some evidence to suggest that hospitalized adolescents suffering from mania tend to have less psychotic symptomatology, higher rates of mixed bipolar disorder, and are less likely to suffer from substance abuse or dependence than are hospitalized adults who suffer from mania.

A major difficulty that occurs in youths with bipolar disorder is dysfunctional behavior associated with the diagnoses of conduct disorder and other disruptive behavioral disorders. For example, youths with bipolar disorder may be physically aggressive or may develop school truancy. What confounds this issue further is that some youths with bipolar disorder may have met symptom criteria for a disruptive behavioral disorder prior to the onset of their mood disorder.

Etiology

Although the etiology of bipolar disorder has not been established, it appears as if both genetic and nongenetic factors may contribute to the development of this syndrome. Evidence that genetics may play a role in the expression of this condition has come from family history studies. For example, it has been shown that there is an increased prevalence of bipolar disorder in the family members of children and adolescents afflicted with this condition. Furthermore, twin studies have revealed that there are higher rates of concordance for bipolar disorder in monozygotic than dizygotic twins. The concordance rates for monozygotic twins has been reported to be as high as 65%, in comparison to only 14% in dizygotic twins. There is evidence that genetic factors may play a particularly large role in the development of pediatric bipolarity. This comes from research that has found that patients with an earlier age at onset have higher prevalence rates bipolarity among family members than patients with later age of illness onset.

Further evidence that biological phenomena play an important role in the development of bipolar disorder comes from reports that there are structural brain differences between young patients with bipolar disorder and youths that do not suffer from bipolar disorder. For example, it has recently been reported that adolescents with bipolar disorder have reduced total cerebral brain volume when compared to a control group of teenagers who do not suffer from any psychiatric condition.

Other factors, such as environmental and social influences, have also been shown to contribute to development of bipolar disorder. For example, the onset of a manic episode often is preceded by a psychological stressor. This is particularly true early in the course of the illness. In addition, studies that have examined the influence of environment on the course of bipolar disorder have suggested that support from family, peers, and close friends might decrease the likelihood that a child will develop the disorder.

Differential Diagnosis and Treatment

There are several syndromes that possess symptoms similar to those that are characteristic of bipolar disorder. For example, attention-deficit hyperactivity disorder (ADHD) may possess symptoms similar to mania. These include hyperactivity, impulsive behavior, and distractibility. However, ADHD may be distinguished from bipolar disorder by ADHD's characteristic earlier age at onset; chronic (as opposed to episodic) course; lack of distinct, unprecipitated mood episodes; and the presence of psychotic symptoms. In addition, either substance abuse or a general medical condition can induce manic symptoms. For example, cocaine or psychostimulants may cause manic symptoms. There are some medications that may also lead to symptoms of mania. These include antidepressants or steroids. Several different types of general medical conditions may also cause manic symptoms. They include neurological, endocrine, metabolic, and infectious diseases. Because many other conditions must be considered before making the diagnosis of bipolar disorder, it is important to obtain a thorough evaluation when faced with a youngster for whom the diagnosis of bipolar disorder is being considered. Such an assessment should examine the nature and severity of the current symptoms, the longitudinal course of the condition, the youth's previous psychological functioning, and a careful familial history.

There are only limited data about the treatment of pediatric bipolarity. However, the mainstays of treatment are medications. Lithium carbonate, carbamazepine (Tegretol®), or divalproex sodium (Depakote®) are the most commonly prescribed treatments for young patients with bipolar disorder.

The available evidence suggests that lithium carbonate may be effective as both acute and maintenance therapy for youths with this illness. The side effects of lithium in children and adolescents are similar to those seen in adults. These include tremors, dyspepsia, nausea, weight gain, polyuria, and polydypsia. It should be noted that very young children may be at particularly high risk for lithium-induced side effects.

Carbamazepine and divalproex sodium also may have mood stabilizing properties in young people with bipolar disorder. Common side effects of carbamazepine include drowsiness, lightheadedness, clumsiness, nausea, and reduced white blood cell counts. Common side effects seen in young patients treated with divalproex sodium include nausea, dyspepsia, sedation, weight gain, and tremors.

In addition to pharmacotherapy, psychosocial interventions are often used in hopes of helping both the young patient and his or her family better understand and manage the disorder. Bipolar disorder can adversely effect a youth in a variety of settings outside of the home. For this reason, it is often useful for close family members and school personnel to be informed about the presence of the illness thereby providing to them a better understanding of how this condition might be affecting a youngster's day-to-day functioning.

Course and Prognosis

Bipolar disorder is a recurrent, cyclic disorder characterized by periods of mania, depression, or mixed states. As an individual grows older, the period between episodes tends to decrease, whereas the severity of episodes tends to increase. It should be noted that those individuals who suffer from psychotic features usually do not develop them until days or weeks after the onset of a mood episode. Conversely, in patients with schizophrenia, psychotic symptoms are prominent even when symptoms of a mood are not present. Patients who do develop psychotic features during a mood episode are at higher risk for developing psychotic features during subsequent episodes.

The specific prognosis for adolescents and children with bipolar disorder has not been extensively researched. However, it is generally thought that earlier age at onset and psychosocial dysfunction prior to the onset of the disorder are risk factors for a poorer prognosis.

SCHIZOAFFECTIVE DISORDER

Kraepelin's work at the turn of the 20th century, in which he distinguished dementia praecox (now known as schizophrenia) from manic depressive illness (bipolar disorder), has been considered one of the most important advances in the nosology of psychotic disorders. However, as time went on, there was an appreciation that some patients experienced symptoms of both schizophrenia and bipolar disorder either simultaneously or during different distinct episodes. The term schizoaffective disorder was introduced to describe this group of patients. According to the *DSM-IV*, schizoaffective disorder is categorized as a distinct psychotic disorder and not a mood disorder. It is approximately twice as prevalent in women as in men. However, because the disorder is less common than schizophrenia, research-based data regarding this condition in children and adolescents are relatively modest.

Symptoms and Psychotic Features

The symptoms of schizoaffective disorder are easily deduced from the name of the illness—the symptoms of schizophrenia and mood disorders occur together. According to the *DSM-IV*, schizoaffective disorder is characterized as an uninterrupted illness during which time criteria for schizophrenia as well as a major depressive, manic, or mixed episode are met. To meet criteria for schizoaffective disorder, a person must experience delusions or hallucinations for at least 2 weeks without the occurrence of mood symptoms. However, for a patient to be diagnosed as suffering from schizoaffective disorder, mood symptoms must be prominent and not transient throughout the duration of the illness. If mood symptoms are not present during most of the illness, then a diagnosis of schizophrenia or another psychotic disorder may be warranted. In addition, it should be noted that to meet symptom criteria for schizoaffective disorder, the mood symptoms that occur during the course of the illness must not be those induced by the presence of psychotic symptoms.

There are two subtypes of schizoaffective disorder: bipolar type and depressive type. Not surprisingly, those patients with schizoaffective disorder bipolar type have at one time met symptom criteria for a manic or mixed episode. Individuals who are suffering from schizoaffective disorder depressive type have met diagnostic criteria for a major depressive episode without ever having experienced a manic or mixed state. In summary, schizoaffective disorder is a combination of symptoms of schizophrenia and either depression or bipolar disorder.

The same diagnostic symptom criteria for schizoaffective disorder that are utilized in adults are also currently applicable to children and adolescents. Although there is a paucity of data, the bipolar subtype seems to be more common in adolescents and young adults, whereas the depressive subtype appears to be more common in older adults.

During an acute episode of schizoaffective disorder, an individual may suffer from psychotic symptoms similar to those seen in schizophrenia. These include delusions, hallucinations, and thought disturbances. The most common type of delusions is the paranoid type, however, other types of delusions may potentially be present. These delusions may be either mood congruent or incongruent. As far as hallucinations are concerned, auditory hallucinations are the most frequent form of hallucinations experienced in schizoaffective disorder. However, other types of hallucinations such as visual, tactile, olfactory, and gustatory may occur.

Age of Onset and Etiology

Schizoaffective disorder generally develops during the second or third decade of life. However, schizoaffective disorder may develop later in adulthood as well.

The precise etiology of schizoaffective disorder has yet to be delineated. As with schizophrenia and the mood disorders, most investigators believe that genetics can impart vulnerability to the development of schizoaffective disorder. The interaction between genes and environment, which was discussed in the section on schizophrenia, has not been as extensively investigated for schizoaffective disorder. However, many investigators and clinicians think environmental factors also play a role in the development of schizoaffective disorder.

Differential Diagnosis and Treatment

Because schizoaffective disorder shares symptomatology characteristic of other disorders such as major depressive disorder, bipolar disorder, and schizophrenia, it is important to consider the potential presence of these disorders prior to making the diagnosis of schizoaffective disorder. For example, during the course of schizophrenia, it is possible that an individual may suffer from a significant mood disturbance that does not meet symptom criteria for either a major depressive episode or a manic episode. Unfortunately, dysphoric mood and suicidal behavior can oftentimes complicate the course of patients with schizophrenia. However, the mood disturbances that are characteristically seen in patients with schizophrenia are relatively brief in comparison to the duration of the other psychotic features.

For those individuals who are having manic or depressive symptoms accompanied by hallucinations or delusions, it is advised that the duration and course of the psychotic symptoms be carefully assessed. By definition, if psychotic symptoms do not persist for at least two weeks in the absence of a mood disturbance, a diagnosis of a mood disorder may be more appropriate. It should be noted that patients who are currently in a manic episode can have symptoms of psychosis that may be difficult to distinguish from the psychotic symptoms observed in schizophrenia. Along this same avenue of thought, it is important for clinicians to remember that patients suffering from major depression with psychotic features may have delusional beliefs as well. If psychotic symptomatology is present only during episodes of a mood disorder, the diagnosis of schizoaffective disorder should not be made.

Two other factors must be considered and ruled out before one gives a patient the diagnosis of schizoaffective disorder. As with other psychotic disorders, the clinician should consider the possibility substance use or abuse may have caused the psychotic symptoms or mood states. In addition, if an individual is afflicted with a general medical condition, its important to exclude it as a possible causal factor.

Schizoaffective disorder shares many symptoms of schizophrenia and affective disorders, therefore, the cornerstone of treatment is pharmacological intervention. As noted earlier in the section on schizophrenia, there is very little controlled treatment research for juvenile schizophrenia. There are even fewer data available regarding the pharmacological treatment of pediatric schizoaffective disorder. However, it appears that much of what applies to the treatment of schizoaffective disorder in adults may be useful when formulating a pharmacological treatment plan for an adolescent suffering from schizoaffective disorder.

Generally speaking, the greatest change in the clinical approach to the adult patient with schizoaffective disorder has been the use of more than one medication at a time. As newer and safer medications have been introduced to treat both symptoms of psychosis and mood disorders, there has emerged a greater tendency to combine medications from the start of treatment. Therefore, it is not uncommon for an adult with schizoaffective disorder bipolar type to be taking both an antipsychotic and a mood stabilizer. The same holds true for schizoaffective depressive type in which patients are often administered both an antipsychotic and an antidepressant. However, it should be mentioned that there is a growing body of evidence to suggest that some of the newer antipsychotics can significantly affect a person's mood. Considering the relative paucity of treatment data, what is our current thinking about medications for schizoaffective disorder in young people?

We feel that the use of the new atypical antipsychotic medications is an important first step in reducing the symptoms of psychosis in young people with schizoaffective disorder. We choose the newer agents rather than the older, traditional medications because of the reduced risk of extrapyramidal side effects and seemingly better acceptability of these new medications. We believe that it is particularly important to be alert for the signs and symptoms of a mood disorder in first episode patients as either depression, mania, or mixed mood symptoms can cause morbidity and even mortality. This may be particularly difficult to do early in the course of treatment because some of the symptoms of schizophrenia may look similar to those of a mood disorder. For example, negative symptoms may be mistaken for depression and vice versa. However, over time, persistent sad mood should alert the clinician to the possibility of the presence of schizoaffective disorder depressed type. On the other end of the mood disorder spectrum, agitation, irritability, or disorganization seen during a period of psychosis might be misconstrued as symptoms of a manic episode. As with depressive symptoms, a clinician should be vigilant for symptoms of mania such as grandiosity and pressured speech.

In young adults, our impression has been that antipsychotic medications alone may reduce symptoms of psychosis for patients with schizoaffective disorder. However, some of these youths may continue to manifest symptoms of continued mood disturbance. For this reason, once the clinician has concluded that schizoaffective disorder is indeed present and has initiated a new antipsychotic medication, the appropriate mood medication should be added. For symptoms of depression, we generally add an SSRI such as fluoxetine, sertraline, or paroxetine. However, other antidepressants such as venlafaxine, nefazodone, or citalopram may also be used. For patients with schizoaffective disorder bipolar type we generally add either lithium carbonate or divalproex sodium (Depakote®) to the pharmacological regimen.

Unfortunately, there is little specific data available regarding psychosocial treatments for patients with schizoaffective disorder. For this reason, we generally adapt what is empirically known about the treatment of psychosis and mood disorders in adults. As a general rule, we feel family involvement in a psychoeducational program is crucial. Attempts at reducing high levels of expressed emotion in the family, may also be appropriate. Individual therapy aimed at problem solving, social skills, and cognitive rehabilitation should all be considered. Group therapies that discuss issues related to self-esteem and emotional support may also be important interventions in the comprehensive approach to the young patient with schizoaffective disorder.

Course and Prognosis

It appears that the prognosis for adults with schizoaffective disorder is better than that for adults with schizophrenia but less optimistic than for adults with mood disorders. However, there are few data about the outcome of schizoaffective disorder in young people. A study that investigated the eventual prognosis of 22 adolescents with schizoaffective disorder reported that a large proportion of patients experienced educational or occupational impairment. Seven years after hospitalization almost half of the patients, by then adults, still lived with their parents and only about a quarter of these patients attained their educational goals. The rest of the sample had moderate to severe difficulties in attaining their educational or career goals. Based on the results of this study, it appears that adolescents with schizoaffective disorder have an outcome that is more comparable to individuals who suffer from schizophrenia than to individuals who suffer from an affective disorder. Considering these pessimistic outcome data, it is important that youths with schizoaffective disorder receive a comprehensive treatment approach in the hopes of improving the prognosis of these young patients.

BEREAVEMENT

Although the symptoms of bereavement can mimic those of major depressive disorder, in the current psychiatric nosology, bereavement is considered within the category of additional conditions that may be a focus of clinical attention. The exact prevalence of bereavement is not known, but it is likely that the condition is fairly common because its onset is triggered by the death of a loved one. However, because bereavement is an important diagnostic consideration in a youth for whom a psychotic disorder is suspected, a description of this condition in children and adolescents is necessary.

Bereavement is the emotional experience of grieving that follows the death of a loved one and it often is accompanied by symptoms of depression. The common depressive symptoms associated with bereavement include sadness, insomnia, decreased appetite, and weight loss. Other symptoms that may occur after a loss that are not part of the typical bereavement process include feelings of worthlessness, psychomotor retardation, pronounced functional impairment, and hallucinations consisting of voices other than that of the deceased loved one. Although the period of bereavement varies in length from culture to culture and person to person, if significant emotional distress persists for longer than a few months, a diagnosis of a major depressive episode may be warranted.

Symptoms and Psychotic Features

Most of the literature on child and adolescent bereavement has considered clinical populations. Therefore, the natural history of bereavement in children and adolescents who did not present for clinical care has not been fully described.

Assessing a youth in whom bereavement is suspected may be difficult. This is not due only to the relative lack of scientific data available about the phenomenon, but is also due to the multiple ways in which bereavement may be expressed in the young. There is clearly a broad range of symptoms that may characterize bereavement. Youths who are suffering from bereavement may become withdrawn, sad, and may lose interest in their favorite activities. Specifically, a youth may begin to decline in school performance and fail courses. The grieving youth may also withdraw from extracurricular activities such as sports and hobbies. Most young people who have suffered a loss will show symptoms of bereavement within the first year following that loss. However, it has been shown that approximately one third of children may have symptoms of bereavement as late as 5 years after the death of a loved one. Studies also indicate that boys tend to manifest more externalizing, potentially disruptive behaviors during bereavement than do girls. Younger children (under the age of 10) may use maladaptive mechanisms to deal with the death such as denying that it occurred or believing that it is reversible. It appears that these maladaptive defense mechanisms are not seen as frequently in older children and adolescents. This may be due in part to the fact that younger children have not reached the level of cognitive development which would enable them to fully understand the exact nature and permanence of death and loss.

Psychotic symptoms do not usually appear during bereavement, rather, their presence should lead the clinician to suspect the development of a more serious condition such as a major depressive episode. However, psychotic features have been associated with severe cases of bereavement. These symptoms typically concern themes of death and may also consist of visual and auditory hallucinations of the deceased loved one. Case studies of children with severe bereavement have suggested that the onset of psychotic symptoms in these youths was secondary to a mourning process that was not complete. Essentially, the child's hallucinations of the deceased were a reflection of the child's wishes to have the deceased return so that the parent-child relationship could be restored.

Etiology

By definition, bereavement is triggered by the loss of a loved one. However, more severe bereavement has been reported to be associated with several environmental factors that were present before the experienced loss. In cases of parental death, family and parental dysfunction, marital conflict, severe parental psychopathology, prolonged or repeated parental absence, the use of guilt by the adult caregivers, negative parent-child relationships, and family isolation have all been thought to adversely influence a child's bereavement process.

In addition to environmental influences that were present prior to the death of a loved one, the emergence of emotional and behavioral difficulties seen in some bereaved children may also be related to factors that occur after the precipitating event. For example, it has been suggested that a surviving parent's inability to share and express feelings of grief with the child after a loss may lead to dysfunction in the grieving child. It is possible that this may be caused, in part, by the surviving parent making it difficult for the child to express his or her own feelings about their own grieving, thereby increasing feelings of anxiety and confusion in the child.

Investigators have considered circumstances that may be associated with the development of depressive symptomatology in children who have lost either a mother or father. It has been found that four factors put bereaved children at higher risk for depressive symptomatology after the death of a parent. These included the death of a father, the presence of an untreated psychiatric disorder prior to parental demise, a family history of depression, and higher socioeconomic status. In addition, it has been described that the level of warmth between the surviving parent and the youth also tended to affect the young person's ability to adjust to a loss.

Differential Diagnosis and Treatment

As mentioned previously, bereavement is diagnosed when an individual has suffered the loss of a loved one through death. However, the possibility of another diagnosis may exist, especially if pronounced symptoms persist longer than 2 months after the loss. At that point, a diagnosis of a major depressive episode, among other disorders, should be considered (and may be justified) if diagnostic symptom criteria are met.

According to current nosology, there are several symptoms that may differentiate a major depressive episode from bereavement. Patients with bereavement complicated by major depressive episodes often have guilt feelings about things that are unrelated to the loss, thoughts of death that are not associated with wanting to be with the deceased person, morbid preoccupation with worthlessness, noticeable psychomotor retardation, prolonged functional impairment, and hallucinatory experiences not related to the deceased loved one. If any of these symptoms are present, it may be useful to consider an alternative diagnosis to bereavement.

Treatments for bereaved youths can occur within the context of individual, family, or group therapies. The use of pharmacotherapy for the treatment of child and adolescent bereavement appears not to be very common and is generally not recommended.

Means by which a child can be helped to cope with a loss of a loved one in psychotherapy have been described. These steps include working with the child to understand and accept both the reality of the death as well as the associated rituals associated with death. This may include explaining to the child how death occurs and why people are often buried in a ceremonial fashion. Another step in the process is allowing the child to mourn or adapt to the permanent loss of the deceased loved one. The last step involves helping the child to resume functioning following the mourning process. Often a child's inability to sufficiently mourn for the loss is what leads to the child's inability to resume normal functioning. A strong support network that instills a sense of safety and security in the child and allows the youth to mourn the loss adequately may facilitate the youth's recovery from the loss.

Consistent with this idea, others have reported that bereaved children who participated in six family therapy sessions that addressed the mourning process exhibited higher levels of functioning following treatment when compared to controls who did not receive therapy. These family therapy sessions focused on increasing communication between the child and the surviving parent and facilitating expression of thoughts and feelings about the deceased loved one. Children who were able to express their grief through crying tended to possess less behavior problems afterwards, suggesting that these young people were better able to adapt to their loss.

Course and Prognosis

The duration with which symptoms of bereavement persist and the outcome of children and adolescents who have suffered from bereavement can vary widely. It has been suggested that the death of a same-sex parent tends to elicit a poor outcome for a bereaved child. There is also evidence to support the assertion that children and adolescents who have lost a parent due to suicide may subsequently have more difficulties than youths who experience the loss of a parent due to other circumstances. It has also been noted that children who suffer from bereavement in early childhood are more likely to develop a psychiatric disorder later on during childhood. In addition, it has been found that bereaved children are five times more likely to develop a psychiatric disorder when compared to the general population.

As can be seen, bereavement can be associated with both acute and long-term consequences for children and adolescents. In some cases, symptoms of psychosis may be present. For this reason, when faced with a youth who is experiencing hallucinations that pertain to a deceased loved one or is having thoughts of death, guilt, or self-reproach, the diagnosis of bereavement should be considered.

4

OTHER PSYCHOTIC DISORDERS

SCHIZOPHRENIFORM DISORDER

Schizophreniform disorder is characterized by the same symptoms as schizophrenia. The difference between schizophreniform disorder and schizophrenia, therefore, is not in measures of phenomenology or severity, but rather in the length of time an individual has been suffering from psychotic symptomatology. In our view, the creation of the diagnosis, schizophreniform disorder, is probably an attempt to reduce over diagnosis of schizophrenia. Although the condition is considered to be part of the differential diagnosis for schizophrenia it has not been a subject of extensive scientific study. Relatively little is known about schizophreniform disorder.

Despite this fact, we feel the issues surrounding schizophreniform disorder are important for clinicians working with children and adolescents because of the large number of people who experience their first symptoms of schizophrenia during the pre-adult years. Because males develop schizophrenia earlier than females, we would estimate that child and adolescent psychiatrists and psychologists might be seeing anywhere from one third to one half of all males as they are initially presenting with symptoms of schizophrenia.

Because there is so little research to date, parameters that could assist in determining whether or not schizophreniform disorder is a specific condition do not exist. Therefore, it is reasonable to question whether schizophreniform disorder is actually an illness or whether it represents the early stages of schizophrenia. The little data gathered on this question generally indicates that the majority of young people who meet symptom criteria for schizophreniform disorder eventually meet diagnostic criteria for schizophrenia.

What, then, are the clinical utility and importance of the schizophreniform disorder diagnosis for child and adolescent mental health professionals? The schizophreniform disorder diagnostic category can be used when the clinician is uncertain whether the diagnosis of schizophrenia is present in a youth with psychotic symptoms. For patients and their families, the diagnosis of schizophrenia is a most difficult one to hear. The use of the diagnosis of schizophreniform disorder may hold hope to a family that a resolution of symptoms is possible. In our clinical experience, the discussion of a diagnosis of schizophreniform disorder at the early stages of psychotic symptoms is a reasonable way to break the news of a youth's psychosis to both patients and their families. On the other hand, we have found that the discussion of schizophreniform disorder may enhance denial in youngsters and families. This may lead to problems later in the course of treatment regarding the use of psychiatric medications or lead to questions regarding whether there is even a psychiatric illness that is truly present. Clinicians, therefore, must consider these issues when working with a young person with psychosis who presents early in the course of an illness with symptoms of schizophrenia.

Symptoms and Psychotic Features

The symptoms of schizophreniform disorder are the same as those listed in the *DSM-IV* for schizophrenia. These symptoms have been reviewed at length in the section on schizophrenia, however, as a brief review, they include hallucinations, delusions of an unusual nature, and thought disorder. Obviously, then, schizophreniform disorder is not to be used for any short-term psychotic illness, but is reserved for those patients with schizophrenia-like symptoms. There are two differences between schizophreniform disorder and schizophrenia. The *DSM-IV* states that the requirement for decreased functioning is not mandatory in order to make the diagnosis of schizophreniform disorder (although diminished function is often present). Secondly, schizophrenia is an illness in which symptoms have been present for at least six months (including prodrome, psychotic symptom state, and residual symptoms). For schizophreniform disorder, the length of time of symptomatology is 1 to 6 months. However, it should be noted that schizophreniform disorder may include any or all of the following phases: prodromal, active, and residual.

The term *provisional* can modify the classification of schizophreniform disorder. This modification is appropriate to use if it is unclear whether the total length of symptomatology will in fact be 6 months. For example, this modification would be used in the case of a young person who has had 3 months of symptoms and these symptoms have not yet resolved. This classification would be modified if symptoms were still present for a period of time longer than 6 months. At that point, such a patient would be rediagnosed as suffering from schizophrenia. In the case of a person who has "recovered," the diagnosis of schizophreniform disorder may be made without modification.

Research on schizophreniform disorder among children and adolescents is minimal. However, research that has focused on the occurrence of schizophreniform disorder in children and adolescents indicates that the symptoms of schizophreniform disorder in the young are comparable to those observed in adults.

People with schizophreniform disorder have psychotic symptoms similar to those with schizophrenia. These symptoms include auditory or visual hallucinations, delusional thinking, and bizarre behavior. It has been suggested that patients with schizophreniform disorder may have less negative symptoms and less of a thought disorder than patients with schizophrenia do.

Etiology

Considering the fact that the symptoms of schizophreniform disorder are very similar to the symptoms of schizophrenia, one would assume that this disorder might be due to the same factors that are hypothesized to cause schizophrenia. The possible etiologic factors that contribute to the development of schizophrenia were reviewed in Chapter 2. Briefly stated, schizophrenia is an illness with a well-proven family aggregation which most clinical investigators believe provides a genetic vulnerability to a psychotic illness under certain environmental factors. Like schizophrenia, genetic and environmental risk factors appear to contribute to the development of schizophreniform disorder.

We are not aware of any research that indicates that the pathophysiology of schizophreniform disorder is any different from that for schizophrenia. However, it is unclear what the pathophysiology of schizophreniform disorder is in those patients who eventually remit and remain asymptomatic off medication. In our opinion, this research question would be most difficult to address because of the small number of cases in whom this occurs. This does not diminish the potential importance of such a research project to understanding the characteristics of patients who make full recoveries.

There has been some debate about the exact relation between schizophreniform disorder and schizophrenia. Although there is evidence that schizophreniform disorder is, indeed, related to schizophrenia, other research has suggested that the disorder may be related to affective disorders. Moreover, other studies have suggested that schizophreniform disorder be considered as its own entity. Because of these uncertainties, others have even questioned the validity of the diagnosis altogether. Due to these unanswered questions, it is clear that schizophreniform disorder should be a topic of further investigation.

Differential Diagnosis and Treatment

As noted in the section on schizophrenia, and of importance for a teenager reporting schizophreniform symptoms, the differential diagnosis of a relatively brief period of psychotic symptoms includes an investigation of potential medical illnesses that might mimic schizophreniform psychosis. This includes an assessment (both clinical history and laboratory based) for substances of abuse. A thorough evaluation of the patient (including a careful family history) regarding the possible presence of bipolar illness as well as major depression with psychotic features should also be performed. The psychosis that can occur in patients with borderline personality disorder or schizotypal personality disorder should also be considered in the differential diagnosis.

There are few data available regarding the treatment of schizophreniform disorder in young people. There is evidence that both typical and atypical antipsychotics are useful in the treatment of adults with this condition. Based on the limited available research and our own clinical experience, if after a careful evaluation the working diagnosis for a young patient is schizophreniform disorder, we generally recommend the use of new, first-line, atypical antipsychotic medications. Our experience in youths having their first psychotic episode is that these newer antipsychotic medications not only effectively reduce symptoms but also provide improved acceptability when compared to the traditional antipsychotic agents. Prior to the introduction of these new medications, there may have been a tendency for the physician to wait to begin antipsychotic medication treatment because of concerns regarding the substantial side effects associated with the older antipsychotic agents. However, recent research has indicated that there may be a substantial negative impact on the longer-term course of a psychotic illness when there is a delay in beginning antipsychotic medication treatment. Therefore, we encourage the use of the atypical antipsychotics when the diagnosis of schizophreniform disorder has been made.

As noted earlier in this section, some clinicians feel that there is a small group of patients who exhibit the symptoms of schizophreniform disorder who then go on to recover and do not require antipsychotic medication treatment. The field continues to struggle with how to identify such people. Some clinical investigators have indicated that a medication-free period after 1 year of treatment may allow the clinician to find those patients who no longer need medicines. However, this strategy remains controversial, as there are very little data about longer-term outcomes when this intervention is employed. We would like to note that if a patient continues to manifest any residual symptoms, even if they are significantly reduced from previous levels, that medication discontinuation should not be encouraged.

The issue of medication discontinuation in schizophreniform stages of schizophrenia is compounded by the practical reality that most young people will surreptitiously try to stop their medications during the first and second years of treatment. Unfortunately, in our experience, this often leads to relapse of symptoms and frequently hospitalization.

Course and Prognosis

It is difficult to describe the course and prognosis of schizophreniform disorder because there are so few studies of its longer-term outcome. As noted earlier, the few studies that have been performed indicate that most patients with this condition go on to be rediagnosed with schizophrenia. Once they receive a diagnosis of schizophrenia, then the course and prognosis is the same for that illness. In many ways, the diagnostic category schizophreniform disorder is somewhat artificial as it may be describing the early phase of schizophrenia.

The *DSM-IV* allows the clinician to assign patients with schizophreniform disorder to either *good* or *poor* prognostic categories. Although clinical investigators are still struggling to define the characteristics of patients with schizophreniform disorder who are at high risk for poor outcome, poor response to treatment, or both, a patient with rapid onset of psychotic symptoms who has been functioning well premorbidly may have a better longer-term outcome.

One concern that exists about the diagnostic category of schizophreniform disorder is that *DSM-IV* is silent on the question of medication treatment as it relates to recovery from psychotic symptoms. In other words, if a young person receives the provisional diagnosis of schizophreniform disorder and has a complete remission of symptoms with one of the new antipsychotic medications, it is unclear whether or not such a patient should be diagnosed with schizophreniform disorder. Clearly further research into this important area is needed.

BRIEF PSYCHOTIC DISORDER

The *DSM-IV* currently has a diagnostic category of *brief psychotic disorder*—a diagnosis to be used when a person has a rapid onset of psychosis which subsequently resolves and allows the person to return to baseline functioning within one month of symptom onset. The previous diagnostic designation for a brief, circumscribed period of psychosis was *brief reactive psychosis*. It is appropriate that this term is no longer used because causality from stress is often difficult to determine. Brief psychotic disorder is one of the least understood of the psychotic disorders. Currently, its prevalence among the general population is unknown.

As with schizophreniform disorder, the designation of brief psychotic disorder is intended to prevent the overdiagnosing of schizophrenia. However, recent studies have shown that patients with a brief psychotic disorder frequently fulfill criteria for schizophrenia at follow up. Therefore, it is important that the diagnosis of brief psychotic disorder be employed judiciously. Just as over-diagnosis of schizophrenia is to be avoided, it is also important not to miss the beginnings of schizophrenia.

What then is the relevance of the diagnosis of brief psychotic disorder when assessing or treating children and adolescents? Youths clearly have many developmentally related tasks to master. These tasks when coupled with other stressors may cause significant distress in a young person. It is possible that some of these children or teenagers who are less well equipped to withstand these vicissitudes may have a brief psychotic episode.

Symptoms and Psychotic Features

According to the *DSM-IV*, brief psychotic disorder is characterized by the sudden appearance of at least one positive psychotic symptom. However, unlike schizophrenia, the type of psychosis present in a patient with brief psychotic disorder is not further clarified. Therefore, a patient with hallucinations, delusions, disorganized behavior, catatonia, or thought disorder would fulfill diagnostic symptom criteria for this condition. By definition, this disorder is a brief psychotic illness. The duration of the disorder typically is between one day and one month after which time the individual with this condition returns to his or her normal state of functioning.

There is not a large amount of phenomenological research that has considered the symptoms of brief psychotic disorder in children and adolescents. However, a recent study described the phenomenology of brief episodes with psychotic features during adolescence. In the 11 teenagers described in this report, paranoia and depressive symptomatology often characterized the episodes that these patients experienced. However, given the small sample size and limited data, it is important not to conclude that these symptoms generally occur in youths who suffer from brief psychotic disorder.

As previously mentioned, the characteristic psychotic features for this disorder are delusions, hallucinations disorganized speech, and disorganized or catatonic behavior.

Age of Onset and Etiology

The age of onset of brief psychotic disorder typically is during young adulthood. The average age of onset is typically either in the third or fourth decade of life.

Several theories exist regarding the cause of brief psychotic disorder. One hypothesis is that either a series of stressful events or one major stressor triggers the onset of the disorder. A corollary to this is that individuals with either preexisting psychopathology or an underlying genetic predisposition are at risk for developing the disorder during stressful periods. It should be noted that for some patients with a brief psychotic disorder, a precipitating stressor can not be identified.

Differential Diagnosis and Treatment

Prior to giving a patient a diagnosis of a brief psychotic disorder, one must consider several other disorders that have symptoms in common with this condition. We have stressed throughout this book that for adolescents suffering from a psychotic episode, a full physical examination and laboratory assessment are required to ascertain whether a general medical condition is causing the psychosis. Because this disorder usually has a very rapid onset, the possibility of substance abuse or a seizure disorder must also be ruled out.

When considering the diagnosis of a patient with brief psychotic disorder, it is essential to ascertain the duration of the condition. If a psychotic episode persists for more than one month, then the possibility of schizophreniform disorder, schizoaffective disorder, or schizophrenia should be considered.

Other disorders that should be considered in a patient with a brief psychotic episode include mood disorders that may be accompanied by psychotic features. The literature on brief psychotic disorder has also noted that brief, sudden psychotic episodes may occur when patients suffer from a personality disorder. Our clinical research indicates that young adults with borderline as well as other personality disorders can suffer from sudden, usually stress-related, psychotic episodes. If there is clear-cut secondary gain, malingering may also be a possibility. However, it is our opinion that the mimicking of psychosis is quite difficult for a teenager or child.

As with schizophreniform disorder, the *DSM-IV* is silent regarding how best to diagnose a patient with a brief psychotic episode whose symptoms resolve with treatment. Therefore, there may be some question about the accuracy of a diagnosis of brief psychotic disorder when a young person had psychotic symptoms, was treated with an antipsychotic medication, and had a complete remission of symptoms within 4 weeks. In such a patient, if the medications were discontinued 6 months later and the patient's psychotic symptoms quickly recurred, that patient would probably more appropriately be diagnosed as having schizophrenia. Therefore, at present, there are some uncertainties about how optimally to diagnose such patients.

However, it is quite clear that there are numerous other conditions that may present in a fashion similar to that of a brief psychotic disorder. Thus, careful consideration of these other conditions is highly recommended prior to making this diagnosis.

At present, there are no proven treatments for this disorder. Our experience in young adults is that a brief psychosis can resolve in a short period of time—frequently during a brief inpatient hospitalization if the patient is at risk for self-harm. Brief inpatient stays can be useful to decrease external stress and provide support and structure. If symptoms resolve within the first 2 days, no medication may be required. In our opinion, when psychotic symptoms are present for longer than 48 hours, or if there is substantial symptom severity, medication should be prescribed. In this instance, we would suggest utilization of new, atypical antipsychotic medications because of their lower rates of side effects.

Course and Prognosis

Brief psychotic disorder, by definition, only lasts for about one month, after which time the individual returns to his or her previous level of normal functioning. Approximately half of the adults who receive an initial diagnosis of brief psychotic disorder will retain this diagnosis at follow-up. However, the other half of these cases will subsequently meet criteria for another diagnosis such as schizophrenia or a mood disorder.

Among the minimal information that exists regarding children and adolescents with brief psychotic disorder, it appears that the eventual prognosis for this cohort tends to vary also. It has been reported that some young patients with brief psychotic episodes suffer from recurrences, others eventually meet criteria for bipolar disorder, and some remain symptom free.

POSTPARTUM PSYCHOSIS

Postpartum psychosis, also known as puerperal psychosis, is a condition which by definition, occurs within the postpartum period. Therefore, this disorder affects adult and adolescent females who are of childbearing age. The prevalence of the disorder is approximately 0.2% in women who have given birth for the first time. For those women who have previously suffered from an episode of postpartum psychosis, the risk of experiencing another postpartum episode of psychosis increases to about 33% after subsequent births. What follows is a description of the characteristics of this syndrome in adult and adolescent females.

Symptoms and Psychotic Features

Although many patients with postpartum psychosis experience symptoms that are characteristic of either a manic, depressive, or mixed episode, the symptoms of some individuals with postpartum psychosis are similar to those seen in patients with schizophrenia. According to current nosology, a mood or a psychotic episode may be considered to be associated with postpartum onset if it begins within 4 weeks of delivery, however, there have been reports of postpartum psychosis developing up to 3 to 4 months postpartum.

Characteristics of postpartum psychosis may include agitation, rapid mood fluctuations, and psychotic features. At first, a teenager may have symptoms of confusion, depersonalization, and insomnia, which are then followed by the emergence of hallucinations and delusions. In addition, an afflicted teenager may suffer from suicidal ideation, obsessional thoughts, poor concentration, disorientation, and agitation. A recent study reported that symptoms of mania and confusion tended to be more prevalent in women who developed the disorder within the first two weeks postpartum than those who had developed the disorder a few months later.

Hallucinations and delusions that pertain to themes regarding the newborn infant typically characterize the psychotic features of postpartum psychosis. The teenager may believe that the infant is possessed or is destined for a terrible fate. She may hear voices that command her to harm the infant. Both the hallucinations and delusions may result in the individual becoming violent toward the infant. Approximately 4% of women with postpartum psychosis will ultimately commit infanticide.

Etiology

Currently, several hypotheses exist as to the cause of postpartum psychosis. However, a definitive etiology has yet to be established. There is a preponderance of evidence to suggest that biological factors contribute to the development of postpartum psychosis.

This assertion is supported by the fact that the prevalence of the disorder appears to be fairly consistent across cultures and over time. For example, several studies have shown that the rates of admission into a mental facility for women who are in the postpartum period have remained stable from the 19th century to the present. In addition, the rates of the illness in both nonindustrialized and industrialized countries are approximately the same. Although changes in hormone levels or alterations in neural transmission have been hypothesized as possible contributors to the pathophysiology of the syndrome of postpartum psychosis, no definitive biological marker has been shown to be associated with the development of the condition.

Further evidence to suggest that biological factors contribute to the development of postpartum psychosis comes from a study that noted a comparable incidence of postpartum psychosis in wartime and times of peace. Because wartime is a significant environmental stressor, the fact that similar rates of postpartum psychosis occurred during both periods suggests that environmental factors do not contribute to the development of postpartum psychosis. More recently, others have also noted that high rates of stress are not associated with the development of postpartum psychosis.

Conversely, there is evidence to suggest that environmental stress may play a role in the expression of postpartum psychosis. A recent study reported that postpartum psychosis was more prevalent in women who had given birth to a female child. It is possible that this may be a reflection of the impact that cultural expectations may have on the development of the disorder. In addition, these investigators found that women who gave birth to an unwanted child suffered from puerperal psychosis more so than did other women.

It has also been suggested that stress may play a more prominent role in the development of postpartum psychosis in those women who are genetically predisposed to developing psychosis. In those high-risk individuals who have family histories of psychotic symptoms, it has been hypothesized that a significant life stressor, such as the birth of a child, may trigger a psychotic episode.

Because there is conflicting evidence about the relation between the emergence of postpartum psychosis and stress, it is possible that some stressors may contribute more to the development of the disorder than do others. Those stressors that may specifically contribute to the development of postpartum psychosis have yet to be definitively established.

Differential Diagnosis and Treatment

Symptoms of nonpuerperal conditions such as bipolar disorder, major depression, schizophrenia, and other psychotic disorders may all be expressed in the postpartum period. For this reason, when faced with a teenager with postpartum psychosis, the clinician is obligated to perform a thorough diagnostic assessment to rule out the possibility of another psychiatric disorder. Key components to the psychiatric assessment should include a detailed past psychiatric history, a thorough family history, and a careful review of the patient's previous psychosocial functioning.

In addition to a psychiatric assessment, the clinician should ensure that all necessary general medical and obstetric examinations and laboratory tests are performed to rule out the possibility that an obstetric complication, another general medical condition, or a substance-related psychosis is an etiology for the patient's psychotic symptoms. Regardless of the diagnosis that is established, it is important to remember that the well-being of two individuals, both the patient and the infant, must be ensured during the assessment process.

There are several different approaches used in the treatment of postpartum psychosis. If indicated, the affected mother should be hospitalized to reduce the risk of her inflicting harm either to herself or to her infant. Pharmacological treatment is aimed at the underlying symptom clusters. If the woman appears to be suffering from a psychotic disorder and not a mood disorder, antipsychotic medications may be prescribed to ameliorate symptom severity. If a bipolar spectrum disorder is present, mood stabilizing medications such as lithium carbonate or anticonvulsant mood stabilizers may also be used. Similarly, if the symptoms are consistent with those of a depressive disorder, antidepressant medications may be considered.

Supportive psychotherapeutic techniques also may be used to help the affected teenager recover from an episode of postpartum psychosis. However, these interventions are usually not implemented until after the antipsychotic medication has begun to reduce the psychotic symptomatology. There is evidence that psychiatric units that allow both the mother and the infant to be hospitalized together may effectively promote maternal-child bonding in addition to providing psychiatric treatment to the mother. In addition to pharmacotherapy and psychotherapy techniques, electroconvulsive therapy may be used to treat some cases of postpartum psychosis. As with other disorders, the utilization of ECT generally occurs when pharmacotherapy has not been shown to be effective or is contraindicated for the individual.

Course and Prognosis

With early intervention, the prognosis for postpartum psychosis is usually good. Symptoms typically disappear within 2 to 3 weeks for those who respond well to treatment. However, even with effective treatment, the teenager is still thought to be at risk for relapse as late as 12 months postpartum. For this reason, maintenance treatment with low doses of antipsychotic medication is generally considered to prevent the recurrence of psychotic symptoms. In addition, because the chances of developing postpartum psychosis after subsequent births is increased in patients who have suffered from a prior episode of postpartum psychosis, the physician should closely monitor a patient's condition following future deliveries.

DELUSIONAL DISORDER

Delusional disorder is relatively uncommon among the general population. According to the *DSM-IV*, the lifetime prevalence rate for the condition is approximately .03%. Evidence has shown that delusional disorder accounts for approximately 1% to 2% of inpatient psychiatric admissions. As far as gender distribution is concerned, delusional disorder appears at equal rates in both men and women. Given the low prevalence rate, it is not surprising that this disorder has not been studied extensively.

Symptoms and Psychotic Features

The primary feature of delusional disorder is the presence of at least one or more persistent, nonbizarre delusions. What distinguishes a nonbizarre delusion from a bizarre delusion is that the former actually has a remote likelihood of occurring, whereas the latter typically does not. Prior to making a diagnosis of delusional disorder an individual's cultural background must be considered. Certain beliefs that are considered plausible in one culture may seem idiosyncratic in another. Therefore, it is important to assess, based on the cultural context of a given patient, whether or not an individual's thoughts are bizarre. It should also be noted that individuals with delusional disorder often tenaciously adhere to their delusions. It is often quite difficult for other individuals to convince the afflicted person about the erroneous nature of their delusion(s).

Auditory or visual hallucinations are not usual features of this condition. If hallucinations do occur, they are not prominent and are typically related to the delusional theme. In addition, as compared with patients with schizophrenia, the psychosocial functioning of an individual with delusional disorder is often not substantially impaired, and his or her behavior is not typically noted to be bizarre or odd. If an individual with delusional disorder has social or occupational dysfunction, it is usually due to the effects of the delusion. For example, an individual with delusional disorder may begin to exhibit odd behavior if he or she is discussing the delusion with another individual or is acting on the delusion. In addition, an individual with delusional disorder may incorporate random occurrences into the delusional theme. Due to the intense feelings that can be generated by these delusional beliefs, mood disturbances may occur in patients with delusional disorder. However, the mood disturbances seen in delusional disorder are typically brief in comparison to the duration of the condition and are usually in reaction to events related to the delusion.

There are several subtypes of delusional disorder. Individuals who have the erotomanic subtype typically have delusions that someone—typically a famous person or one who possesses a higher socioeconomic status—is in love with him or her. Often the afflicted individual may try to seek contact with the loved person.

People who suffer from the grandiose subtype of delusional disorder may believe that they possess a great talent that is yet to be recognized. They may also believe that they have a large amount of insight or have made an important discovery.

Those who suffer from the jealous subtype believe that their mate is being unfaithful. This belief is typically founded on little or no evidence. Affected individuals frequently confront their spouses about their fidelity or conduct extensive investigations based on their beliefs of unfaithfulness.

Individuals who suffer from the paranoid subtype believe that they are being spied on, conspired against, followed, or harassed. They may claim that trivial things are supportive of their beliefs. In turn, they may decide to take legal action to halt this perceived harassment. Similarly, those with this subtype of delusional disorder may become angry or bitter to the point of becoming violent toward others.

People with the somatic subtype often possess delusions related to their bodies. These may be characterized by the belief that their bodies are emitting foul odors, that there is an infestation of insects underneath their skin, or that they have an internal parasite. Individuals may also believe that certain parts of their bodies are deformed or not functioning properly.

Not all individuals with delusional disorder can be diagnosed as suffering from one of these five subtypes of delusional disorder. If this is the case, then the patient should be diagnosed either as suffering from a mixed subtype or an unspecified subtype of delusional disorder. People with the mixed subtype of delusional disorder have clear delusions that are not circumscribed to a single specific theme. Patients should be diagnosed with the unspecified subtype of delusional disorder when they have many delusional themes and one or two dominant themes cannot be clearly delineated.

Few studies have focused primarily on the symptoms of delusional disorder in children and adolescents. One report described the symptoms and eventual prognosis of an adolescent who had presented with a somatic delusion with distinct obsessional features. This individual was 17 years old at the time when the symptoms began. Based on this one case study, it appears that delusional disorder may manifest itself similarly in adolescents and adults. There is yet to be a clear description of how the disorder may affect children, however.

In addition to delusions, individuals with this disorder may also suffer from hallucinations. However, hallucinations that occur during the course of this illness are usually infrequent and are not a prominent component of the condition. The most common type of hallucination seen in patients with delusional disorder is auditory, but visual hallucinations may occur as well. Tactile or olfactory hallucinations may also be present, especially if they are related directly to the delusional theme.

Age of Onset and Etiology

Typically, individuals do not develop delusional disorder until they reach adulthood. However, the symptoms can potentially begin as early as adolescence.

The cause of delusional disorders has not been completely elucidated. Social isolation, internal conflicts, being an immigrant, and having low intelligence may be risk factors associated with the development of the condition. However, there is some evidence to support that genetics may have a role in the expression of the disorder. Some research has shown that individuals with delusional disorder have family members who are more suspicious, jealous, secretive, and paranoid than are families of controls. In addition, it has been reported that individuals with delusional disorder are more likely to have family members with paranoid or avoidant personality disorder than are individuals with schizophrenia or normal controls.

Differential Diagnosis and Treatment

Needless to say, delusional disorder is characterized by prominent delusions. If hallucinations are present they are infrequent. When faced with a patient with these symptoms, it is important for the clinician to remember that substance abuse or general medical conditions may precipitate the emergence of the delusional symptoms. For example, patients with either delirium or dementia may develop delusions. Similarly, patients with amphetamine abuse may become delusional.

To make an accurate diagnosis, delusional disorder should be differentiated from both schizophrenia and schizophreniform disorder. This can be readily accomplished because the delusions of schizophrenia or schizophreniform disorder are often bizarre and are commonly accompanied by other symptoms such as hallucinations, disorganized speech, negative symptoms or catatonic behavior. In addition, people who suffer from schizophrenia or schizophreniform disorder generally have significantly more impairment in functioning in both occupational and social areas when compared to those patients with delusional disorder.

Along with psychotic disorders, one must also consider the possibility of a mood disorder, such as major depressive or bipolar disorder, as the potential causal factor in a patient with delusions. To delineate whether or not a patient is truly suffering from a mood disorder, one must take into consideration the temporal relationship between the occurrence of mood symptoms and the development of the delusions. If the amount of time that mood symptoms are present is brief when compared to the duration of the delusional beliefs, a diagnosis of a mood disorder may not be warranted.

In addition, one must consider the possibility of somatoform disorders such as body dysmorphic disorder or hypochondriasis when determining whether or not a patient has a somatic delusion. For patients with body dysmorphic disorder or hypochondriasis, excessive concern and preoccupation about either physical appearance or physical well-being, respectively, are present. However, for patients with hypochondriasis, the intensity of the fear of being ill is not as great as that seen in the somatic type of delusional disorder. Similarly, the intensity of the concern that patients with body dysmorphic disorder have about their body is generally less pronounced than seen with patients suffering from the somatic form of delusional disorder.

There is no single definitive means by which patients with delusional disorder should be treated. Because individuals with this condition often do not believe that they are suffering from a psychiatric illness, developing a therapeutic alliance with the patient can be the most challenging part of the treatment process. Psychosocial interventions that are considered for patients with delusional disorder include supportive and cognitive-behavioral-based psychotherapies. Talking treatments may also focus on the consequences and the distress associated with the condition. Individuals with delusional disorder will often feel demoralized, isolated, and rejected. These feelings can be addressed during psychotherapy. In addition, the treatment may focus on how social isolation and stress can adversely affect the individual.

Medications have also been employed in the treatment of delusional disorder, however, there are few data regarding the pharmacotherapy of delusional disorder during adolescence or childhood. The antiobsessional agent clomipramine has been reported to be useful for adults as well as adolescents with delusional disorder. Similarly, other antiobsessional agents may be effective with some patients. Although typical antipsychotics have also been reported to be of potential use in some patients with delusional disorders, these agents' salutary effects may be limited. For this reason, clinicians have begun to explore whether or not atypical antipsychotics may have a role in the treatment of delusional disorder. There are case reports of symptom amelioration in adult patients with delusional disorder treated with clozapine or risperidone.

Individuals with delusional disorder do not normally need to be hospitalized for treatment, and the interventions described above are generally conducted on an outpatient basis. However, there are select circumstances in which hospitalization may be warranted. These include individuals who are violent or hostile toward others or those patients with poor impulse control. Patients who are at risk for suicide may also be candidates for hospitalization.

Course and Prognosis

The course and eventual prognosis for delusional disorder is variable. It appears that the more acute and earlier the onset of the delusional disorder, the better the prognosis. It appears that individuals suffering from the persecutory and jealous subtypes may have better outcomes than do individuals who suffer from other subtypes of this condition. Demographic factors such as martial status and gender also appear to be associated with differences in outcome. For example, it has been reported that married women tend to have a better prognosis than other patients do. It should also be noted that for some individuals, the disorder might be a chronic one. This is especially true for older individuals who develop the disorder.

SHARED PSYCHOTIC DISORDER

Shared psychotic disorder, or *folie à deux*, is an infrequent phenomenon characterized by one individual adopting the psychotic or delusional thinking of another individual. According to the *DSM-IV*, research on the disorder is extremely minimal. The condition is most common among women and usually occurs among people who live within the same household. Shared psychotic disorder may occur between spouses, siblings, and within a parent-child dyad.

Symptoms and Psychotic Features

The primary feature of shared psychotic disorder is that a delusion emerges within an individual (secondary case) who has a close relationship with another person (primary case) who is afflicted with a psychotic disorder and delusions. The delusions and symptoms of the shared psychotic disorder usually resemble those of delusional disorder. The delusions in the secondary case are typically identical in content to the delusions of the primarily affected individual. Usually, the delusions will diminish or disappear when the secondary person is separated from the primary case. In shared psychotic disorder the primary individual may be suffering from one of several psychotic illnesses. The delusions may be nonbizarre, bizarre, mood-congruent, or mood-incongruent. Aside from possessing delusional beliefs, the secondary individual typically does not manifest any unusual behavior unless it is associated with the delusion itself. In addition, the secondary individual does not necessarily possess a psychotic disorder per se prior to developing the disorder. The secondary individual is generally not as severely impaired by the delusional beliefs as is the primary individual. Despite the fact that a secondarily affected patient does not generally suffer from psychosis prior to developing these delusions, he or she may maintain a belief in the shared delusion(s) with intense conviction. Exposure to the primarily affected individual, who also possesses the delusion or finds the delusion to be reasonable, often reinforces this belief.

In shared psychotic disorder it is generally noted that the primarily affected individual is often in a position to profoundly influence the secondary individual. For example, the primary individual may be either more intelligent or domineering than the secondary individual. The secondary individual may be more passive and suggestible in such a dyad. However, shared psychotic disorder is not always limited to two individuals. The disorder may potentially affect an entire group of individuals, such as a family.

Considering that children are often impressionable, it is not surprising that this disorder has been reported to occur in parent-child dyads. However, there does not appear to be an abundant amount of information that specifically addresses how the disorder affects children and adolescents. Not surprising, case reports have described adverse consequences of this condition in children and adolescents.

Age at Onset and Etiology

Shared psychotic disorder is capable of being present across the life cycle. It may occur in young children and elderly adults. However, due to its rareness, specific information regarding the age of onset for this condition is not available.

Shared psychotic disorder is induced by one individual essentially adopting the psychotic symptoms of another individual. The exact manner by which this transpires still is unknown. It has been hypothesized that the appearance of a psychotic illness in the primary individual triggers the onset of the disorder in a genetically or biologically predisposed secondary individual. However, clinical evidence suggests that psychosocial factors may play a role in the development of shared psychotic disorder. This evidence comes from the observation that shared psychotic disorder typically appears in socially isolated dyads where the primary individual is more dominant than the secondary individual.

Differential Diagnosis and Treatment

Due to the uniqueness of this disorder, the differential diagnosis for this condition is not as extensive as in other psychiatric illnesses. The key to making the diagnosis of a shared psychotic disorder is the identification of similar delusions in both a primary individual and a secondary individual. When examining a patient in whom a shared psychotic disorder is suspected, it is important to note when the delusions appeared in the presumed secondary individual. If it is evident that psychotic symptoms emerged prior to the onset of the shared delusions, an alternative diagnosis may be warranted. Also, one may consider the possibility that another psychotic disorder is present if both the psychotic symptoms and delusions do not disappear after the secondary individual is separated from the primary individual. Disorders such as schizophrenia, delusional disorder, schizoaffective disorder, and mood disorder with psychotic features should all be considered. Finally, as in all patients for whom a psychotic disorder is suspected, it is essential to rule out the possibility that the delusions may be due to substance abuse or a general medical condition.

Given the fact that shared psychotic disorder is generally believed to be caused primarily by the psychosocial influences of one individual on another, this disorder usually is treated by separating the secondary individual from the primary individual. After the separation occurs, close monitoring as well as emotional support is generally provided to the secondary individual to see if the delusional symptoms disappear. If the symptoms do not disappear within a short amount of time, then antipsychotic medication is usually considered. Of course, the primary individual must also be treated. Treatment for the primary case is predicated on treating the underlying diagnosis that is responsible for this individual's psychotic symptomatology.

Other approaches that are typically utilized in the treatment of shared psychotic disorder include incorporating other nondisordered family members into the therapeutic process. The main purpose of this intervention is to educate family members about the nature of the disorder as well as to inform family members how they may become actively involved in preventing a relapse. Family members would be encouraged to develop an improved support system so that the primarily affected individual has a less influential role on the secondarily affected person's environment. In addition, the family may be asked to facilitate socialization of the affected family members outside of their own family to prevent isolation.

Course and Prognosis

The overall outcome of shared psychotic disorder appears to be fairly good. If the proper treatment techniques are implemented, it appears as if the symptoms possessed by the secondary individual will eventually disappear. However, the amount of time that it takes for the symptoms to diminish varies across individuals. However, rapid recovery without seque-lae is quite possible. Not surprising, factors that may affect outcome include whether or not the primary individual is effectively treated and whether or not family interventions, environmental interventions, or both are properly implemented.

5

PERSONALITY DISORDERS

During the last 50 years, it has been observed that some people who have personality disorders may have short periods of psychotic symptomatology. *Borderline states* was a condition described in the early 1950s as a means to characterize patients who were not suffering from schizophrenia or bipolar illness, but who had brief psychotic episodes when under stress. Throughout the following decades, patients who had impulsivity, identity disturbances, self-injurious behavior, and impulsive aggressive acts were noted also to have periods of either paranoia or confusional states. According to the *DSM-IV*, borderline personality disorder (BPD) is characterized by a persistent combination of emotional, behavioral, and identity disturbances. Approximately 2% of the general population suffers from this disorder.

The previous conditions described in this book are categorized by the *DSM-IV* as Axis I disorders. The personality disorders (including BPD and schizotypal personality disorder) are considered Axis II conditions. This distinction may convey to some that these illnesses are inherently less severe than Axis I disorders. This is not the case. BPD can be a debilitating and potentially lethal illness. For example, the majority of patients with BPD have attempted suicide at some point in their lives. Moreover, the risk of completed suicide associated with BPD approximates the risk of suicide seen with MDD.

Some might consider it inappropriate to make the diagnosis of a personality disorder in a person younger than 18 years of age. It is certainly true that part of the task of adolescence is to clarify issues of identity. It is also the case that some adolescents without any psychiatric illness may on occasion have some difficulties similar to those seen in patients with personality disorders. However, the chronic pervasive difficulties associated with personality disorders are not part of normal development. Therefore, when carefully considered, it is appropriate to consider the diagnosis of a personality disorder in a young person.

Symptoms and Psychotic Features

According to the *DSM-IV*, the characteristic features of BPD are a "pervasive pattern of instability of interpersonal relationships, self-images, and affects, and marked impulsivity that begins by early adulthood and is present in a variety of contexts" (p. 650). In adult patients with BPD, self-injurious behavior, manipulative suicide attempts, impulsive behavior, affective instability and brief psychotic episodes can all occur. Those who have BPD also often try to avoid a sense of real or imagined abandonment. Individuals with BPD often have relationships that are unstable, tumultuous, and intense. In addition, the person with BPD may have a persistent unstable self-image.

The impulsive behavior seen in individuals with BPD may be manifested in a variety of ways. For example, people with BPD may gamble, spend money irresponsibly, binge eat, abuse substances, engage in unsafe and promiscuous sexual activities, and drive recklessly. The affective lability seen in patients with BPD is frequently characterized by intense, rapidly fluctuating mood states that vary in their quality. Other subjectively experienced emotional disturbances may include persistent feelings of emptiness, having difficulties controlling one's anger, and becoming easily bored. Angry outbursts can be followed by feelings of guilt or shame. Both the impulsive behaviors and the affective disturbances seen in people with BPD can have profound adverse consequences for them.

The diagnostic criteria for BPD in children and adolescents are identical to those used for adults. As noted previously, there is some skepticism as to whether or not BPD (or any other personality disorder) may be diagnosed in a young person. This is primarily due to the fact that personality traits in adults are presumably more stable than in children and adolescents and by definition a personality disorder is chronic and enduring.

It has been reported that BPD symptomatology in children and adolescents is characterized by symptoms similar to those seen in older people. These include a pattern of unstable and intense interpersonal relationships in which the affected individual alternates between the extremes of idealizing and devaluing other people in their lives as well as distorting the overall nature of their relationships. In addition, other symptoms may include potentially self-damaging and reckless risk taking. These acts may include running away, substance abuse, and sexual promiscuity. As with adults, young people with BPD may also have affect instability and mood shifts. A person's mood may rapidly become depressed, angry, or irritable. Youths with BPD have also been reported to have difficulties with impulse control. They may make suicidal threats, gestures, or perform self-mutilating acts. Youths with BPD typically have problems with self-perception that may affect their sense of identity, friendships, and career plans. As seen in adults, youths with BPD often may feel chronically empty or bored and also may have an intense fear of abandonment.

Prior to developing BPD, many children and adolescents are considered to be temperamentally difficult, cranky, and hard to soothe. For example, as infants they may have had high activity levels, poor adaptability, negative mood, and problems settling into rhythmic patterns of sleep and feeding. By preschool age, youths who eventually develop BPD are often hyperactive and have frequent temper tantrums. Others may be very clingy and fearful of separations from their caregivers. Many of these youths may meet diagnostic criteria for attention-deficit hyperactivity disorder (ADHD), conduct disorder, separation anxiety disorder, or a mood disorder.

Psychotic features can occur in individuals with BPD and often are manifested during times of extreme stress. For example, the precipitating stressor may be the development of a sense of real or imagined abandonment. These symptoms may include paranoid ideation (with associated anxiety), confusion, or dissociative symptoms. Less often, an individual with BPD may develop more pronounced psychotic symptoms such as hallucinations, body image distortions, and ideas of reference.

Age of Onset and Etiology

BPD typically begins in young adulthood. However, it is capable of appearing as early as middle childhood.

Genetics and environmental influences appear to be important risk factors for the development of BPD. Patients with BPD often have high rates of depression, substance abuse, and other forms of psychopathology in their families. The high rate of depressive illness in family members of patients with BPD is one of the reasons that some consider BPD to be a mood disorder spectrum disorder. Although the specific biological factors that predispose a patient to developing BPD have not been identified, there is evidence that the pathophysiology of BPD in young people may involve central nervous system dysfunction.

The fact that patients with BPD have a higher prevalence of psychopathology among their family members than do youths without BPD does not rule out the possibility that environmental factors may also contribute to the expression of this disorder. Some researchers have speculated that parents of children with BPD, who themselves suffer from a psychiatric illness, may expose their child to a more disruptive, less stable, and less empathic home environment. It is this stressful upbringing that may contribute to the development of BPD. Some evidence also supports the hypothesis that physical or sexual abuse may be risk factors for BPD. It has been reported that adults with BPD were more frequently neglected, physically abused, and sexually abused as children than were controls. In summary, these data support the supposition that environmental factors may contribute to the development of BPD in children and adolescents.

Differential Diagnosis and Treatment

Given the fact that a personality disorder diagnosis is indicative of a persistent condition, it is important to consider the temporal nature of a youth's symptoms before making the diagnosis of BPD. This is important because episodic conditions, such as mood disorders, may be characterized by symptoms similar to those of a personality disorder. It is also important to consider whether a person's emotional and interpersonal difficulties may be due to the abuse of illicit substances. In addition, alterations in a person's personality may occur as a result of a general medical condition or as the sequelae of a medication-induced adverse event. In addition, there are many different personality disorders that have symptoms similar to those seen with BPD. These conditions must also be considered when faced with a patient with chronic affective, interpersonal, and behavioral dysfunction.

As noted above, patients with BPD may develop psychotic symptoms. For this reason, it is important to realize that the psychotic symptoms seen in people with a psychotic disorder (such as schizophrenia) are different from those seen in patients with BPD. The psychosis of schizophrenia is often characterized by multiple voices, voices commenting on the patient's behavior, unusual or bizarre delusions, and a thought disorder. Paranoia, anxiety, and possibly some confusion characterize the acute psychotic episodes associated with BPD. Patients with BPD do not generally experience bizarre delusions or a formal thought disorder.

Psychosocial interventions, and occasionally medications, are used in the treatment of young patients with BPD. For adults, the current treatment of choice for BPD appears to be a combination of medication and psychosocial interventions. This is not to say that every adult or youth with BPD requires medication, but it has been shown that medications can have salutary effects in adults treated with this condition.

Serotonin selective reuptake inhibitor antidepressants, anticonvulsant mood stabilizers for impulsive and aggressive patients, and low doses of antipsychotics for brief psychotic episodes have all been described as being associated with salutary effects. Recently our group reported that low doses of atypical antipsychotics such as risperidone and olanzapine may be of benefit to patients with BPD.

Psychosocial interventions that have been employed for adolescents with BPD include family therapy, individual therapy, parent therapy, pharmaco-therapy, hospital and milieu therapy, and behavioral therapy. Often, a combination of these different methods is implemented throughout the course of treatment. The development of reality testing appears to be a key component in the treatment of individuals with BPD, reducing anxiety and abandonment fears and correcting cognitive misperceptions. Considering the diversity of symptoms that may occur in a patient with BPD and the paucity of treatment data, it is difficult to assert that there is a single modality that is best for treating the disorder. Therefore, when caring for a patient with BPD, clinicians must be flexible in regard to the types of intervention that should be incorporated into a treatment plan.

Course and Prognosis

According to the *DSM-IV*, the course of BPD is extremely variable. Individuals typically suffer from chronic dysfunction during their early adult years. However, as individuals become older, their symptoms may diminish. Regrettably, there appears to be minimal information on the outcome of BPD in children and adolescents. However, youths with BPD who are admitted to a psychiatric hospital appear to be at high risk of readmission. There is evidence to suggest that although youths with BPD may not meet symptom criteria for this condition later in adolescence or as adults, they are, in fact, likely to meet diagnostic criteria for another disorder later in life.

SCHIZOTYPAL PERSONALITY DISORDER

Schizotypal personality disorder (SPD) is believed to affect approximately 3% of the general population. Like other personality disorders, SPD is a chronic condition. SPD is considered to be a *schizophrenia spectrum* disorder because it is characterized by many of the symptoms seen in persons with schizophrenia. Although SPD has not been extensively studied in children and adolescents, there is evidence that the disorder does occur during the preadult years. SPD appears to occur more commonly in boys than in girls.

Symptoms and Psychotic Features

According to the *DSM-IV*, SPD is characterized by an ongoing pattern of social and interpersonal deficits. Adult patients suffering from SPD often have symptoms consisting of ideas of reference, magical thinking, cognitive distortions, active social avoidance, and delusions. Such psychotic-like symptoms appear to be consistently present and are not episodic such as the psychotic symptoms seen in patients with BPD.

Symptoms seen in children and adolescents with SPD include social isolation, poor peer relationships, social anxiety, poor academic performance, hypersensitivity, peculiar thoughts and language, and bizarre fantasies. Others may view children and adolescents with SPD as being odd or eccentric. It has been noted that children with SPD tend to have significant communication deficits when compared to normal children. Specifically, children with SPD rarely used referential cohesion or conjunctions within their spoken sentences. They also frequently interrupted their flow of conversation with another individual to refer to themselves or to their surrounding environment. For this reason, listeners may have difficulty determining exactly what these children are talking about and may have difficulty following their train of thought. In addition, young people with SPD may have illogical thinking and loose associations. It has been found that adolescents with SPD are significantly more likely to drop out of school than are adolescents with other personality disorders.

The psychotic features that are present with SPD are not associated with the same degree of dysfunction and are not as pronounced as the psychotic features found in primary psychotic disorders such as schizophrenia. Those with SPD may have perceptual alterations characterized by hearing murmuring voices or sensing that another person is present. Often, an individual may be suspicious and have paranoid ideation. In addition, as already noted, the speech of a person with SPD may have idiosyncratic phrasing and construction. An individual with SPD may apply words and concepts in an unusual way and respond to questions in an abstract manner. It should be noted that more pronounced and profound psychotic symptomatology might develop in patients with SPD after a particularly stressful life event. However, these exacerbations of psychosis are typically transient. Although it appears that psychotic episodes are not common in young people with SPD, because of the chronic psychotic-like symptoms that are present with this syndrome, some clinicians may erroneously diagnose such a person as having a major psychotic illness during these brief periods of psychotic decompensation.

Age of Onset and Etiology

SPD typically develops during early adulthood. However, the disorder can be identified in elementary school aged youths.

There is evidence from genetic studies that SPD may be related to schizophrenia. For example, SPD is commonly found within the offspring and other relatives of patients with schizophrenia. Likewise, there is evidence that children with schizophrenia and children with SPD share some of the same symptoms. It has been reported that both children with schizophrenia and children with SPD exhibit significantly more illogical thinking and loose associations than normal controls. In addition, according to descriptions, children with either schizophrenia or SPD can have significant impairments in premorbid functioning. Children with SPD or schizophrenia have also been reported to have difficulties with passivity, poor concentration, peer rejection, and impairments in emotional rapport.

However, there is also evidence that there may be a genetic relationship between affective disorders and SPD. This is based on the finding that affective disorders are common among relatives of children with SPD.

Differential Diagnosis and Treatment

Prior to making a diagnosis of SPD, one of the clinician's main considerations needs to be an awareness of the chronic nature of the symptoms. Certain disorders, including brief psychotic disorder, schizophreniform disorder, or a mood disorder with psychotic symptomatology, may have features similar to SPD. However, with these other diagnoses, their duration or symptomatology is relatively brief when compared to SPD. However, disorders such as schizophrenia, although more severe and potentially more debilitating, may be more difficult to distinguish from SPD because they are often characterized by a more chronic course. As with other disorders in which brief periods of psychosis may occur, the possibility of a substance abuse disorder or a general medical condition being present must also be considered.

SPD also shares symptoms with some of the other personality disorders. Both paranoid personality disorder and schizoid personality disorder may be characterized by detachment and restricted affect. However, unlike SPD, these two disorders are usually not accompanied by idiosyncratic or eccentric behavior.

Information regarding the treatment of SPD in children and adolescents is quite minimal. There is some support that antipsychotic medications may be helpful for the treatment of the disorder.

Course and Prognosis

There are few data about the course of SPD in young people, however, it appears that most patients with SPD do not develop schizophrenia or another psychotic disorder. It has been reported that only 6% of adolescents with SPD still meet symptom criteria for the condition two years after an initial diagnosis is made. However, it appears that youths with SPD continue to have persistent symptoms of the disorder. Youths with SPD who were followed longitudinally have been reported to remain eccentric, but appear to achieve some degree of social adaptation during adulthood.

6

DISORDERS WITH PSYCHOTIC SYMPTOMATOLOGY

SUBSTANCE INDUCED PSYCHOTIC DISORDER

The prevalence of substance abuse among children and adolescents is alarmingly high. Recent statistics report that by age 13, approximately one third of boys and one fourth of girls have tried alcohol. By the age of 18, most teenagers have used alcohol, and approximately 4% report using alcohol daily. In addition, the use of drugs such as marijuana is quite prevalent among adolescents with reports indicating that about 40% of high school seniors have tried the drug, and about 2% use marijuana daily. According to the *DSM-IV*, there are several substances that can lead to disorders associated with abuse. Other than caffeine and nicotine, these include alcohol, amphetamines, cocaine, hallucinogens, inhalants, opioids, phencyclidine, and sedative/hypnotics. Substance related disorders are serious conditions affecting many facets of society. For example, alcohol alone may be responsible for over 50% of the violent crimes committed in this country.

It has been known for decades that substances of abuse such as alcohol, opioids, and cocaine could lead to symptoms of psychosis. The following will describe the symptoms that may occur during adolescent substance abuse as well as the psychotic features that may accompany the abuse of these drugs.

Symptoms and Psychotic Features

The *DSM-IV* considers the substance-related disorders to include substance dependence, substance abuse, substance intoxication, and substance withdrawal. Criteria for a substance dependence disorder are met when an individual is found to be suffering from cognitive, behavioral, or physiological symptoms, and that person continues to use the substance in question despite the presence of drug-related difficulties. Symptoms associated with substance dependence include an excessive consumption of the given substance, the development of tolerance to the substance, an inability to diminish or control the use of the substance, a disruption of social or occupational activities as a result of the substance use, and symptoms of withdrawal. An individual suffering from a substance dependence disorder is aware that the substance is causing impairment, but still does not cease using it. A physiological dependence on the substance may occur, but this does not need to be present to meet the requirements for substance dependence. An individual who suffers from a substance abuse disorder also may suffer from clinically significant impairment or distress as a result of the substance abuse, but does not experience all the difficulties that occur in patients with substance dependence.

An individual who is suffering from substance intoxication develops a substance-specific syndrome that is caused by excessive use of the agent. Typically, an individual will have clinically significant maladaptive behavioral or psychological changes while intoxicated. When an individual stops using the substance, substance withdrawal symptoms may then appear. As with substance intoxication, the characteristics of the substance withdrawal are specific to the drug in question. The symptoms of substance withdrawal may result in clinically significant distress, physiological perturbations, or impairment in one's occupational or social functioning.

Many nonspecific behavior changes can occur in adolescents who are abusing substances. These youths may become involved in a variety of high-risk behaviors and as noted above may experience perturbations in intrafamilial and peer relationships. Teenagers with substance abuse disorders may also have significant academic dysfunction. In addition, changes in personal hygiene and dress may occur in these youths. Because changes associated with substance abuse are nonspecific and may occur within the context of many other circumstances besides substance abuse, other possibilities must be reviewed when faced with a young person for whom the diagnosis of a substance abuse disorder is being considered.

There is clear evidence that psychotic features may result from the use or abuse of a substance. Therefore, when an individual presents with psychotic symptoms, there is always a possibility that the symptoms may be substance-induced. Some typical psychotic symptoms produced by the use of substances include hallucinations and delusions. However, it should be noted that bizarre delusions and thought disorder are more common in schizophrenia than in substance abuse disorders. It is also important to realize that substance abuse disorders commonly occur comorbidly in patients with psychotic conditions. In fact, substance abuse disorders are quite prevalent in patients experiencing their first episode of psychosis.

At times it is difficult to ascertain whether a substance abuse disorder, a psychotic disorder, or both are contributing to the clinical symptoms in a patient with psychosis. Often the individual is not aware that the hallucinations or delusions that they are experiencing are a result of the substance use. Moreover, the temporal relationship between the substance misuse and the development of psychotic symptoms can be quite variable. Psychotic symptoms can occur while the individual is intoxicated or suffering from withdrawal. In addition, a psychotic state can last up to several weeks during a withdrawal period.

Age of Onset and Etiology

It is clear that the prevalence of substance use and abuse is quite high among young people, especially adolescents. Based on recent statistics, older adolescents abuse drugs at higher rates than both younger adolescents and children.

Although the specific causes of substance abuse disorders have not been delineated, both genetic and psychosocial determinants have been identified as risk factors for the development of substance abuse. Studies with twins have illustrated a stronger concordance rate between monozygotic than dizygotic twins for alcoholism. Similar concordance rates have also been reported for the use of drugs other than alcohol.

There is evidence that environmental factors such as inadequate parental supervision and monitoring during the elementary school years increases the likelihood that children will experiment at earlier ages with substances such as alcohol or other drugs including marijuana, cocaine, and inhalants. Likewise, some studies have shown that adolescents who abuse substances typically come from family environments that are dysfunctional. In some cases, adolescents may begin using substances at home with their parents who are also substance abusers.

The presence of life stressors may also trigger substance abuse among adolescents. It has been noted that some high school seniors claim that they use drugs and other illicit substances to escape their problems and troubles. Another important risk factor for substance abuse is the presence of a comorbid psychiatric disorder. Recent findings have shown that, among adolescents who use alcohol, up to 80% meet criteria for another psychiatric disorder. Typically, the alcohol abuse follows the onset of the comorbid condition. Often individuals who are afflicted with a psychiatric disorder will begin using a substance as a maladaptive way to minimize the challenges and vicissitudes of living with their mental illness. Consistent with this finding, research has indicated that there is a strong relation between having a family history of mental illness and eventually developing a substance abuse disorder. For example, it has been reported that the rate of substance abuse is greater among children who had a family history of panic disorder than among those who did not have a family history for the disorder. Evidence has also shown that offspring of depressed or bipolar individuals are at high risk for abusing substances. This body of evidence highlights the need for the clinician to consider comorbid psychiatric conditions when faced with an adolescent suffering from a substance abuse disorder.

There are several substances that can potentially induce psychotic features. According to the *DSM-IV*, these substances include alcohol, amphetamines, cannabis, cocaine, hallucinogens, inhalants, opioids, phencyclidine, and sedatives.

- *Alcohol (ethanol)*. Alcohol, which is a central nervous system depressant, may induce psychotic symptoms during a withdrawal period. Throughout withdrawal, an individual may experience vivid, persistent, and typically unpleasant hallucinations. The symptoms of psychosis usually develop about 48 hours following the cessation or reduction of chronic alcohol use or dependence. The most common form of hallucinations are auditory, and they are normally characterized by derogatory or threatening voices. Tactile and visual hallucinations may occur as well. While experiencing the psychosis, the individual usually is not aware that the hallucinations are the result of his or her alcohol abuse.

- *Cocaine*. Cocaine abuse can induce emotionally distressing experiences such as suicidal thoughts, irritability, anxiety, depression, and paranoid ideation. Approximately half of the individuals who use cocaine experience paranoid delusions and hallucinations at some point while using this drug. However, whether or not psychotic symptoms will occur depends on the amount of cocaine used, the duration of abuse, and the user's sensitivity to the substance. Besides hallucinations, other perceptual changes can also occur associated with cocaine abuse. These include visual or tactile hallucinations. For example, an individual may have the sensation that bugs are crawling over his or her skin (formication). The presence of psychotic symptoms, especially the paranoid delusions, may prompt the individual to become aggressive or violent.

- *Amphetamines*. High doses of amphetamines and related substances can lead to feelings of dysphoria, social withdrawal, and depression. Persistent use can also lead to psychotic symptoms similar to those seen in patients with paranoid schizophrenia. However, the presence of amphetamine-induced psychosis can be differentiated from paranoid schizophrenia in several ways. Visual hallucinations, an appropriate affect, hyperactivity and hypersexuality are more characteristic of amphetamine-induced psychosis. It is less common to see a formal thought disorder during amphetamine psychosis and this finding is much more characteristic of schizophrenia.

- *Cannabis.* The most common form of cannabis that is abused is marijuana. It is possible for a person to develop psychotic symptoms from the use of this substance. Paranoid ideation appears to be more common than frank hallucinations or bizarre delusions. Cannabis-induced psychotic symptoms are usually more prevalent when large doses of cannabis are abused or when the cannabis is tainted with other psychotomimetic substances.

- *Lysergic acid diethylamide (LSD).* This hallucinogenic drug is capable of producing disturbances in sensory functions that may include perceptual disturbances and hallucinations. Hallucinations typically occur at higher doses, whereas at lower doses, perceptual distortions and disorganization of thinking may occur. In addition, affective responses, ability to recognize reality, and ability to communicate or relate to others can all be compromised at lower doses.

The psychological effects of LSD can vary from individual to individual. Some people experience bizarre thoughts and feelings. This may prompt the person using LSD to manifest dangerous behaviors because of beliefs that he or she can fly or has the power to stop moving vehicles. In other cases, users of LSD have reported that the drug has allowed them to develop new insights. Some people who use LSD report that LSD induces a sense of peacefulness yet others report that LSD use can lead to a disquieting sensibility. Perceptual alterations that occur during LSD use can be visual, auditory, or tactile in nature, and they may involve extreme misperceptions of the physical environment. In addition, the person may experience synesthesia, which is the transportation of experiences across the senses. People with synesthesia, for example, may state that they are able to "see sounds" or "feel colors."

Some of the more aversive effects of LSD include dysphoric reactions or *bad trips.* Bad trips typically occur when the individual takes a larger dose of LSD than usual. The person experiencing an LSD-induced dysphoric reaction may feel as if he or she is going to lose control and never return to normal. During these reactions, other people or objects may become visually distorted so that they look grotesque and threatening. Some individuals may also experience anxiety, panic, or paranoia, which may result in violent behavior. Typically, acute effects disappear in 6 to 12 hours. However, some individuals have reported that dysphoric symptoms may last for days or weeks. In rare cases, the symptoms of a dysphoric reaction can last for months. Some individuals who have abused LSD also report experiencing flashbacks. These flashbacks are brief episodes, which are similar to the LSD-induced state, that occur several weeks or months after taking the drug. These flashbacks are often visual in nature and may include visual disturbances.

- *Phencyclidine (PCP)*. PCP is considered a dissociative anesthetic and is commonly referred to as angel dust. Typically, those who suffer from PCP-induced psychosis have delusions, hallucinations, or both. The PCP-induced psychosis usually lasts no more than several days.

- *Opioids*. Opioids induce analgesia and euphoria in those who use the substance. The most common type of opioid is heroin, which is often injected intravenously. Opiate abuse can lead to symptoms of psychosis such as hallucinations, delusions, or both.

- *Inhalants*. The most common types of inhalants are solvents, glues, fuels, and aerosol propellants. Inhalants act as central nervous system depressants. The most common inhalant-induced psychotic symptoms include paranoid states. Individuals also can suffer from hallucinations or delusions during inhalant abuse.

- *Sedative, hypnotics, and anxiolytics*. This class of drug includes antianxiety agents such as benzodiazepines and barbiturates. Usually, the types of psychotic features that are associated with abuse of these substances include hallucinations and delusions.

- *Medications*. In addition to illicit drugs, several different types of prescribed medications also have the potential for causing psychotic symptoms. These include digitalis, isoniazid, dopamine agonists (such as L-DOPA), reserpine, corticosteroids, and over-the-counter cold preparations containing ephedrine/pseudoephedrine and dextromethorphan.

Differential Diagnosis and Treatment

Delineating whether or not a substance-induced psychotic disorder is present in a patient presenting with psychotic symptoms is an important part of the assessment process. For many patients, the psychotic symptoms are caused solely by the abuse of a substance and not by the existence of psychotic disorder such as schizophrenia. To determine whether or not the psychotic symptoms a young person is experiencing are due to substance abuse or a psychotic disorder, it is necessary to obtain a comprehensive psychiatric history. This history should carefully assess for the difficulties that are currently present, but also incorporate a longitudinal assessment of functioning and symptom development. If the individual had been exhibiting psychotic symptoms prior to the development of substance abuse, a primary psychotic disorder should be more strongly considered. Conversely, it is more likely that a primary substance abuse disorder is present if it is clear that the psychotic symptoms developed well into the course of the substance abuse.

However, it is also quite clear that patients may suffer from both a primary psychotic disorder as well as a substance-related disorder. When faced with an adolescent with idiosyncratic behavior or psychosis, it appears that many clinicians more readily consider the presence of a substance-related disorder than the possibility of a psychotic disorder. This generally leads to having the youth undergo drug screening. Even if the drug screen is positive, considering the high rates of comorbidity between substance abuse and psychotic disorders, that does not mean that substance abuse is the sole explanation for the youth's difficulties. In other words, a positive toxicology screen does not mean that a psychotic disorder (or even another psychiatric disorder) may not be present as well. Therefore, it is essential for the clinician to vigilantly consider the presence of comorbid psychiatric conditions when faced with a young patient with a substance abuse disorder.

Several methods have been implemented to treat children and adolescents with substance abuse problems. Some of the most common treatment methods include individual psychotherapy, drug-specific counseling, and self-help groups. Individuals with substance abuse disorder may also be treated in a variety of settings such as inpatient units, residential treatment facilities, group homes, or outpatient settings. Considering that substance abuse problems are often accompanied by another mental health disorder, the clinician must carefully assess all the needs of the individual prior to beginning treatment. If another psychiatric disorder is present, it is often necessary to treat the psychiatric disorder as well as the actual substance abuse problem.

There is evidence to suggest that treating the comorbid psychiatric disorder may lead to reductions in substance use in these dually diagnosed patients. For example, it has been found that lithium treatment led to less substance abuse and better global functioning when compared to placebo in a group of adolescents with bipolar disorders who had secondary substance dependency. It has been recently reported that treatment with fluoxetine was effective in reducing both alcohol use and depressive symptomatology in depressed alcoholic adults. Considering the high rates of comorbidity between depression and substance abuse in adolescents and the fact that teenagers with both depression and substance abuse disorders may be at particularly high risk for suicide, scientifically tested interventions need to be developed for this adolescent group.

Pharmacological interventions may also be used in the treatment of certain substance abuse disorders. Disulfiram has been utilized in the treatment of adults and teenagers with alcohol abuse. However, disulfiram has several shortcomings. First, its utility can be compromised if it is not taken as prescribed. Moreover, if alcoholic beverages are consumed while on this drug, an aversive reaction occurs which can be quite severe. Some medications have been used to diminish the reinforcement effects of the abused substance. Naltrexone has been prescribed to help individuals decrease opioid and alcohol use. In addition, methadone may be prescribed to replace the abused substance for patients with opiate addiction. When faced with a patient with a substance-related psychosis, the use of an antipsychotic agent may be necessary to address the hallucinations and delusions that are present.

Course and Prognosis

The eventual prognosis of adolescents who have substance abuse problems varies. In general, it appears that those individuals who have the strongest motivation to quit misusing substances have the best prognosis. It also appears as if peers and family members can significantly influence the course and prognosis of a youth with a substance abuse disorder for either the better or the worse.

PSYCHOTIC DISORDER DUE TO A GENERAL MEDICAL CONDITION

As a result of general medical conditions, patients can develop symptoms of psychosis similar to those seen in patients with psychotic disorders. The exact prevalence of this type of disorder is not clear, however, it occurs often enough to warrant its own separate diagnosis in the *DSM-IV*. Psychotic symptoms may occur in individuals who are afflicted with a wide variety of general medical conditions. These conditions include, but are not limited to, neurological, metabolic, or endocrinologic conditions.

Symptoms and Psychotic Features

Even in the 19th century, it was noted that psychotic features are capable of occurring in a variety of different general medical conditions. What follows is a description of several types of conditions that may induce a psychotic episode or symptoms of psychosis.

Traumatic Brain Injury. Those who suffer from a traumatic brain injury may potentially develop psychotic symptoms. Often, brain injury may be the result of an accident, which may have involved either blunt or penetrating head trauma. Besides psychosis, several other sequelae can occur in a person who has experienced a traumatic brain injury. These include depression, increased impulsivity and aggression, and changes in personality.

Some researchers have noted that individuals with traumatic brain injury may be at reasonably high risk for subsequently developing psychotic symptoms. For example, it has been reported that out of approximately 3,000 war veterans with moderate to severe brain injury, 25% suffered from some form of psychiatric disturbance. The types of disturbances included delusional psychosis, paranoid schizophrenia, and paranoid schizophreniform disorder. In addition, other studies have described case series of brain injured patients who developed postinjury psychosis. There is recently published evidence to suggest that there are identifiable risk factors associated with the development of new-onset psychopathology within the first 3 months after a traumatic brain injury in children and adolescents. These include increasing severity of injury, the presence of preinjury psychopathology in the youth, a family history of a psychiatric disorder, lower preinjury intellectual functioning, and family dysfunction.

Brain Lesions of the Central Nervous System and Cerebral Hypoxia. Brain lesions and tumors, such as metastatic masses, primary cerebral tumors, and subdural hematoma, may all induce psychotic symptoms. In addition, other general medical conditions associated with reduced cardiac output, pulmonary insufficiency, and carbon monoxide toxicity may cause psychotic symptoms as well.

Neurological Diseases. There are several different disorders of the basal ganglia that can be associated with symptoms of psychosis. These include Parkinsons's disease, Huntington's disease, and Wilson's disease. However, these disorders are considered to be relatively uncommon in children and adolescents.

Epilepsy is considered one of the most prevalent neurological diseases in the United States, affecting approximately 1% of the overall population. Although young patients with epilepsy may be at higher risk for psychosocial difficulties, it is rare for a young person with epilepsy to suffer from psychosis as a result of their epilepsy.

An individual with epilepsy may suffer from various types of seizures, which include generalized seizures and partial seizures. Although it is more common in adults, children and adolescents may also suffer from complex partial seizures of the temporal lobe (sometimes referred to as temporal lobe epilepsy). Some of the most common symptoms of this disorder include confused behavior, alterations in consciousness, and a wide variety of other clinical disturbances. It is believed that this type of epilepsy is the form of epilepsy most likely to induce psychotic symptoms. For example, it has recently been reported that approximately 10% of individuals who have complex partial seizures also suffer from psychotic features. The most typical psychotic symptoms include hallucinations and paranoid delusions. The hallucinations are usually auditory. In addition, individuals may have delusions. Individuals with this form of seizure disorder also may suffer from thought disorder, which is usually characterized by circumstantiality. For this reason, patients with this form of seizure disorder are occasionally misdiagnosed as suffering from schizophrenia. Distinguishing between the two conditions requires the clinician not only to focus on the presenting symptomatology, but also to consider the longitudinal course of the illness and to inquire about past seizures.

In addition, an aneurysm, a collagen vascular disease, hypertensive encephalopathy, an intracranial hemorrhage, or any other conditions that can lead to perturbations of the cerebral vascular circulation may put a person at risk for developing secondary psychotic symptoms.

Infectious Diseases. There are several infectious diseases that can result in psychotic symptomatology. Herpes simplex encephalitis often includes symptoms of insomnia, olfactory and gustatory hallucinations, personality changes, and bizarre or psychotic behaviors. Other forms of encephalitis and postencephalitic states have also been reported to potentially cause psychotic symptoms. Neurosyphilis can result in personality changes, poor judgment, and irritability. In addition, approximately 10% to 20% of individuals who suffer from neurosyphilis may experience delusions of grandeur. A rare condition that occurs primarily in children and adolescents called subacute sclerosing panencephalitis may also lead to symptoms of psychosis. Other central nervous system infections that have been reported to cause psychotic features include brain abscesses, malaria, meningitis, and the human immunodeficiency virus.

Endocrine Disorders. There are many endocrine disorders that potentially can cause psychotic symptoms. For example, patients with thyroid disorders may develop psychotic features as the result of their endocrinological disorder. Patients who suffer from adrenal disorders, such as

Addison's disease, can develop secondary symptoms of depression or psychosis. Those with Cushing's syndrome, another disorder of the adrenal gland, may also develop symptoms of a mood disorder. A small number of these individuals may develop psychotic symptomatology as well. Along with these endocrine conditions, other endocrine disorders that have been reported to be associated with psychotic features include pituitary insufficiency and diabetes mellitus.

Metabolic Disorders. There are also metabolic disorders that can potentially lead to psychotic symptoms. These include hypoglycemic encephalopathy and acute intermittent porphyria. Individuals who are afflicted with the former can experience disorientation, confusion, and hallucinations. Those who suffer from acute intermittent porphyria typically suffer from anxiety, insomnia, lability of mood, depression, and psychosis. Disorders associated with calcium and other electrolyte imbalances, uremia, and hepatic failure can all lead to symptoms of psychosis.

Nutritional Disorders. Individuals who have a vitamin B_{12} deficiency may suffer from apathy, depression, irritability, and moodiness. In addition, these people may develop delirium, hallucinations, dementia, and paranoid features. Those who have niacin (pellagra) or thiamine deficiencies may also develop psychotic symptomatology.

Metals. Poisoning from metals can lead to symptoms of psychosis. Lead, mercury, iron, bromide, and manganese poisoning all can contribute to psychotic symptoms.

Some of the more common psychotic features that are associated with a general medical condition include hallucinations or delusions. Usually the individual is unaware that his or her psychotic symptoms are a result of the general medical condition. According to our current nosology, there are two subtypes of psychosis that are due to a general medical disorder. The first subtype is diagnosed when only hallucinations are present or when hallucinations predominate over the other psychotic features. In these instances, various types of hallucinations may occur. The second subtype is diagnosed when only delusions are present or when the delusions predominate over the other psychotic features.

At times, it is difficult to determine whether a delusion or hallucination is clearly secondary to the general medical condition or if it is the result of a previously undetected psychiatric disorder. If this occurs, it is prudent to consider the psychotic symptoms as likely being due to the general medical condition unless there is evidence to the contrary. However, to more clearly either confirm or refute whether the symptoms of psychosis are truly due to a general medical condition, a longitudinal history of the patient's symptoms is necessary. When psychotic symptoms are truly the result of a general medical condition, there is generally a direct temporal correlation between the onset, pervasiveness, severity and remission of the psychotic symptoms with the signs and symptoms of the general medical condition.

Some of the specific types of hallucinations that individuals may suffer from during a psychotic disorder induced by a general medical condition include visual, olfactory, gustatory, tactile, or auditory hallucinations. Various types of delusions may also occur (such as somatic, grandiose, religious, and persecutory).

Etiology

By definition, a psychotic disorder due to a general medical condition is caused by the presence of the general medical condition. However, the pathophysiological mechanisms that underlie the psychoses associated with these various general medical conditions have yet to be fully elucidated.

Differential Diagnosis and Treatment

The symptoms of psychosis that can occur secondary to a general medical condition are similar to those seen in other disorders in which psychotic symptomatology is manifested. Of course, several other disorders should be considered before a diagnosis of psychotic disorder due to a general medical condition is made. Several prescription and over-the-counter medications can elicit symptoms of psychosis. A careful review of all medication that a patient is taking should be made in a medically compromised patient who is presenting with hallucinations or delusions.

Clearly another potential cause of the psychotic symptoms that should be considered is substance abuse. In addition, before making the diagnosis of psychosis due to a general medical condition, one must also eliminate the potential of a primary psychotic disorder such as schizophrenia, schizoaffective disorder, or delusional disorder as the cause of the psychotic symptomatology. The presence of a primary psychotic disorder is more probable if there is a family history of psychotic illnesses, evidence of premorbid psychosocial dysfunction and asociality, or if the longitudinal course of the illness is similar to that of schizophrenia. This usually can be determined by assessing for the presence of psychotic symptoms or the existence of impaired behavior prior to the onset of the medical condition.

Because psychotic symptoms may occur in affective illnesses, the possibility of a mood disorder being present must also be considered.

Various methods may be utilized to treat the psychotic features resulting from a medical condition. Other than assuring that the general medical condition causing the psychosis is being treated, the most common form of treatment for psychosis due to a general medical condition is pharmacotherapy. Antipsychotic drugs often are used successfully to treat the psychotic symptoms.

DELIRIUM

Delirium is a condition characterized mainly by a disturbance of consciousness and a change in cognition. Delirium typically develops over a short period of time. Because there are many different physiological causes that may be responsible for the development of delirium, it is not a single disorder per se but a syndrome associated with characteristic symptoms.

Symptoms and Psychotic Features

According to the *DSM-IV*, those who suffer from delirium often are not clearly aware of their surrounding environment and may have difficulty focusing, sustaining, or shifting their attention. They often are easily distracted, which can make it difficult to engage them in conversation. Other cognitive impairments also exist when a patient is suffering from delirium. These impairments are usually manifested as memory difficulties, disorientation, or language disturbance. Memory problems may be described as the inability to register, retain, or recall facts. Individuals who are disoriented may not be able to recognize others who are close to them such as family members and other loved ones. The language difficulties of delirium are often characterized by rambling and irrelevant or incoherent speech.

Other symptoms that are often associated with delirium include sleep disturbances and perturbations in activity level such as restlessness or sluggishness. The psychomotor disturbances may be quite variable in their manifestations and activity levels may shift from one extreme to another during the course of a delirium. While delirious, an individual may also suffer from any number of emotional disturbances such as anxiety, fear, depression, irritability, anger, euphoria, and apathy. Again, individuals may rapidly shift from one emotional state to another.

It is often difficult to diagnose delirium in young people because this condition affects a patient's cognition and the cognitive capacities in this age group are changing throughout their development. The clinician sometimes needs to become familiar with the premorbid cognitive capacities and emotional functioning of a young patient to determine whether or not a particular youth is truly suffering from delirium. Some symptoms of delirium that may be specifically characteristic of children and adolescents include uncooperative behavior and difficulty becoming soothed. However, most of the symptoms of delirium that are evident in adults are also evident in children and adolescents.

Psychotic symptoms may be present during an episode of delirium. Some of the common psychotic features that may occur include perceptual disturbances such as misinterpretations, illusions, or hallucinations. The perceptual misinterpretations may occur in different sensory modalities including visual, auditory, tactile, or olfactory. Visual or auditory misperceptions are the most common. It should be noted that when a patient is delirious, delusions may also be present.

Often, during the course of a delirium, a patient's psychotic features may develop rapidly and may wax and wane over the course of the day. Sometimes, the hallucinations or delusions may prompt an individual to become extremely fearful and react strongly to them. The person may lash out, scream, or even try to escape from the hospital ward. Extreme reactions, such as these, typically occur at night when environmental stimulation or sensory cues are lacking.

Etiology

As stated above, delirium does not have its own cause, rather it is a result of a general medical condition or medication toxicity. One of the most common times that delirium may develop is during the postoperative period. Delirium that develops postoperatively may be the result of the stress from surgery, postoperative pain, insomnia, analgesics, electrolyte imbalances, fever, or hypovolemia.

Conditions such as epilepsy, traumatic brain injury, meningitis, and encephalitis, as well as neoplasms and vascular disorders, may all potentially cause delirium. It has been reported that in a sample of 750 brain injured war veterans, almost one in five eventually developed delirium.

Extracranial causes of delirium include drugs, poisons, endocrine dysfunction, diseases of nonendocrine organs, nutritional deficiency diseases, metabolic derangements (such as electrolyte imbalances), systematic infections, or extracranial trauma. There are many types of drugs that can potentially cause delirium. These include both medications and illicit drugs such as opiates and anabolic steroids. Some poisons that may induce delirium include carbon monoxide and heavy metals. Diseases that lead to dysfunction of the liver, kidney, lungs, or cardiovascular system all have the potential to lead to delirium. Furthermore, severe deficiencies of thiamine, niacin, vitamin B_{12}, or folic acid can also lead to delirium. Risk factors for the development of delirium include age (young children and the elderly are particularly vulnerable), preexisting brain injury, a prior history of delirium, sensory impairment, and malnutrition.

Differential Diagnosis and Treatment

When delirium with psychotic features appears to be present, it is important to consider the possibility that the psychotic symptoms are being caused by a different disorder. These include brief psychotic disorder, schizophrenia, schizophreniform disorder, and a mood disorder with psychotic features. These conditions can usually be ruled out when a history is obtained that suggests that the individual is suffering from either a general medical condition or substance abuse complications (intoxication or withdrawal) and that the symptoms of psychosis are circumscribed to the period of delirium. Other than a temporal assessment of symptom development, it is also important to assess whether the symptoms of psychosis that are present are those typically seen during the course of a psychotic disorder. The psychotic features that are typical of delirium are usually fragmented and disorganized and accompanied by memory impairment. As noted before, a waxing and waning of cognitive impairment and disorientation are not part of the natural history of schizophrenia and other psychotic disorders. In summary, it is important to conduct an extensive medical examination and to obtain both cross-sectional and longitudinal information regarding an individual's history to determine whether or not a medically compromised patient with psychosis is suffering from delirium.

Delirium is usually treated by addressing the underlying cause of the delirium. However, during the treatment of the condition that is causing the delirium, the patient should be provided with a supportive environment that will reduce emotional distress. This usually includes modifying the amount of stimulation that the person receives so that there is neither sensory deprivation nor overstimulation. In addition, having a familiar family member or friend present is often helpful for a patient suffering from an episode of delirium. Pharmacological treatments also may be implemented for some patients. If an individual is suffering from psychotic symptoms, an antipsychotic agent may be considered in hopes of alleviating the symptoms of psychosis. In addition, benzodiazapines or other hypnotics may also be used to treat insomnia or anxiety.

Course and Prognosis

Delirium often develops during a short period of time, usually overnight or within a few hours. The delirium may potentially resolve within a few hours or may persist for a few weeks. Typically, the delirium remits once the underlying cause has been treated. It should be noted that the presence of delirium may be considered a risk factor for a poor prognosis during the course of a general medical condition.

DEMENTIA

Dementia is a condition that is characterized mainly by the existence of multiple cognitive deficits, which typically involves memory impairment. Dementia may affect an individual's memory, language, problem solving, orientation, attention and concentration, judgment, and social abilities. The condition primarily affects individuals over the age of 65. However, dementia does not occur only in elderly individuals. Young and middle-aged adults, as well as children and adolescents, may also be affected by this condition.

Symptoms and Psychotic Features

Typically, the cognitive deficits that occur in dementia are severe enough to lead to a recognizable and significant decline in a person's previous level of social and occupational functioning. During the early stages of dementia, memory impairment is likely to be the most readily noticeable symptom. This is manifested mainly by an individual's reduced ability to learn new material as well as to remember previously learned material. During the later stages of the illness, the afflicted individual may become unable to recognize familiar objects or family members. In addition to memory impairment, when a person is suffering from dementia, his or her language abilities may also deteriorate. This may be manifested by an individual's inability to provide names of familiar people and objects. The person's speech may become vague or digressive. A person with dementia may have difficulty comprehending words with which he or she was previously familiar. A person with dementia also may exhibit disinhibited or inappropriate behaviors, anxiety, mood, or sleep disturbances.

Individuals with dementia may develop psychotic symptomatology during the course of their dementia. Some of the symptoms may include hallucinations and delusions. Considering the often disturbing nature of the psychotic symptoms, those who are suffering from psychosis may potentially become aggressive or violent toward others.

Fortunately, dementia is quite rare in both children and adolescents. However, when it is diagnosed, it is generally the result of a general medical condition (often a neurodegenerative disorder). The dementia may present as a significant deterioration in functioning or delay in normal acquisition of developmentally appropriate milestones. Deterioration in school performance may be an early sign.

Etiology

There are several different general medical conditions that can lead to the emergence of dementia. The most common causes of dementia in adults include Alzheimer's disease, dementia with Lewy bodies and cerebral vascular disease. Fortunately, these conditions do not occur in young people. However, there are other, less common conditions that may affect children and adolescents and lead to dementia.

According to the *DSM-IV*, there are several different disorders that are associated with dementia. These include traumatic brain injury, brain tumors, anoxia, infectious disorders (such as those caused by HIV), endocrine conditions, vitamin deficiencies, immune disorders, hepatic diseases, and metabolic and neurological conditions. In addition, substances such as alcohol, cocaine, inhalants, and hallucinogens, all potentially cause dementia. Exposure to toxic or poisonous substances may also lead to the development of dementia.

Differential Diagnosis and Treatment

Considering the myriad of potential symptoms that may occur in dementia and the fact that the condition can be accompanied by psychotic features, it is important to conduct an extensive medical examination and to obtain information regarding the individual's psychological and familial history before making this diagnosis. This is necessary with children and adolescents because it is essential to make every effort to identify the cause of the dementia and the psychotic symptoms.

One of the main conditions that must be considered when evaluating a youth for whom the diagnosis of dementia is being considered is the diagnosis of delirium. The two conditions are able to be distinguished from each other by the fact that the symptoms that characterize delirium typically fluctuate. On the other hand, the symptoms of dementia usually are more stable over the short term.

There are several other conditions that must be ruled out before a diagnosis of dementia is given to a young patient. Substance abuse-related disorders (such as intoxication or withdrawal) may mimic some of the cognitive deficits that are characteristic of dementia. The possibility that a primary psychotic disorder such as schizophrenia may be present must also be examined because dementia may be characterized by psychotic symptoms. On occasion, those who suffer from major depressive disorder have complaints of memory loss or impairment, difficulty thinking or concentrating, and a reduction in intellectual abilities. Thus, the possibility that a patient is suffering from depression must also be reviewed.

In many cases, dementia is the result of an irreversible general medical condition and therefore cannot be "cured." In cases were the underlying cause of dementia is treatable, however, different treatment approaches may be utilized depending on the causal disorder. The treatment approach for a patient with dementia usually entails providing adequate medical care to the patient, giving emotional support to the patient and his or her family members, and prescribing pharmacological treatment for specific symptoms. Anxiolytics and sedative/hypnotics may be administered in hopes of alleviating anxiety and insomnia, respectively. Similarly, antidepressants may be used to treat depressive symptomatology. In addition, antipsychotic medications may be prescribed to treat delusions and hallucinations as well as agitation.

Course and Prognosis

According to the *DSM-IV*, dementia is a condition that can take a variable course. Depending on the underlying cause, the dementia can be progressive, static, or remitting. Neurodegenerative disorders often have a progressive course. The cognitive deficits that occur as the result of brain injury are typically stable over time. For those patients in whom the underlying cause of dementia is reversible, the dementia may remit once the therapeutic interventions are implemented. Some of these reversible disorders that may have symptoms of dementia associated with them include hypothyroidism and brain tumors.

PSYCHOTIC DISORDER NOT
OTHERWISE SPECIFIED

Psychotic disorder not otherwise specified (NOS) is a diagnostic category in the *DSM-IV* that is used to describe those individuals who are suffering from psychotic symptomatology but for whom there is not sufficient or consistent evidence to warrant a diagnosis of another specific disorder. Given the fact that psychotic disorder NOS is not a clearly defined syndrome with specific symptoms, its prevalence within the general population or within children and adolescents is not known. In addition, because there has only been a relatively modest amount of research on patients meeting symptom criteria for this particular disorder, there are relatively few data about other aspects of this condition.

Symptoms and Psychotic Features

According to the *DSM-IV*, the symptoms that characterize psychotic disorder NOS are delusions, hallucinations, and thought disorder. For example, psychotic disorder NOS may be diagnosed in a patient who has a prominent symptom of psychosis (such as persistent auditory hallucinations) that is not accompanied by other features of a psychotic illness. Similarly, if enduring, nonbizarre delusions are present in a person, then these symptoms may warrant a patient being given a diagnosis of psychotic disorder NOS. This diagnosis may also be used if the clinician is initially unable to determine whether or not a patient's psychotic symptoms are the result of either a substance-related disorder or a general medical condition.

The psychotic features that characterize psychotic disorder NOS are essentially the features that are manifested in other psychotic disorders. These features include hallucinations, delusions, negative symptoms, and thought disorder. These symptoms may be persistent or may change over time.

As with adults, the symptoms of psychotic disorder NOS in children and adolescents are not clearly defined and have not been extensively researched. However, there are two groups of youths who have multiple developmental difficulties and also have psychotic-like symptomatology as part of their clinical presentation.

One cohort of youths that has been described and classified by investigators under the rubric of *multiple complex developmental disorder* (MCDD; sometimes referred to as *multiplex developmental disorder*). Youths with MCDD are described as having pervasive difficulty in three domains. Areas of dysfunction include problems with regulating affect (particularly anxiety), difficulties with interpersonal interactions, and impaired cognitive processing. Manifestations of this last group of difficulties may include delusions, magical thinking, difficulties in distinguishing reality from fantasy, and loose associations. Due to their impairments in social functioning, emotional states, and cognitive processing, youths with MCDD often are described as suffering from an autistic spectrum disorder.

The other group of youths who suffer from a variety of difficulties that have been described as having multiple impairments, as well as psychotic symptoms, are those described as having *multidimensionally impaired disorder* (MID). Interestingly, young people with MID have similar difficulties to those seen in young people with MCDD. However, investigators have described the youths with MID as possibly suffering from a variant of schizophrenia. Whether or not MCDD is truly distinct from MID remains to be seen and should be a topic for future investigation. Further research is also necessary to establish whether these conditions should be considered within the autism- or schizophrenia-spectrum of illnesses.

Age of Onset and Etiology

Considering the heterogeneity of psychotic disorder NOS, it is difficult to assess the average age of onset. The disorder has been reported in children under the age of 12 years as well as in adolescents.

Bearing in mind the heterogeneous presentation of psychotic disorder NOS and the paucity of information available about this diagnosis, it is understandable that a precise etiology for this condition is not yet known. It should be noted that high rates of psychopathology, particularly psychotic disorder, have been described in family members of youths and adults suffering from psychotic disorder NOS. These results suggest that genetic factors may contribute to the development of psychotic disorder NOS. Furthermore, these family history data also suggest that schizophrenia and psychotic disorder NOS may be related conditions. There is also evidence that environmental factors, such as recent life stressors, may have a role in the development of psychotic symptoms for patients with psychotic disorder NOS.

Differential Diagnosis and Treatment

Psychotic disorder NOS effectively is a residual diagnostic category that should be used only for patients with symptoms that do not appear to meet symptom criteria for well-established syndromal conditions. For this reason, prior to making the diagnosis of psychotic disorder NOS, the clinician should carefully review other diagnostic possibilities. As can be seen from earlier chapters, there are numerous psychiatric illnesses, substance abuse disorders, and general medical conditions that must be ruled out. Therefore, a careful psychiatric and thorough medical assessment (including laboratory tests and a physical examination) are indicated for patients for whom the diagnosis of psychotic disorder NOS is being considered.

Generally, psychotic disorder NOS should be diagnosed only in two types of patients. One is a patient who does not meet all the symptom criteria necessary to allow for another diagnosis to be given. The other type of patient is one who has an unclear clinical presentation for whom a more definitive diagnosis would be premature. It is our clinical experience that the diagnosis of psychotic disorder NOS is sometimes used inappropriately by clinicians to describe patients who are clearly suffering from another psychotic syndrome. The diagnosis of psychotic disorder NOS is used due to the clinician's concern about possibly stigmatizing the patients in question. However, it is generally recommended that if a youth is truly suffering from a clearly defined psychiatric syndrome, the young person and his or her family be accurately appraised of this fact so that appropriate information about prognosis and treatment can be shared.

There are no definitive treatment strategies available for young people suffering from psychotic disorder NOS. The research that has focused on the treatment of these youths has described only small groups of patients. With these limited data, we generally recommend that the treatment regimen for youths suffering from psychosis NOS specifically address the individual needs of the patient.

If needed, hospitalization may be considered to ensure a patient's safety as well as to provide close observation and supervision. Should a patient be aggressive or destructive, hospitalization may be necessary to prevent a patient's impulsive or assaultive behavior from harming others.

For an individual who has significant hallucinations and delusions, we have found that pharmacotherapy may be quite beneficial. As with other psychotic disorders, we generally recommend initially treating such patients with the newer atypical antipsychotic agents. We recommend these medications due to their apparent improved tolerability when compared to older drugs.

Nonpharmacological interventions such as individual, group, or family therapy may also be helpful in treating these youths. In addition, social skills training may be beneficial to the patient. However, none of these interventions have been proven to be effective in the treatment of a young person with psychotic disorder NOS. Therefore, the clinician should create a psychotherapy regimen based on the specific needs of the individual.

Finally, it is important to note that the clinical picture of patients suffering from psychotic disorder NOS may evolve over time. For example, patients with psychotic disorder NOS can eventually meet diagnostic symptom criteria for schizophrenia. For this reason, careful follow-up assessments should be conducted to monitor thoroughly the patient's clinical status and course of illness.

Course and Prognosis

Minimal research exists regarding the eventual prognosis of those individuals who suffer from psychotic disorder NOS. Some investigators have suggested that patients with psychotic disorder NOS will continue to meet symptom criteria for this condition over time. However, other studies have suggested that patients initially diagnosed with psychotic disorder NOS often will meet diagnostic symptom criteria for another psychiatric condition at follow-up. Due to the clinical heterogeneity of patients with psychotic disorder NOS and the limited amount of research done in this patient population, it is difficult to describe the eventual prognosis of young patients suffering from this condition. It is clear that more research regarding the eventual prognosis of patients diagnosed with this disorder is needed.

HALLUCINATIONS ASSOCIATED WITH DISSOCIATIVE DISORDERS AND POSTTRAUMATIC STRESS DISORDER

Psychotic symptomatology may be present in young patients who suffer from dissociative disorders as the result of traumatic events. Youths who suffer from posttraumatic stress disorder may also suffer from symptoms of psychosis. Although the phenomenology of psychotic symptoms in these populations has not been researched extensively, the occurrence of hallucinations appears to be more common in traumatized youths that suffer from dissociative disorders than in traumatized youths who do not dissociate.

The current nosology (*DSM-IV*) lists several different types of dissociative disorders. These include dissociative amnesia, dissociative fugue, dissociative identity disorder, depersonalization disorder, and dissociative disorder not otherwise specified. However, *dissociative hallucinosis*, a dissociative disorder accompanied by hallucinations, is not considered a specific disorder or condition within the current psychiatric nosology.

Although the lifetime prevalence rate for these dissociative disorders is difficult to accurately determine, the current diagnostic manual reports that these conditions are uncommon. For example, the lifetime prevalence for dissociative fugue disorder has been estimated to be as low as 0.02%. Moreover, there is even less information regarding the prevalence of dissociative disorders among children and adolescents.

Similar to the dissociative disorders, the precise lifetime prevalence of posttraumatic stress disorder has yet to be definitively established. For example, the lifetime prevalence of posttraumatic stress disorder has been reported to range from 1% to 14%, depending on the population studied. Moreover, research that has examined individuals who have been exposed to many traumatic experiences have reported prevalence rates of posttraumatic stress disorder ranging from less than 5% to almost 60%. What follows is a review of the existing literature regarding the occurrence of psychotic symptomatology among individuals with dissociative symptoms, posttraumatic stress disorder, or both.

Symptoms and Psychotic Features

There are many different symptoms that characterize the dissociative disorders. The main features include a disturbance in consciousness, memory, identity, or perception of the environment. These disturbances may vary in regard to duration as well as the nature of their onset. Dissociative amnesia is characterized mainly by an inability to remember important personal information. This forgetfulness is typically severe enough to differentiate the disorder from normal, everyday memory lapses. Dissociative amnesia is usually the result of a traumatic event or stressor.

An individual who is suffering from a dissociative fugue may unexpectedly travel away from his or her place of employment or residence. During this time, the patient is usually unable to remember his or her past. A person suffering from a dissociative fugue may be confused about his or her own identity, and may even assume a new one.

Patients who are diagnosed with a dissociative identity disorder often have two or more separate identities or personalities that alternate in controlling their behaviors. Depersonalization disorder is often described as having a recurring feeling of being detached from one's mental processes or body, but this sensation is usually accompanied by an intact sense of reality. Finally, dissociative disorder not otherwise specified is characterized by dissociative symptoms that do not specifically fulfill the complete diagnostic criteria of the other dissociative disorders.

As noted above, children and adolescents who suffer from these conditions also may experience dissociative hallucinosis. Youths who suffer from dissociative hallucinosis typically experience episodes of altered consciousness. This altered state can lead to the youth experiencing memory lapses. Youths may appear as if they are in a dream or a trance. Conversely, a youth that is experiencing an episode of dissociative hallucinosis may appear fearful, angry, and agitated. The youth also may express fear of being attacked or loosing control.

During periods of dissociative hallucinosis, a young person may act quite impulsively. They may become suicidal or manifest other forms of self-injurious behavior. On the other hand, youths with dissociative hallucinosis may become aggressive toward others. These behaviors often are associated with the young person's desire to relieve tension or to combat feelings of psychic numbness.

Along with dissociative disorders, trauma-related disorders such as posttraumatic stress disorder have been reported to be accompanied by psychotic symptomatology. According to the current diagnostic criteria, posttraumatic stress disorder is triggered by an exposure to one or more traumatic stressors such as violence, abuse, or physical injury. Many children and adolescents have developed posttraumatic stress disorder as the result of either experiencing or witnessing a stressful event. Often, the youth will respond to the stressor with intense fear or horror. After a traumatic event, a youngster with posttraumatic stress disorder may develop mood lability. A youth who is suffering from posttraumatic stress disorder may also become either physically aggressive or develop self-injurious behavior.

Following the stressful event, the young person may reexperience the trauma in a variety of forms such as nightmares or flashbacks. Nightmares experienced by youths with posttraumatic stress disorder may contain threatening content such as monsters or may focus on themes of rescue from hazardous circumstances. Children who have been traumatized may also relive their traumatic experience through imaginative play. In addition, youths with posttraumatic stress disorder may try to avoid any stimuli that can trigger memories of the traumatic event.

Young patients with posttraumatic stress disorder also may have symptoms of intense hyperarousal. Symptoms of hyperarousal may include difficulty falling asleep, a heightened startle response, or an excessive sense of vigilance. Patients with posttraumatic stress disorder may also experience *psychic numbing* in which they may feel emotionally detached from their environment and have a reduced emotional responsiveness. Youths may no longer take pleasure in previously enjoyable activities. To meet full symptom criteria for posttraumatic stress disorder, these symptoms should last at least one month and should cause significant distress and functional impairment.

It is essential to note that psychotic symptoms are not the primary feature of either dissociative disorders or posttraumatic stress disorders. Because the symptoms of psychosis that can occur in these conditions can be so disturbing and distressing to both the child and his or her parents, these symptoms occasionally lead to clinical consultation or may become the focus of clinical attention later during the course of treatment.

Psychotic symptoms in adult patients with dissociative disorders have been more fully studied than psychotic symptoms in children and adolescents with similar conditions. However, there is evidence to suggest that psychotic symptoms may occur in adults with dissociative disorders. For example, it has been noted that adults who suffered from dissociative identity disorder had scores on the Minnesota Multiphasic Personality Inventory (MMPI-2) that were indicative of psychosis. Similarly, a subsequent study reported that dissociative detachment was related to psychotic symptoms in adults with these conditions.

Analogously, there is evidence to suggest that adults with posttraumatic stress disorder also may experience symptoms of psychosis. When combat veterans with posttraumatic stress disorder were compared to combat veterans without posttraumatic stress disorder, patients with posttraumatic stress disorder were noted to suffer from significantly more hallucinations, delusions, and bizarre behavior when compared to those veterans without posttraumatic stress disorder. The psychotic features were often found to relate to wartime experiences and were primarily auditory hallucinations.

Among children and adolescents, the experiencing of psychotic features related to dissociative states or trauma appears to be similar to that of adults. Auditory hallucinations do occur in adolescents who dissociate. The auditory hallucinations experienced by a youth with dissociative hallucinosis are often described as threatening to the individual. Oftentimes these auditory hallucinations are also pejorative in nature in which derogatory comments are being made about the youth. It has also been reported that sometimes the hallucinations may command the person to commit self-injury.

Children and adolescents with posttraumatic stress disorder may experience hallucinations, which can be either visual or auditory in nature. Similar to dissociative hallucinosis, youths with posttraumatic stress disorder may experience command hallucinations to harm others. In addition, these youths may have hallucinations that are derogatory in content or threatening in nature. Young people with posttraumatic stress disorder may also experience command hallucinations to inflict harm on themselves. A youth with posttraumatic stress disorder and auditory hallucinations may report hearing the voices from either inside or outside of his or her head. Usually, youngsters with posttraumatic stress disorder will not experience other features of psychosis such as delusions, inappropriate affect, or a formal thought disorder.

It should be noted, however, that for a variety of different reasons, a child's account of an actual incident of abuse may seem either bizarre or fantastic. For this reason, when children's reports of abuse seem improbable and have a bizarre quality to them, they may be inappropriately considered delusional.

In addition, some youths, whether or not they have suffered from a traumatic incident, may suffer from nightmares. Children who have been traumatized often experience their hallucinations at night. These experiences should also be differentiated from either hypnagogic or hypnopompic hallucinations. Hypnagogic hallucinations occur at sleep onset and hypnopompic hallucinations occur at the termination of sleep. These hallucinations can either be auditory, visual, olfactory, or haptic. Patients with hypnagogic or hypnopompic hallucinations may find it difficult to distinguish reality from the hallucination. Therefore, these experiences can be quite terrifying.

Youths with dissociative hallucinosis may also appear thought disordered. Those youths who do experience disorganized thinking usually have thoughts that are characterized by terror or immense fear. The disorganization also may be accompanied by feelings of disorientation.

Age of Onset and Etiology

Both dissociative hallucinosis and posttraumatic stress disorder can develop at fairly young ages. It has been reported that posttraumatic stress disorder can occur in preschool aged children. However, many more cases of posttraumatic stress disorder have been reported in both older elementary school-aged children and in adolescents.

The etiology of dissociative disorders and posttraumatic stress disorder both have been reported to be triggered by either single or multiple traumatic life experiences. However, considering that many individuals experience trauma but do not manifest dissociative or posttraumatic stress disorder symptomatology, some research that has focused on these conditions has considered factors that may predispose a person to develop these syndromes after they experience trauma.

Some describe a variety of risk factors that may contribute to the development of posttraumatic dissociative symptomatology in children and adolescents. These include a family history or an inherited tendency to develop dissociative symptomatology, a disrupted childhood characterized by a chaotic home environment, an insecure attachment to a caregiver, the presence of sexual or physical abuse in the home, and a family that fails to either acknowledge or to help the vulnerable child cope emotionally with the abuse. The combination of some or all of these factors may make it necessary for the child to develop ways to escape from unpleasant thoughts, feelings, or experiences. When the child's desire to escape from his or her environment becomes the major priority in the child's life, dissociative symptoms are likely to become noticeable.

The development of posttraumatic stress disorder symptoms after a traumatic event or events is typically associated with the increasing severity, duration, and proximity of the traumatic event to the afflicted individual. In addition, environmental factors such as social support, family history, childhood experiences, personality variables, and the existence of other mental disorders may either foster resilience or promote the development of the disorder.

Differential Diagnosis and Treatment

Because both dissociative disorders and posttraumatic stress disorders may have psychotic symptoms that are characteristic of many other primary psychiatric disorders, one must carefully assess whether or not the traumatized individual was suffering from another psychiatric disorder prior to the development of the trauma-related diagnosis. In addition, it is important that the clinician inquire about the longitudinal course of the individual's level of functioning both prior to and after the onset of trauma-related symptomatology. In this way the clinician can assess the extent to which the trauma is affecting the youth's life. The clinician should obtain a careful family history to assess whether or not the patient has a family history of psychiatric illnesses. This is important because there is evidence to suggest that genetics may play a role in the development of posttraumatic symptomatology and family history may be a risk factor for dissociative disorders. Finally, the clinician should include a thorough medical examination and consider obtaining laboratory tests during the evaluation process. These should be done to screen for ongoing abuse, general medical conditions, or substance abuse.

Some of the disorders that should be considered prior to giving a trauma-related diagnosis to a patient with psychotic symptomatology include schizophrenia and other schizophrenia spectrum disorders such as schizophreniform disorder. One way to distinguish between a dissociative disorder and schizophrenia is by observing the patient's affect. Often the emotions that are exhibited by an individual with a dissociative disorder will be congruent with the trauma and emotional turmoil caused by a specific event. In contrast, those youths who are suffering from a psychotic disorder more typically display a grossly inappropriate affect that is not necessarily congruent with the individual's thoughts or behaviors.

Another means to help a clinician distinguish between the two types of disorders is by the nature of the symptom onset. Typically, schizophrenia has a gradual onset characterized by poor premorbid functioning and premorbid asociality. However, dissociative symptoms usually have a more rapid onset that may be clearly associated with the occurrence of a traumatic event.

In addition, the hallucinations and delusions that are commonly associated with schizophrenia are not typical of the type of hallucinations and delusions that individuals with dissociative disorders experience. For example, individuals with schizophrenia often have delusions of thought insertion, delusions of influence, or delusions of reference. Yet, those patients with dissociative disorders rarely have bizarre delusions of this nature and typically have hallucinations that are a reflection of their traumatic experience. The hallucinations of a patient with schizophrenia often are described as having no particular relationship to any given event and may involve conversations between two or more individuals. Finally, those patients with schizophrenia may seem disinterested in interacting with other individuals and are often withdrawn. Conversely, people with dissociative disorders usually desire interpersonal contact and may often appear to desperately seek attention from others.

Along with the primary psychotic disorders, when faced with a patient in whom a trauma-related hallucinosis is being considered, a clinician must also investigate the possibility that the individual may be suffering from substance abuse or a general medical condition. Often the trance-like states that are associated with dissociative disorders and posttraumatic stress disorder can be similar in presentation to those seen in general medical conditions such as delirium and temporal lobe epilepsy. These disorders should be considered and investigated as appropriate. In addition, as noted above, the individual should be screened for substance intoxication or withdrawal because these conditions may induce psychotic symptomatology.

Depending on the severity of the patient's symptomatology, the clinician may choose to admit an individual with a trauma-related condition into a hospital setting. This may be advised if the youth is at risk for self-injury, suicide, or reckless behavior. Typically, inpatient treatment for these individuals should include the presence of a supportive and nurturing staff, which is conducive to successful treatment. Once a young person is admitted for treatment, both psychotherapy and pharmacotherapy may be considered as part of a comprehensive treatment plan.

Several psychotherapy techniques that may be used with children who are suffering from dissociative symptomatology have been described. Individual psychotherapy is one of the ways to approach treatment for these youths. Typically, the initial sessions focus on having the clinician develop a rapport with the child. This is important so the youngster feels more comfortable sharing the details of the traumatic experience, as well as describing the emotions associated with it. The treatment may then progress with the clinician providing desensitization and coping techniques in hopes of helping the child deal with emotions related to the trauma. Some other psychotherapeutic techniques that may be used include art therapy, reframing of certain emotions (such as guilt or shame) that are associated with the trauma, interactive story telling, gestalt dialogues, dreams, and role playing. The possibility of success with individual psychotherapy may become diminished if the youngster is suffering from symptoms of other conditions or has environmental factors that are contributing to the propagation of the dissociative symptoms. These may include eating disorder symptoms, disruptive behaviors (such as lying), and the lack of outside social support from parents or other family members.

In addition to individual therapy, group and family sessions may be beneficial. Sharing experiences with peers who have had traumatic experiences and are now experiencing similar difficulties often may help the child confront his or her problems more confidently and effectively. Likewise, family members can also play an important role in treatment. This is particularly true if the family members are educated about the dissociative disorder and are taught how to communicate more successfully with their child. Family therapy may also be used to build a stronger emotional bond between the child and other family members. This may help alleviate some of the dysfunctional patterns that may promote dissociative symptoms.

Along with psychotherapy, a clinician may find it useful to consider pharmacotherapy. There is little empiric research regarding the pharmacotherapy of children with dissociative symptoms and posttraumatic stress disorder. However, medications that have been noted to be of potential therapeutic benefit in these conditions in adults include benzodiazapines, tricyclic antidepressants, serotonin selective reuptake inhibitors, nefazodone, beta blockers, and alpha-2-adrenergic agonists. These agents may be effective in reducing symptoms related to hyperarousal, depression, insomnia, and intrusive, repetitive thoughts. There is also evidence to suggest that propranolol, carbamazepine, and alpha-2-adrenergic agonists may have salutary effects in children with posttraumatic stress disorder. Because the majority of research on the pharmacotherapy for the treatment of dissociative symptoms and trauma has been conducted on adults, the clinician must use caution when deciding on the proper medication regimen for the treatment of children and adolescents with any of these conditions.

Course and Prognosis

The development of dissociative symptomatology among children and adolescents typically has a rapid onset and a brief duration. A dissociative episode can last for 1 hour, or as long as 1 week. In addition, dissociative episodes have the potential to recur if they are not treated properly.

Likewise, the emergence of posttraumatic stress disorder symptomatology typically occurs within the first 3 months of the traumatic event(s). However, some youths may have a delayed onset of symptomatology, and the posttraumatic symptoms may not develop for several months or several years after the trauma. It should be noted that although symptoms of posttraumatic stress disorder often diminish with time in some youths, many other young people may experience trauma-related symptoms for more than a year after the precipitating event(s).

7

PSYCHOTIC SYMPTOMS RELATED TO OTHER CONDITIONS

As can be seen from earlier sections of this book, both psychotic and nonpsychotic disorders can be associated with psychotic symptoms in children and adolescents. However, it is also important to note that hallucinations may be present in a variety of other conditions and may even be present in nonpathological states. What follows is a review of several other diagnostic possibilities that should be considered by the clinician when faced with a young person who is experiencing hallucinations or other symptoms of a psychotic illness.

DISTINGUISHING FANTASIES FROM TRUE HALLUCINATIONS

Childhood play is often characterized by imaginative play, which is not only a very normal activity, but is an essential component of development. However, there are times when children may appear to possess bizarre thoughts or claim to perceive things that are out of the ordinary. When this occurs, it is important to determine if these thoughts or perceptions are indicative of a developing psychotic illness or merely the result of normal childhood imagination.

In general, children are reporting an age-appropriate fantasy if the experiences that they are recounting lack the characteristics of a true perception. A child who is fantasizing will generally be able to acknowledge that their fantasy is part of pretending and play and will be capable of distinguishing their inner experiences from the reality of their external world. However, it is important for the clinician to realize that some children state that their fantasies are indeed "real." Because these fantasies truly do exist in the minds of these youths, such fantasies are, as far as the youngster is concerned, truly "real." In such instances, when not psychotic, these children will be able to distinguish between the reality of their inner thoughts and the reality of their external experiences.

Youths without psychiatric disorders may have other experiences that can be misconstrued as possibly being a manifestation of psychotic symptomatology. Some of the most typical of normal imagery that children experience include imaginary companions, eidetic imagery, night terrors, and other hypnagogic and hypnopompic phenomena. However, young children who possess less mature cognitive capabilities may have more difficulty communicating the nature of their experiences. For example, research conducted on the development of perception has shown that children under 6 years of age have difficulty attending to the most salient and important components of a stimulus.

Similarly, children, teenagers, and even adults who suffer from developmental disabilities or mental retardation may be improperly diagnosed as suffering from a psychotic illness when in fact they are not psychotic at all. For example, many individuals, including teenagers and adults, talk to themselves. This may be improperly interpreted as evidence that the person is experiencing hallucinations. Likewise, many youths or adults with developmental disabilities or mental retardation who are not delusional may have imaginary friends. In such instances these imaginary friends are a means by which these youths may deal with chronic social isolation and peer rejection. For these reasons, if someone with developmental disabilities or mental retardation either talks to him- or herself or has imaginary relationships, this does not necessarily mean that the person in question is suffering from a psychotic disorder.

TRUE HALLUCINATIONS
IN NONPSYCHOTIC YOUTHS

Nonpsychotic youths who suffer from hallucinations differ from psychotic children and adolescents who experience hallucinations in a number of ways. As noted previously, psychosis is a syndrome characterized by a variety of symptom clusters. Therefore, the presence of hallucinations does not necessarily imply that the youth experiencing them is psychotic. Because both the treatment and prognosis of these two groups of patients are so different, it is important to be able to accurately identify those children who, although they may be experiencing true hallucinations, are not psychotic.

Youths who are not psychotic but experience hallucinations generally have their hallucinations within the context of a clear consciousness. Not surprisingly, this usually promotes significant anxiety, distress, and fear. These experiences are particularly frightening because the young person who is experiencing these events is often unable to control or change the hallucinations. However, some nonpsychotic youths with hallucinations have been shown to have insight regarding the unreality of their hallucinatory experiences.

Because hallucinations can be so distressing, it is fortunate that most young patients seen within treatment settings do not experience these phenomena. For example, in a retrospective chart review study of 4,767 clinically referred children and adolescents without psychotic disorders, only about 1% of these young people were noted to have experienced hallucinations. The most common form of hallucinations was auditory hallucinations. This occurred in 85% of the nonpsychotic youths who had hallucinations. Of these young patients who experienced hallucinations, 40% of them had visual hallucinations and 15% had olfactory hallucinations. Thirty percent of these youths had more than one type of hallucination. Among those children who suffered from the auditory hallucinations, about three quarters of them reported that they heard voices addressed to them. Half of them claimed that the voices were telling them to do something wrong. In addition, about a third of the children with auditory hallucinations described the hallucinations as being unpleasant or threatening in nature. The origin of the voices differed among these young patients. Some of them stated that the voices were coming from within their bodies, whereas other youths reported hearing the voices outside of their bodies. Older children tended to report the voices coming from outside of their bodies, whereas younger children described the voices as coming from inside of their bodies. Of those youths who described experiencing visual hallucinations, some of them described seeing frightening objects such as skeletons or ghosts. Others claimed that they saw recently deceased individuals.

In another report that described the hallucinations in 11 nonpsychotic children ages 7 to 12 years old, another group of investigators found similar results. These investigators also observed that the most common type of hallucination in nonpsychotic children was auditory. They reported that the hallucinations experienced by nonpsychotic children were coherent and that the content of those experiences was often a reflection of current events or circumstances in these children's lives.

Other types of auditory and visual hallucination reported by nonpsychotic children included hearing animal sounds and seeing animals. In addition, others have described that nonpsychotic children can also experience haptic hallucinations. Young patients without psychotic illnesses described that they felt as if bugs were crawling on them. Often the children would try frantically to tear off their clothing in a desperate attempt to remove the bugs.

There are a variety of heterogeneous features that have been reported as being common in young patients who are suffering from hallucinations but do not suffer from psychotic disorders. These include disturbances in affect such as moodiness, irritability, depression, and feelings of guilt. The presence of disruptive behaviors has also been reported in this population. These behaviors include restlessness, agitation, impulsive behavior, inappropriate sexual behavior, tics, and stereotypical movements. Conversely, other nonpsychotic youths with hallucinations have been noted to be passive, and seem to have psychomotor retardation. Other behaviors, such as social withdrawal, social ineptness, and sleep disturbances, have been reported in these youngsters. Many nonpsychotic young people with hallucinations have been noted to suffer from anxiety or phobic disorders. In addition, some of these youths have been described as possessing irrational fears, especially regarding school. Migraine headaches have also been described as being commonplace in this group of youths.

As can be seen, there is no typical clinical presentation for a nonpsychotic youth with hallucinatory experiences. This is because these patients can suffer from a wide variety of comorbid difficulties. However, it should be noted that some youths with nonpsychotic hallucinations do not suffer from significant coexisting conditions.

Age of Onset and Etiology

The occurrence of nonpsychotic hallucinations has been documented in children as young as 3 years of age. However, most of the research has focused on children between the ages of 7 and 13 years. However, nonpsychotic hallucinations do occur in older adolescents.

One factor that appears to be consistently associated with the appearance of nonpsychotic hallucinations in children is the presence of a stressor within the child or adolescent's home environment. It has been noted that nonpsychotic hallucinations are often precipitated by stressful life changes. These stressors include transferring to a different school, being admitted to a hospital, parental separation, or experiencing the death of a friend or a loved one. Other studies have shown that children who suffered from nonpsychotic hallucinations often have intrafamilial stressors that may include parental substance abuse and low socioeconomic status. As noted in a previous chapter, hallucinations also can occur in patients who have suffered from either physical or sexual abuse.

In addition, parental characteristics such as being overly hostile or controlling, anxious or insecure, and disinterested or rigid have been described as possibly being associated with the development of hallucinations in young patients who are not psychotic. More than one study has reported an increased prevalence of affective and mood disturbances in the families of young patients with hallucinations. Histories of depression, anxiety, bipolar disorder, and panic disorder have been described as quite prevalent among the family members of children with nonpsychotic hallucinations.

Some have hypothesized that nonpsychotic children and adolescents hallucinate because the hallucinations serve as an escape mechanism for a youngster who is experiencing intense fears and anxieties regarding a stressful environment in which they are placed. In addition, nonpsychotic youths are believed to hallucinate because the hallucinatory experiences provide a more acceptable way for them to express their thoughts and feelings of hostility or aggression. Finally, it has been hypothesized that nonpsychotic children may hallucinate because they are experiencing feelings of guilt and fear of punishment. Overall, these hypotheses infer that nonpsychotic hallucinations may be the result of the inability of youth to sufficiently express or experience certain disturbing emotions.

Treatment

Different types of therapeutic interventions have been considered for the treatment of nonpsychotic hallucinations in young people. It has been reported that children with nonpsychotic hallucinations respond favorably to psychotherapy involving both the parents and the children when it also incorporates environmental interventions within the home and at school. Others have noted that brief supportive therapy tends to help children whose hallucinations appeared to be a result of a significant life stressor. However, others have observed that some children responded better to more long-term individual psychotherapy.

Along with nonpharmacological interventions, it has been noted that if identified, treating the underlying etiology for the nonpsychotic hallucinations with medications may be effective. Young people who suffer from posttraumatic stress disorder and who have hallucinations may respond well to pharmacological treatment of their anxiety disorder. In addition, for those children who suffer from migraine headaches and nonpsychotic hallucinations, Periactin® (cyproheptadine) can be helpful in reducing both the migraines and the hallucinations. In short, pharmacological interventions should be considered in those patients in whom an existing clinical syndrome might respond to medication. However, it should be clearly stated that treatment with antipsychotics does not appear indicated in these youths.

Course and Prognosis

In some studies, nonpsychotic hallucinations generally appear to be transient phenomena and are not likely to persist for an extensive period of time. It has been noted that the hallucinations in a small sample of nonpsychotic children generally last for only several hours to several days. Consistent with this finding, others have described the hallucinations in nonpsychotic children as remitting quite rapidly, generally disappearing within a few weeks or months. In some of the cases, hallucinatory symptoms have been reported to diminish spontaneously without any specific therapeutic intervention.

Conversely, there is evidence to suggest that it is possible for nonpsychotic hallucinations to last for several years. A follow-up study of adults who suffered from nonpsychotic hallucinations as children reported that more than half of the participants reported having hallucinatory experiences during the time of follow-up. In addition, it has been reported that approximately half of children who suffered from nonpsychotic hallucinations at an initial intake assessment, also suffered from them during a follow-up period approximately 4 years later.

Although the natural history of the hallucinatory experiences seems to be quite variable, some research has described an optimistic outcome for some youths who suffer from nonpsychotic hallucinations. After the precipitating environmental stressors among a sample of children with nonpsychotic hallucinations were identified and then addressed, favorable outcomes for these youths were observed. In addition, others have noted that the short-term prognosis for young people with nonpsychotic hallucinations was generally very good, provided that the emotional disturbances associated with these phenomena were understood and remedied effectively.

In summary, it appears that the longitudinal course of nonpsychotic hallucinations in young people is quite variable. Some youths have a more benign course, whereas others may have persistent hallucinatory experiences. It is likely that the differences in outcomes across samples may be related to the heterogeneity of the underlying causes for the hallucinations in different groups of patients.

8

CULTURAL INFLUENCES AND PSYCHOSIS

There has been little research devoted to the study of cultural influences on the expression of psychosis. This is unfortunate for several reasons. First, an understanding and appreciation of the culture from which a young person and his or her family come can help the clinician during both the assessment and the treatment of a youth in a variety of different ways. For example, in a youngster in whom a psychotic disorder is suspected, cultural influences can affect how psychiatric symptomatology may be expressed. In addition, culture can affect how families communicate and interact with mental health professionals.

An appreciation of the culture from which a youth comes is also important because there are culture-specific syndromes that can present with symptomatology that may be considered psychotic. These culturally bound syndromes are disturbances in which the expression of psychosocial dysfunction is specifically manifested within the context of a particular culture, but is absent from the framework of general Western culture. Whereas some of those suffering from these culturally bound conditions meet diagnostic criteria for a psychotic disorder, others may not. Several of these culture-specific psychoses were once classified under the rubric of atypical psychosis.

Appreciation of cultures other than one's own is important because different cultures may conceptualize and describe psychotic symptomatology among the members of their society in different fashions. In fact, the manner in which a member of Western culture may interpret psychotic behavior may be quite different from the way that Eastern and African cultures may view the same behavior. In fact, what may be considered maladaptive or unusual behavior or thinking in a particular culture may not be considered dysfunctional or idiosyncratic in other cultures.

The following section will discuss how cultural distinctions may influence the means by which different peoples approach, understand, and seek treatment for a youth who might be considered psychotic. With an appreciation of these topics, a clinician can have a better understanding of how to approach those clinical situations in which culturally sensitive issues are present.

WHAT IS CULTURE?

There are many ways in which culture can be defined. Culture has been referred to as "the complex patterns of learned behavior, values, and belief systems shared by members of a designated group. These patterns are generally transmitted through generations, creating a blueprint not only for thought and action but also for physical illness and its presentations, for psychopathology, and for models of treatment" (Neppe & Tucker, 1989, p. 843). Others have defined culture as "the functional design for living worked out by an identified community over the course of its history. It is composed of organized systems of knowledge that are learned, shared, and continually renegotiated to adapt to changing conditions and new opportunities" (Edwards & Kumru, 1999, p. 409). A consideration of these definitions leads one to appreciate that the means by which a member of a particular culture interprets certain behaviors is based in part on the experiences and teachings passed on from previous generations. Culture, therefore, provides the basis and context for the understanding of oneself and one's surrounding environment. For this reason, a clinician should consider culture when formulating a diagnosis and developing a treatment plan for a patient.

CULTURALLY INFLUENCED PHENOMENA

One of the ways in which cultural influences should be considered when working with a young patient in whom a psychotic disorder is suspected is to appreciate that not all cultures view psychopathology as an experience that originates from within the individual. For example, some cultures use the process of projection, which is a common and acceptable practice in many cultures other than our own. Projection is just one example of the different ways in which certain cultures may conceptualize and express the presence of psychopathology among members of their society.

Via the mechanism of projection, members of a certain culture tend to place shame and blame on individuals, objects, or things rather than themselves. Because negative attributions are not internalized, but rather projected externally, aggressive behavior toward others may be manifested as a means by which psychological distress is expressed. In addition, because certain cultures believe that external forces are the source of difficulties, persons in those cultures may perform ritualistic ceremonies to address these external forces. These rites are intended to ward off outside influences, which may be of supernatural origin, that are to blame for the presence of psychopathology and emotional distress among members of their society.

Just as belief in the supernatural may have a role in the projection mechanism that occurs in some cultures, there are some cultures in which beliefs in mysticism and the supernatural are quite prevalent and acceptable. For example, the practice and belief in both witchcraft and sorcery is thought to be part of every day life within many cultures. These beliefs may serve a religious or spiritual role in certain cultures. Belief in other spiritual practices such as shamanism may be misinterpreted by a clinician as a manifestation of a psychiatric disorder. As another example, some religious beliefs involve communicating with the dead, spirits, or other supernatural forces. In addition, an acceptance of other phenomena such as trances and possession may also occur within the context of a particular culture. A clinician who is not aware that these types of practices are sanctioned and accepted within certain cultures may very well interpret them as manifestations of psychosis.

In addition to religious or spiritual beliefs and practices, other factors such as social or political influences may lead to the presence of thoughts and behaviors in individuals that could be misconstrued as expressions of psychosis. For example, people who have experienced intense discrimination or racism may develop suspiciousness or paranoia. These thoughts can at times be considered delusional in quality and intensity. The presence of this type of thinking or behavior may make an accurate interpretation of a clinical presentation more complicated for the clinician unless he or she is mindful of the social experiences of the young person in question.

The phenomena discussed above provide a general description of why cultural influences should be considered when one is working with a youth in whom the diagnosis of a psychotic disorder is being considered. As mentioned above, there are several culturally specific phenomena that also occur. These conditions are not limited to one geographic locale, but occur throughout the world. Because travel across the globe is becoming increasingly common, the possibility that a clinician may be asked to care for a young person experiencing one of these culturally bound syndromes is becoming more and more likely. For further reference, the *DSM-IV* provides detailed descriptions of many more cultural phenomena that will be only briefly summarized here.

Disorders of Africa

Boufee Delirante. The main symptoms of this particular condition are sudden outbursts of aggression, agitation, and confusion. Some with this condition may experience visual and auditory hallucinations or paranoid ideation. Boufee delirante has been described in West Africa and Haiti and its presentation is similar to that of a brief psychotic disorder.

Brain Fatigue. This culturally bound syndrome generally occurs among high school and college students in West Africa. It is an expression of emotional distress and is often the result of educational pressures. Cognitive symptoms of *brain fatigue* that could be confused with psychosis include difficulties with concentration, remembering, and thinking. Somatic complaints such as fatigue, visual disturbances, as well as pain, pressure, and tightness around the head and neck are also characteristic of the condition. Other than psychosis, "brain fag" has many symptoms of anxiety, depressive, or somatoform disorders.

Zar. This syndrome is reported among North African and Middle Eastern cultures. Among these cultures, this is not considered a pathological condition. Zar is characterized by the belief that supernatural spirits possess an individual. In fact, the person, usually a woman, may believe that she has developed a long-term relationship with a possessing spirit. The person with zar may experience anxiety, restlessness, dissociative symptoms, shouting, laughing, singing, crying, and even convulsions. Other symptoms may also include refusal to attend to routine activities and responsibilities.

Disorders of East and Southeast Asia

Amok. Amok is of Malayan origin and translated means to "engage furiously in battle." The condition begins with a period of solemn behavior followed by unprovoked aggressive and violent outbursts that lasts several hours. These outbursts can either be directed at other people or objects. The condition is mostly prevalent in men, and is often triggered when the individual is insulted. This phenomenon is seen in Southeast Asian cultures and may occur in people with chronic psychotic disorders. In addition, a similar clinical picture has been reported in Puerto Rican and Navajo cultures and are called mal de pelea and iich'aa, respectively, in these regions.

Koro. This particular phenomenon is reported in southern and eastern Asia, but also has been reported to occur in India. In men it is characterized by intense anxiety or fear that the penis will retract into the body, leading to the afflicted person's death. In women koro is associated with fear relating to internal recession of the vulva or nipples. Clinicians should recognize that koro is a culturally based syndrome that is considered an illness within the patient's culture. However, patients with koro should not necessarily be considered to be manifesting a delusional symptom by the Western clinician.

Latah. Although a phenomenon of southeast Asia, the clinical picture of latah has been reported in many other areas of the world. The characteristic symptom of this particular condition is a hypersensitivity reaction to a sudden fright. People with latah may experience echopraxia or echolalia, use obscenities, and exhibit dissociative-like behavior. Due to the idiosyncrasies in behavior that may be manifested in patients with latah, patients suffering from this condition may resemble a patient with schizophrenia and catatonic symptoms. In many cases it is a habit and is a coping mechanism. Less frequently, it is consciously performed to obtain secondary gain.

Qi-gong Psychotic Reaction. This condition occurs within the Chinese culture. It is characterized by dissociative, paranoid, or other psychotic symptoms. This particular phenomenon is generally brief in duration and typically develops after participation in a Chinese health-enhancing activity called Qi-gong.

Shame (or Face). This syndrome has been reported to occur within the Filipino culture and is most common in young adolescent females. Symptoms of the condition include insomnia, anorexia, social withdrawal, suicidal ideation, and auditory hallucinations. Although this syndrome may have symptoms of a psychotic disorder, it is generally the result of the afflicted individual having been publicly humiliated or shamed, thereby losing face. When a clinician is asked to treat a young person with this condition, specifically addressing feelings of shame with the teenager is likely to be of greatest benefit.

Shin-Byung. This syndrome occurs within the Korean culture. The afflicted individual expresses somatic symptoms which are accompanied by anxiety. The somatic complaints may include weakness, anorexia, dizziness, sleep, and gastrointestinal problems. Subsequently, these symptoms are replaced by dissociative symptoms and by the afflicted person's belief that he or she is possessed by spirits.

Taijin Kyofusho. This condition occurs within the Japanese culture. In many ways it resembles social phobia. Taijin Kyofusho is characterized by worrying that one's appearance, facial expressions, gestures, or body odor will somehow be displeasing or offensive to other people. It is important that this syndrome be distinguished from a somatic delusion or body dysmorphic disorder.

Disorder of Europe

Mal de Ojo. The literal translation is the *evil eye.* This condition is reported among Mediterranean cultures. It is characterized mainly by disturbed sleep, crying for no apparent reason, diarrhea, vomiting, and fever.

Disorders of Latin America

Ataque de Nervios. This particular phenomenon is common in the Caribbean and Latin American regions. Ataque de nervios generally is an acute response to an intrafamilial stressor, such as a death in the family or marital conflict that lasts for only a brief period of time. It is a manifestation of a distress response. Ataque de nervios is characterized by shouting, crying, trembling, as well as verbal or physical aggression. In addition, some individuals with this condition may experience dissociative episodes, seizures, or fainting. The afflicted may exhibit self-injurious or suicidal behaviors as well as perceptual disturbances. The symptoms of ataque de nervios frequently begin while in the presence of relatives where the affected individual is able to receive psychological support and to relinquish social responsibility.

Individuals who experience ataque de nervios are likely to be older, less educated, and female. People who experience this syndrome may also meet criteria for anxiety or mood disorders. However, the symptoms of this condition also resemble those of a brief psychotic disorder.

Locura. This condition is used to describe a persistent psychosis among Latinos both in the United States and Latin America. The symptoms of this condition are similar to those that may be seen in psychotic disorders. They include incoherence, agitation, auditory and visual hallucinations, and unpredictable or violent behaviors.

Nervios. This condition, which was first described in Costa Rica, is now commonly referred to among the Latino culture in both the United States and Latin America as a means of describing emotional upset. The primary symptoms of nervios include those of psychological distress and somatic symptomatology. Patients with this condition may complain of neurological symptoms such as headaches, trembling, tingling sensations, and dizziness. People with nervios also may describe irritability, anorexia, dyspepsia, sleep disturbances, anxiety, tearfulness, disorientation, as well as difficulties concentrating. This particular condition, unlike ataque de nervios, is thought to be a chronic problem. Nervios may occur by itself or it may occur in patients who meet diagnostic criteria for anxiety, depressive, dissociative, somatoform, or psychotic disorders.

Disorders of North America and the Caribbean

Ghost Sickness. This phenomenon is reported among members of Native American tribes. A person with this condition becomes preoccupied with either thoughts of death or with thoughts about a person who is deceased. Symptoms of ghost sickness include nightmares, a sense of foreboding, anxiety, anorexia, fainting, dizziness, hallucinations, and confusion. Due to the perceptual and cognitive disturbances that may occur in an afflicted individual, these patients may appear psychotic.

Piblokto. This condition, reported among arctic and subarctic Eskimo communities, is also known as *arctic hysteria.* It occurs most commonly in women and is attributed to evil spirits. Characterized by a period of irritability that may last hours or days, it is then followed by a period of up to 2 hours of intense excitement. During this period of excitement, inappropriate or dangerous behavior may occur. These acts include tearing off one's clothes, running, screaming, breaking furniture, shouting obscenities, and eating one's feces. This period of excitement may culminate in seizures that are then followed by a deep sleep. After the episode has subsided, the person may not by able to recall what had occurred.

Spell. Reported primarily among African American and European American cultures from the southern United States, this particular condition is characterized by a trance-like state in which the afflicted individual is believed to be communicating with either deceased relatives or spirits. A spell may be mistaken as a brief psychotic episode.

Windigo. This culture-bound syndrome occurs in Native Americans of Canada and is believed to be due to witchcraft. Windigo is characterized by an affected person's fear that he or she may become a cannibal due to possession by a monster. After a period of anorexia and depression, the afflicted individual may experience suicidal or homicidal ideation or behaviors.

GUIDELINES FOR ASSESSING
AND TREATING YOUTHS
OF DIFFERENT CULTURES

Because there are multiple disorders that are unique to different cultures, it may be quite difficult for a clinician to formulate an accurate diagnosis for a young person who is expressing psychotic symptomatology. As can be seen, it is important to understand that some cultures may consider psychotic symptomatology to be attributable to evil spirits, witchcraft, or even cultural norms. Therefore, the description of the psychotic symptomatology by a youth or the youth's family may be influenced by the culture to which the family belongs. However, despite the fact that a family may believe that external or supernatural influences may be the cause of their child's condition, the clinician must consider other possibilities such as syndromal mental illnesses or substance abuse. Because schizophrenia is a disorder that has been reported throughout the world, an adolescent who shows the signs of schizophrenia may very well be suffering from this condition.

Therefore, to formulate an accurate diagnosis, it is important for the clinician to acquire both an understanding of the type of behaviors that the youth is engaging in and the manner in which the culture usually appreciates the presenting symptoms. Various cultures have different expectations and attitudes toward children and adolescents. Behavior that may be culturally sanctioned by one group may be considered pathological in another. However, it should also be remembered that cultural influences may effect the expression of psychotic symptomatology in people with mental illnesses. Therefore, just because it may become clear to the clinician that a youth's culture is influencing the manifestations of his or her condition, does not necessarily mean that the young person in question is not psychotic.

Moreover, because the means by which psychotic conditions are generally managed within various cultures do not always include traditional medical interventions, the implementation of a traditional treatment regimen that might be successful in alleviating the patient's symptoms may be viewed with skepticism or suspicion. In some cases, the clinician may chose to modify the way that he or she interacts with a patient and the family to accommodate their cultural practices or beliefs.

Given that there are various cultural influences that may influence the expression of psychotic symptoms in a youth, a clinician may find him- or herself pondering many diagnostic possibilities while trying to formulate a diagnosis. The clinician may wonder if behaviors or symptoms that may appear idiosyncratic to the clinician are common or expected among adolescent individuals of a particular culture. In addition, the clinician may also be thinking about the specific role that culture plays in the development, maintenance, and treatment of certain symptoms. Fortunately, guidelines that may be helpful for assessing and treating psychotic features in individuals from a different culture have been previously described in detail.

Communicate Properly

One essential component to a successful diagnosis is the clinician's ability to foster communication with the patient in a culturally sensitive fashion. Having a clinician who not only understands the patient's language but is also familiar with the individual's culture can facilitate this. The main reason why this is important is because it affords the clinician a clearer understanding of the patient's psychotic symptomatology within the context of the patient's culture. If a clinician who speaks the patient's language is not available, culturally sensitive communication through an interpreter trusted by the patient and his or her family can facilitate the assessment and treatment processes.

By being aware that attitudes about seeking professional help may vary between cultures is another key means to foster proper communication among the patient, the patient's family, and the clinician. Often, people with mental health difficulties are shunned in certain cultures. For this reason, the patient or the patient's family may be reticent about disclosing the precise nature of the afflicted person's symptoms to the clinician. Similarly, if a person who comes from a culture in which patients with mental illnesses are stigmatized, it is important for the clinician to keep in mind that it is likely that a patient's symptoms and difficulties may be quite severe at the time of initial consultation. At times, only the presence of severe symptomatology or dysfunction will cause a family to seek out help from a mental health professional because of the fear of their child being stigmatized.

Obtain a Complete History

To make a correct diagnosis, it is important to obtain a careful history. Because psychotic disorders are often associated with disturbances in premorbid functioning, it is important to ascertain whether the patient's premorbid functioning was considered appropriate for that given culture. When faced with a youth with psychotic symptoms, it is important to ascertain how the condition may be affecting the youth's functioning within the context of their own culture. The clinician should obtain information regarding not only the duration of the symptoms but also the intensity of the symptoms. One should ascertain how disruptive the youth's difficulties are to their everyday life. The clinician also should ascertain which aspects of the youth's life are being affected by the illness. In addition, influences of family (other than genetic vulnerability) and peers may affect the expression of psychotic symptomatology. Because youths can be quite impressionable or mimic what they have seen others express, whether or not a friend or family member is having difficulties similar to those seen in the youth in question should be determined.

As part of a careful history, it is crucial to consider that the youth's culture may influence the way in which his or her psychotic symptoms are expressed. For example, certain cultures may describe these symptoms in religious terms. Other cultures may provide a more mystical explanation of the symptoms. Therefore, the clinician should gain a clear appreciation of how members of an individual's culture recognize and understand the symptoms. To collect a more complete assessment of the youth within the context of his or her culture, if it is acceptable to the patient and the patient's family, the clinician may want to work with other important figures in the young person's life. Interviews with other adults may provide further information regarding diagnosis and treatment from within the context of a young person's culture.

Do Not Overgeneralize

One of the primary mistakes that a clinician can make when working with patients from other cultures is that they might make a judgment about a young person based on the youth's outward appearance. In addition, the clinician may erroneously assume that because a young patient is a member of a certain group that the youth and the youth's family ascribe to the practices and beliefs of that culture. However, an individual's or a family's beliefs may not necessarily be congruent with what is accepted by the majority of members in a youth's culture. For these reasons, it is crucial that each patient be carefully evaluated not only as a member of a culture, but also as an individual.

Have Confidence

Assessing and treating a child or adolescent from another culture can be quite challenging for a clinician. However, it is important for a clinician to maintain confidence in his or her ability to properly diagnose and treat a particular individual from any culture. A clinician may feel tempted to refer a case to another clinician who may be from the same cultural background as the patient or who may be more familiar with the patient's culture. Probably the only time that a clinician should refer a case to another clinician is if he or she feels that it is not possible to establish a working relationship with the patient and members of the patient's family. Fortunately, the presence of cultural differences is generally not an insurmountable obstacle to the development of a therapeutic relationship among a clinician, a young patient, and a youth's family.

SUMMARY

As can be seen, the assessment and treatment of psychotic features in individuals who are from other cultures may be quite challenging for the clinician. By consulting with the patient, the family, and other health professionals, both an accurate diagnosis and an effective treatment plan can be formulated for the child or adolescent in question. Considering that many cultures place a stigma on seeking professional help for mental health issues, it is essential that the clinician treat both the patient and his or her family with respect and remain sensitive to their needs and concerns. In addition, when working with an adolescent patient, the clinician especially may want to consider the role that contextual factors play in the manifestation of the symptoms. Consulting with family members about whether the young patient's condition is having an adverse effect on developmentally and culturally expected functioning may be the most effective way to approach diagnosis and treatment.

9

EVALUATION OF PSYCHOTIC SYMPTOMS AND ANTIPSYCHOTIC SIDE EFFECTS

The proper detection and diagnosis of psychotic symptomatology among children and adolescents can be challenging for clinicians. As noted previously, this is due to a variety of reasons. First, there are numerous symptoms of psychosis. These include hallucinations, delusions, thought disorder, inappropriate affect, and catatonia. Therefore, to ascertain appropriately whether or not a psychotic disorder is present or absent, all of these symptoms need to be carefully considered as part of the assessment process. In addition, even if a symptom of psychosis is present, the differential diagnosis of each symptom of psychosis is extensive. For this reason, it is often difficult to decide whether or not a symptom that could be a manifestation of a psychotic disorder is actually a part of a psychotic process. For example, as previously described, not all hallucinations occur within the context of a psychotic illness.

In addition, it may be difficult to ascertain whether or not a distressing and intrusive thought is part of a delusional system. Although youths with obsessive-compulsive disorder do have intrusive thoughts that may be quite distressing to them, youths with obsessive-compulsive disorder do not have the myriad of other symptoms or the same longitudinal course as youths who are afflicted with a psychotic disorder. The ability to distinguish between obsessive-compulsive disorder and a psychotic illness is important because the treatment and outcome of both conditions are so different. For this reason, if a youth has intrusive, unpleasant thoughts or concerns about cleanliness and contamination, it is essential to delineate whether or not these thoughts are part of a delusion that is occurring within a psychotic state or are the manifestations of obsessive-compulsive disorder.

Furthermore, symptoms of psychotic disorders can be present in a variety of psychotic and nonpsychotic psychiatric disorders, general medical conditions, and nonsyndromal states. Further complicating the assessment process of a youth in whom a psychotic disorder is suspected is that much less research has been performed in children and adolescents with psychotic disorders than adults. Unfortunately, a group of procedures that could be considered a gold standard assessment battery for youths with a suspected psychotic disorder has not been clearly established.

Finally, another difficulty with the assessment of a young person in whom a psychotic disorder is being considered is that the clinician needs to be mindful about whether or not the youth in question is functioning within the range of age and cognitively appropriate developmental norms. For all these reasons, it is understandable that the assessment of psychotic symptoms in children and adolescents may be more challenging than the assessment of psychosis in adults.

To ensure that an accurate diagnosis is made, it is generally recommended that both the patients and their parents are interviewed. Furthermore, because youths with psychosis may have difficulties in a wide variety of settings, it is suggested that information that encompasses a broad range of the child's current and previous mental health history be considered. Typically, this may involve obtaining school reports, previous neuropsychological test data, speech and language evaluations, and the results of neurological and genetics consultations. In addition, information regarding the onset of the condition, changes in the child's academic and social functioning, and developmental and family history should all be obtained. Therefore, to optimize the detection and diagnosis of psychotic symptoms in children and adolescents, there is a need for the clinician to have data about a young person's functioning, strengths, and shortcomings in a wide variety of domains.

A fair amount of research has also been devoted to the development of reliable and valid psychometric instruments that may be used with children and adolescents. Some are used as diagnostic measures. Others are employed to quantify and describe symptomatology in children and adolescents. In addition, there are psychological assessment measures that can be used to describe a young person's level of functioning. There are several measures that are commonly used for these purposes. A discussion of the characteristics of some of the most frequently used psychometric measures employed with children and adolescents with psychotic symptomatology follows.

In addition, because neurological side effects such as tardive dyskinesia, Parkinsonism, and akathisia may all occur during the course of antipsychotic pharmacotherapy, it is often important for the clinician to monitor for the possibility of these adverse events. Numerous instruments are used to this end. Several of the most commonly used measures will also be reviewed. It should be noted that although not all of the psychometric instruments or neurological rating scales that will be described were specifically developed for use in children and adolescents with psychotic disorders, these measures often have utility in the assessment and treatment of youths who suffer from these conditions.

It is also important to remember the shortcomings of these assessment scales and diagnostic instruments. Although rating scales may have an important role in the assessment and treatment of youths with psychosis, it is important to recognize that no single instrument or battery of question-naires should be used to either definitively confirm or definitively refute the presence or absence of a psychotic disorder in a youth. For example, pro-jective tests occasionally have been used in the past as diagnostic tools in child and adolescent psychiatry. Some of these projective tests may, at times, be able to distinguish dysfunctional children from those without psychological disturbances. In addition, projective tests may provide valuable information about the thoughts and feelings of young people with psychological disturbances. However, there are no data to support the use of these instruments as diagnostic tests or outcome measures. Despite this fact, it is not uncommon for patients to come for clinical assessment whose parents were informed that the presence or absence of a psychotic disorder was tested for with a projective test.

At present, a clinician should only diagnose a youth as suffering from a psychotic disorder based on his or her judgment and skill in incorpo-rating all available clinical information. No single instrument or battery of instruments can integrate information and judge the nature of information obtained from a variety of sources as a skilled clinician is able to. Conver-sely, just because psychometric instruments alone should not be used to confirm or refute the presence of a psychotic disorder, it does not mean that these measures may not provide useful information to the clinician.

DIAGNOSTIC INTERVIEWS

Several diagnostic interviews have been developed to ascertain either the presence or absence of diagnostic criteria for many of the major psychiatric disorders in children and adolescents. These include structured and semi-structured diagnostic interviews.

Probably the most commonly employed structured diagnostic instrument in child and adolescent psychiatry is the Diagnostic Interview Schedule for Children (DISC). It can be administered to the parent, the child, or both by either a computer or a lay interviewer. Because the DISC is not designed to be administered by a skilled clinician, and as noted above, the ascertainment of information about the presence or absence of psychotic symptomatology is not a simple one, the DISC has not been used in studies that have focused on child and adolescent schizophrenia.

The Diagnostic Interview for Children and Adolescents (DICA), a clinician-rated instrument, was the first structured psychiatric interview developed for children. It has two separate interviews, one for the child and one for the parent. The DICA has been used as a diagnostic instrument in child and adolescent schizophrenia research. However, there is no method for aggregating information from the parent and child interviews with the DICA. Due to the imperfections of the DICA and the DISC, the most commonly used diagnostic assessment instrument being used in pediatric mood and psychotic disorder research studies is the Schedule for Affective Disorders and Schizophrenia for School-Age Children (K-SADS). The most recent iteration of the K-SADS is the Present and Lifetime version of this instrument, otherwise known as the K-SADS-PL.

Schedule for Affective Disorders and Schizophrenia for School-Age Children

The Schedule for Affective Disorders and Schizophrenia for School-Aged Children, Present Episode Version (K-SADS-P) is a semistructured diagnostic instrument that was first developed to assess affective illnesses in children and teenagers using DSM-III nosology. This measure was intended to be utilized primarily by skilled individuals with clinical experience.

The K-SADS-PL was developed to address shortcomings of the K-SADS-P and to incorporate *DSM-IV* criteria. One of the drawbacks of the K-SADS-P was that it did not assess for some of the major psychiatric diagnoses. In addition, the K-SADS-P did not examine previous psychiatric history. The K-SADS-PL addresses these shortcomings by including questions about most major psychiatric diagnoses that occur during childhood and adolescence. The K-SADS-PL also considers both current and lifetime symptomatology for most of these conditions. For both instruments, the parent and the child are interviewed separately, and a summary score for each item is derived based on the rater's clinical impression of both interviews.

The K-SADS-PL is comprised of seven different components, which can detect the presence of most *DSM-IV* Axis I child and adolescent psychiatric diagnoses. The administration of the K-SADS-PL includes an introductory interview (to build rapport), a screen interview (to obtain preliminary information regarding diagnostic criteria), and five diagnostic supplements (to further explore the presence of certain psychiatric symptomatology). Each item in the K-SADS-PL is rated on a 3-point scale.

Psychometric Properties. The psychometric properties of the K-SADS-P have been studied among a sample of Israeli adolescent inpatients. It was found that the instrument demonstrated fairly strong interrater and temporal stability (kappa = .78 and .78, respectively). In addition, the measure was also found to have adequate consensual validity (kappa = .64). These findings indicate that a reliable diagnosis can be made in acutely and severely disordered adolescents using the K-SADS-P.

It was also noted that mother and child agreement on the K-SADS-P was quite low (kappa = .42). It has been hypothesized that the low agreement between the mothers and children were the result of the mothers' tendency not to report symptoms of depression, anxiety, and other internalizing problems in comparison to their children. Mothers did, however, agree with their children regarding externalizing symptoms such as conduct problems.

Two recent studies investigated the psychometric properties of the K-SADS-PL. One study reported an average of 98% agreement among raters regarding the assignment of lifetime diagnoses. In addition, this study found high kappa coefficients for many of the different Axis I disorders when investigating the measure's temporal stability. This study also noted that the K-SADS-PL demonstrated good concurrent validity with the Child Behavior Checklist. The K-SADS-PL has also been tested among a group of Israeli inpatient and outpatient adolescents. It was found that the measure had adequate interrater reliability (kappa = .87) and consensual validity (kappa = .80). The high agreement between raters was thought to be a result of the systematic structure of the K-SADS-PL, which is comprised of clearly focused probes. As with the K-SADS-P, it was found that there was low agreement between mothers and children (kappa = .54) on the K-SADS-PL. The scales that yielded lowest mother-child agreement included depression, dysthymia, mania, phobia, oppositional-defiant disorder, and drug abuse. Higher agreement between mothers and children were related to the more externalizing symptoms such as eating disorders, conduct disorders, enuresis, psychosis, and obsessive-compulsive disorder.

MEASURES OF PSYCHOTIC SYMPTOMATOLOGY

Once a diagnosis of a psychotic disorder for a youngster has been established, there are several reasons that the clinician may wish to measure psychotic symptomatology with a standardized rating scale. Certainly, the particular symptoms of psychosis that are present in each individual may vary. By ascertaining which psychotic symptoms are present and which are absent, the clinician can then identify target symptoms for treatment. In addition, by having the psychotic symptomatology measured in terms of severity, clinicians can assess, longitudinally and in an objective fashion, the effectiveness of their interventions for a young person with a psychotic disorder. There are several rating scales that can be used to measure psychotic symptomatology in young people.

Brief Psychiatric Rating Scale

The Brief Psychiatric Rating Scale (BPRS) is a global scale that is useful for evaluating any type of psychotic disorder (including psychosis associated with mania or depression). The BPRS has been utilized in both inpatient and outpatient settings, and is designed to be administered by a trained clinician. According to some researchers, it is considered the best and most researched instrument in psychiatry. The measure consists of 18 items and there are subscales within the BPRS that can be used to measure thought disorder, behavioral disturbance, mood disorder, and anxiety. Scores on each individual item on the BPRS range from 0 to 6 and clinicians assign a score based on a clinical interview that addresses each scale item. The total score can then be used to monitor outcome and to determine the severity of a youth's difficulties.

Psychometric Properties. Most of the research on the BPRS has focused on adult populations. A recently conducted study examined the psychometrics of the positive symptom, negative symptom, and depression scales subscale scores in a sample of 101 middle-aged and elderly outpatients with schizophrenia. The positive symptoms subscale includes items such as disorganized speech, hallucinatory behavior, and unusual thought content. The negative symptoms subscale consists of questions that probe for emotional withdrawal, motor retardation, and blunted affect. The depressive subscale contains questions that consider anxiety symptoms, guilt feelings, and depressed mood. The interrater reliability for all three of these scales was found to be very good (all of the scales had an intraclass correlation coefficient of greater than .77). In addition, the scales also showed good construct validity.

An expanded 24-item version of the BPRS (BPRS-E) has also been utilized. One of the main purposes for creating the expanded version was to better assess the long-term prognosis of patients with schizophrenia. This expanded measure has been used primarily for assessing relapse rates and the recurrence of symptoms. One study, which assessed the component structure of the BPRS-E on a sample of both general psychiatric inpatients and adolescent patients with schizophrenia spectrum disorders, found that the measure is comprised of five different factors. The first factor consists of items indicative of positive symptoms such as hallucinations, delusions, and unusual thought content. The second factor is comprised of items that reflect depressive symptomatology. The third factor contains negative symptoms such as an absence of drive or affect. The fourth factor has items associated with conceptual disorganization or formal thought disorder as well as items characteristic of mania. The fifth factor only has two items— disorientation and mannerisms. However, this last factor has a low internal consistency due to the fact that it has so few items (alpha = .55). The other factors have acceptable to good internal consistency (positive factor, alpha = .74; depression factor, alpha = .75; negative factor, alpha = .76; thought disorder factor, alpha = .64). It has also been found that the BPRS-E possesses only fair discriminant validity in its ability to distinguish different diagnostic subgroups (schizophrenia, schizophreniform, schizoaffective) from one another. Therefore, one may conclude that the BPRS-E may be best suited for assessing the longitudinal course of certain symptom clusters, as opposed to distinguishing across diagnostic subgroups.

Positive and Negative Syndrome Scale

The Positive and Negative Syndrome Scale (PANSS) was initially developed to assess positive and negative symptomatology in adults with schizophrenia. The measure includes 30 items that are considered to best represent the positive and negative symptoms of the disorder. Each item is rated on a scale from 1 (*absent*) to 7 (*greatest*), measuring frequency, prominence, and behavioral disruption. There are approximately seven factors that have been identified for the PANSS. These include negative, positive, excited, depressive, cognitive dysfunction, suspiciousness, and stereotypic thinking factors. These factors are incorporated into three subscales—the negative, positive, and general psychopathology subscales. Seven items constitute the negative subscale. These items include blunted affect, emotional withdrawal, poor rapport, passive-apathetic social withdrawal, difficulty with abstract thinking, poverty of thought and spontaneous activity, and stereotyped thinking and behavior. The items that make up the positive subscale are delusions, conceptual disorganization, hallucinatory behavior, excitement, grandiosity, suspiciousness, and hostility. The sum of the remaining 16 items make up the general psychopathology subscale.

Positive and Negative Syndrome Scale for Children

In addition to the PANSS, a version of the measure called the Positive and Negative Syndrome Scale for Children (Kiddie-PANSS) was created for administration to young people to account for the unique developmental issues that affect child and adolescent psychopathology. As in the original PANSS, the Kiddie-PANSS contains the negative, positive, and general psychopathology subscales. However, it also has a prepatient interview that is useful for obtaining information from the primary caregiver. It also has a 25 minute patient interview that involves the administration of both semi-structured and structured sections. These additional components compensate for the limitations of children's communicative abilities regarding their symptomatology.

Psychometric Properties. The PANSS has good interrater reliability, high internal consistency (positive scale alpha = .80, negative scale alpha = .82, and general psychopathology scale alpha = .82), and appropriate temporal stability. In addition, it has adequate construct validity. Several studies have reported that the PANSS has sufficient internal consistency. Good interrater reliability has also been reported (positive subscale ICC = .72, negative subscale ICC = .80, and general psychopathology subscale ICC = .56) for the PANSS. In addition, strong concurrent validity with the Scale for the Assessment of Positive Symptoms (SAPS) and the Scale for the Assessment of Negative Symptoms (SANS) have also been described. The correlation coefficients with these two scales were $r = .70$ and $r = .81$, respectively.

The Kiddie-PANSS has good interrater reliability among trained raters. In addition, both the negative and general psychopathology subscales showed good internal consistency, with alpha levels of .82 for the negative subscale and .78 for the general psychopathology subscale. The positive subscale yielded a moderate alpha level of .61. The Kiddie-PANSS also has been described as having criterion-related validity.

It is clear that both the PANSS and the Kiddie-PANSS are reliable and valid measures for assessing both positive and negative symptoms of schizophrenia. Considering each measure's excellent psychometric properties, both instruments may be valuable when assessing psychotic symptoms among children and adolescents.

The Scale for the Assessment of Negative Symptoms and the Scale for the Assessment of Positive Symptoms

The Scale for the Assessment of Negative Symptoms (SANS) and the Scale for the Assessment of Positive Symptoms (SAPS) were developed to assess for the presence of negative and positive symptoms in individuals with schizophrenia. However, these measures have been used for schizoaffective disorder, schizophreniform disorder, and organic psychoses as well. Using the two instruments together provides a more comprehensive symptom profile, allowing a clinician to readily measure changes in symptomatology. The SAPS and the SANS have both been suggested as useful in the assessment of psychotic symptoms among children and adolescents. In fact, both the SAPS and the SANS have been used extensively with adolescent samples.

The SAPS was created specifically to judge the existence of positive symptomatology characteristic of schizophrenia within the month prior to assessment. The instrument is comprised of a semistructured clinical interview that is conducted by a trained rater. Each item is rated on a scale from 0 to 5 and belongs to one of four subscales, which include hallucinations, delusions, bizarre behavior, and disrupted speech. The SANS, which is a completely separate instrument from the SAPS, was designed to assess the presence of negative symptoms of schizophrenia based on behavioral observations. The measure is comprised of five subscales. These include alogia, affective flattening (which includes motor disturbances), avolition-apathy, anhedonia-asociality, and attention.

Psychometric Properties. The SAPS has demonstrated good interrater reliability for all four subscales (intraclass correlation coefficients, or ICCs, range from .70 to 1.00). When one obtains low interrater reliability while using the SAPS in adults, it is usually the result of the raters not being provided with sufficient training or experience in the administration of the instrument. In addition, it has been found that the SAPS has good interrater reliability (ICC = .80) and appropriate internal consistency (Cronbach's alpha = .71). The SAPS also has been shown to have good convergent validity with the positive symptom scale of the BPRS ($r = .66$).

The SANS has also been shown to possess good psychometric properties. It has been reported that the instrument has good reliability provided that the raters administering the instrument have received adequate training. In addition, it has been demonstrated that the internal consistency for the five subscales of the SANS are fairly high (alpha coefficients range from .67 to .90). However, the attention subscale is, overall, possibly less reliable and possibly less valid when compared with the other four subscales. Investigators have cautioned that negative symptomatology characteristic of schizophrenia, such as anhedonia and avolition, sometimes may be confused with depressive symptomatology and that this should be taken into consideration while using the instrument. Also, the SANS has been shown to possess fairly robust interrater reliability (ICC = .72) and internal consistency (alpha coefficient = .81). Moreover, it has also been reported that the SANS possesses good convergent validity with the negative symptom scale of the BPRS ($r = .71$).

Although the SAPS and the SANS have not been extensively used in young patients, considering that these instruments both demonstrate excellent psychometric properties in adults, this lends support for their use in assessing psychotic symptomatology in children and adolescents. In addition, because the two instruments are well established and have been utilized extensively, they may be helpful when comparing symptomatology in young people to the symptomatology manifested by adults with psychosis.

FUNCTIONAL ASSESSMENT

Although a variety of symptom domains characterize the psychotic disorders, when assessing and treating a young person with a psychotic disorder, it is important not only to measure the severity of the symptomatology but also to consider the youth's overall level of functioning. Psychotic disorders can lead to patient distress, intrafamilial dysfunction, academic underachievement, and failure to maintain developmentally appropriate responsibilities. Several measures are available that can be useful to the clinician who wishes to measure this domain.

Children's Global Assessment Scale

The Children's Global Assessment Scale (CGAS) is an instrument used by clinicians to obtain ratings of functional impairment for children and adolescents 4 to 16 years of age. Essentially, this measure condenses the comprehensive knowledge that has been obtained about the psychiatric and social disturbances of a particular individual and allows a rater to assign one single score. The CGAS was adapted from the Global Assessment Scale (GAS), which assesses adult levels of functional impairment. The scale measures the level of adaptive functioning and ranges from 1 (*most impaired*) to 100 (*healthiest*). Individuals who score greater than 70 on this measure are considered to be functioning within the normal range. It is composed of paragraph descriptors that depict certain behaviors. Each descriptor contains behaviorally oriented examples that are typical for children or adolescents. The rater assigns a score to each descriptor based on his or her knowledge of the child's psychological and social functioning.

It has been suggested that the CGAS may be broken down into the following two subscales: one that targets the global severity of psychopathology and the other that focuses on global competence and adaptive skills. Although the CGAS does not specifically target psychotic symptoms, it may be useful within a clinical setting because it adds a functional dimension to the symptomatic picture that is usually not considered by measures that primarily assess psychotic symptomatology.

Psychometric Properties. Since the development of the CGAS, numerous studies have focused on the reliability and validity of the clinician-rated version of this measure. However, several nonclinician versions of the CGAS have been created recently. One is a nonclinician CGAS in which global impairment is rated by a nonprofessional. Another has a rater obtain information from the parent and assign a global assessment score (PIC-GAS). There is also a youth informant CGAS (YICGAS) in which the rater obtains information from the affected child or adolescent to create a global assessment score. Finally, there is a parent-report CGAS (PCGAS) in which the parent assigns a global score of the child's functioning. The real difference between the clinician-rated version of the CGAS and the nonclinician rated versions of the CGAS is that the descriptors have been simplified within the nonclinician versions to facilitate the scoring process. A description of the psychometric properties of each of these four measures will be provided.

The clinician-rated version of the CGAS has been reported to be a useful and reliable instrument for assessing global ratings within clinical settings. Among a sample of 10 children, the CGAS demonstrated high interrater reliability with an intraclass correlation coefficient among 10 raters found to be .93. Likewise, several studies that examined the interrater reliability of the CGAS. These studies have found intraclass correlation coefficients of .84 and .87. As for the temporal stability of the CGAS, correlations of .85 and .83 have been described. However, it has been indicated that levels of temporal stability on the CGAS appear to vary based on the nature of the diagnosis. Specifically, when comparing the follow-up assessment (6 to 8 weeks after the first assessment) with the initial assessment, the stability of the ratings appeared to be the strongest for cases that were diagnosed with either a severe psychological disturbance or with a single diagnosis. Yet, for those cases that had a less severe dysfunction or that manifested symptoms characteristic of more than one disorder, the level of temporal stability was not as strong.

The clinician-rated measure of the CGAS has also been shown to possess very good discriminant validity and is able to distinguish those youths who are suffering from severely disabling disorders from youngsters who have more modest difficulties. Overall, the clinical cut off score of 70 appears to differentiate minor from more significant degrees of psychopathology. In addition, it has been found that the CGAS is able to distinguish a clinical from a nonclinical sample of children. The CGAS also was able to differentiate severely impaired, moderately impaired, and unimpaired individuals from one another. It should be noted, however, that the anchor points at the lower end of the CGAS may not be as clearly defined as the anchor points at the upper end of the measure. For this reason, it is possible that difficulties may arise when trying to differentiate the functional status of more impaired individuals from one another.

Strong concurrent validity has been reported for the CGAS. It has been found that CGAS scores were significantly related to indicators of child competence. In addition, the CGAS appears to be highly reflective of the presence of psychiatric symptomatology. However, ratings on the CGAS are described as being related to teachers' ratings of school and activity competence as well as the milieu staff's ratings of a child's capacity for social relations. Taken as a whole, these findings might suggest that clinician ratings on the CGAS could reflect levels of cognitive and social competency rather than actual psychiatric symptomatology, thereby providing an index of the youth's strengths.

The CGAS also has been shown to be useful as a treatment outcome measure. For example, the CGAS was able to detect therapeutic change from hospital admission to discharge as well as at a five-month follow-up assessment. CGAS ratings have been reported to be the strongest predictor of a child's level of functioning during a follow-up period.

It does not appear necessary that an experienced professional who has extensive training or experience in the mental health professions needs to complete a clinician rated CGAS for accurate utilization of this measure. No differences in CGAS scores are found when raters from different mental health professions and raters with different degrees of clinical experience rate youths with this measure.

In comparison to the clinician version of the CGAS, there has not been extensive research on the nonclinician versions of the CGAS. However, a comprehensive study investigated the psychometric properties of the nonclinician versions of the CGAS, the PICGAS, the YICGAS, and the PCGAS. Preliminary investigations have reported that the temporal stability for the nonclinician CGAS measures is comparable to the clinician CGAS ($r = .83$). In addition, nonclinicians appear to agree with one another to the same degree that clinicians agree with one another.

As for the PICGAS, the YICGAS, and the PCGAS, both the PICGAS and the PCGAS have strong agreement with other measures of dysfunction. However, the YICGAS did not agree as well with other measures. All three instruments were moderately correlated with clinician ratings on the CGAS. Yet, the parent measures (PICGAS and PCGAS) appear to have stronger concurrent validity in comparison to the youth measure (YICGAS).

The discriminant validity for all three of the measures appear to be fairly strong. Each measure differentiated those individuals who had psychiatric symptoms involving behavioral or emotional disturbances that required professional attention within the last 6 months from those who did not suffer from these symptoms. However, both parent measures tended to differentiate these two groups more clearly than did the youth measure.

The cutoff scores for some of the nonclinician versions of the CGAS differ from those of the clinician version. The PICGAS has a cutoff score of 68 which signifies that any score below this value is indicative of impairment. However, the PCGAS has a cutoff score of 80 which is noticeably higher. This may be due to the fact that parents, overall, tend to score their children higher on global functioning when compared to other raters.

The Child Behavior Checklist

The Child Behavior Checklist (CBCL) is a broad-band instrument that was developed to assess emotional and behavioral problems in children. It is likely the most frequently used assessment instrument for this purpose. It has been utilized successfully in both inpatient and outpatient settings. The CBCL also has been reported to be useful in residential treatment settings. Although it may not be the ideal instrument for assessing psychotic symptoms in children and adolescents, it may be very helpful in helping the clinician obtain a more comprehensive symptomatic picture of the youth being assessed. In fact, there are preliminary data to suggest that the CBCL may be useful as a quality of life measure for adolescents with schizophrenia.

The most recent version of this measure assesses children and adolescents between 4 and 18 years of age. The measure is completed by a parent and consists of 20 competence items and 120 problem items. Of the 120 problem items, 118 assess specific behavioral and emotional problems and 2 are open-ended items for reporting additional difficulties. For each item, the parent is required to rate the child based on his or her behavior over the past 6 months. Each item is rated using a 0 to 2 point scale. An item is assigned a 0 if it is not true of the child, a 1 if it is somewhat or sometimes true of the child, and a 2 if it is very true or often true of the child. Based on factor analyses, the items comprise different behavior problem scales and two broad band scales that target internalizing and externalizing behaviors. The internalizing scale targets problems such as anxiety, depression, social withdrawal, and communication difficulties. The externalizing scale focuses on aggressiveness, delinquency, and hyperactivity. In addition, there is also a social competency scale and a total problem or summary scale. The CBCL is scored using separate profiles for boys and girls at ages 4 to 11 and 12 to 18.

Psychometric Properties. There are various studies that have investigated the psychometric properties of the CBCL. Often, the research has focused on the reliability and validity of certain scales of the CBCL. It has been reported that the CBCL shows high temporal stability (test-retest) at 1 week with the CBCL problem scales ranging from .82 to .95, with a mean of .89 (Pearson r). A study that investigated the psychometric properties among a sample of Dutch children and adolescents (age range 4 to 16 years) investigated the temporal stability of problem, syndrome, externalizing, and internalizing scales of the CBCL. This study found that the Pearson r coefficients after a 2-year and 6-year follow-up were .67 and .56, respectively, for the total problem scale scores. For the syndrome scales (10 total), stability ratings (Pearson r) ranged from .19 to .67 for the 2-year follow-up and from .17 to .55 for the 6-year follow-up. Likewise, the Pearson r correlation coefficient was .48 for the externalizing scale and .55 for the internalizing scale at the 6-year follow-up. In addition to adequate reliability, the CBCL also has illustrated strong validity. It has been shown that the CBCL successfully differentiated between nonreferred and referred children. Referred children scored significantly higher than nonreferred children on 113 of the 118 items of the CBCL. This is indicative of strong discriminate validity. Likewise, it has been found that the CBCL externalizing and total scales illustrated strong concurrent validity in samples of emotionally disturbed adolescents.

Considering that the CBCL is a measure that has been widely used in various settings, it is clear that it may provide very useful information regarding a child's emotional and behavioral adjustment. Because the measure targets symptoms that have spanned the course of a 6-month period, it may be especially helpful in providing the clinician with a better assessment of a child's level and quality of life both prior to the emergence of psychotic symptomatology and after the development of a psychotic illness. In addition, the CBCL may be beneficial for assessing the presence of any current externalizing or internalizing symptomatology.

PROJECTIVE TESTS

In addition to some of the more traditional assessment instruments that may be used to detect psychotic symptomatology, the use of projective tests such as the Rorschach Inkblot Test, Thematic Apperception Test (TAT), and the Children's Apperception Test (CAT) may be of potential use in the assessment of a youth in whom the diagnosis of a psychotic disorder is being considered. In addition, the Draw-A-Person (DAP) is another projective instrument that may be utilized. One of the main reasons that projective tests may be used for assessing psychotic symptomatology is because they allow for open-ended answers from the youth who is being assessed.

In addition, projective tests such as these may provide a clinician with insights regarding the patient's ability to communicate his or her thoughts clearly. Considering the potential utility of projective tests, the following will describe three instruments that have been used for this purpose. The psychometric properties of each instrument will be discussed as well. However, it is important to reiterate that these tests are not diagnostic instruments. Therefore, these tests should not be used as means by which the presence of a psychotic disorder is either established or refuted.

Rorschach Inkblot Test

The origin of the Rorschach test dates back to the 1920s when Hermann Rorschach, a Swiss psychiatrist, developed a system to assess introverted and extroverted personality characteristics. The test was comprised of a series of ambiguous inkblot images that allowed an individual to create his or her own interpretation of each picture. From a psychoanalyst's perspective, the meaning that the individual associated with each inkblot provided insight regarding the individual's unconscious thoughts and emotions. However, even with the advent of many other psychological disciplines, the

Rorschach is still being utilized in various settings for different purposes. Various scoring systems, including Exner's, have been created since the development of the Rorschach to establish a more valid and reliable way of interpreting responses.

The Rorschach is comprised of 10 cards, each of which contains one inkblot. The examiner shows an individual one card at a time and asks the person to provide an open-ended response regarding the inkblot. The examiner then documents every detail of the individual's response regarding each inkblot, how long it takes the individuals to make a first response regarding the inkblot, and the total time spent on each inkblot. The examiner also notes the position of the card (upside down, sideways, etc.) in addition to any other spontaneous remarks that the individual may make during each card's presentation. Following the administration of all of the 10 cards, the examiner then returns to each card, reminds the person about the response that he or she provided, and asks the individual what prompted the response. Going over the responses to each card gives the person an opportunity to clarify or elaborate on any of his or her previous responses.

Most of the scoring systems that are used for interpreting responses on the Rorschach focus on three characteristics. The first is the location of the individual's response, which refers to the area of the card that the person focuses on during his or her interpretation. The individual may have incorporated the entire inkblot into his or her response or may have focused on just one aspect of it. In addition, whether or not the individual includes some of the small or large details of the blot into the interpretation impacts on how the response is scored. Along with the location of the person's response, the content of the individual's answer is also important. This refers to the actual object or scene that the person describes in his or her response. Another aspect of an individual's response that is incorporated into the scoring process is the specific determinants or components of the inkblot that elicited the person's reply. Some of these may include the form, color, texture, or shading that is contained in the inkblot. The commonality or popularity of a person's response based on the relative frequency of this type of answer within the general population is sometimes included in the scoring process also. The actual scoring of the Rorschach may vary. Sometimes, the examiner may look primarily at the number of determinants that are used in a given response, or he or she may be interested in the proportion of one type of response to another type of response. How the examiner chooses to score each response may depend entirely on the nature of the scoring system that he or she is using in addition to more idiosyncratic reasons.

Psychometric Properties. The psychometric properties of the Rorschach have been investigated numerous times over the course of the past decades. As with other subjective projective tests, it is difficult to obtain reliability and validity coefficients that are comparable to objective measures. One of the major drawbacks of the Rorschach is the fact that because individual responses vary so widely from subject to subject, it is difficult to obtain a sound assessment of reliability. Although some research has illustrated the validity of the Rorschach to be around .42 and the test-retest reliability to be in the mid-.80s, there is still some skepticism regarding the accuracy of these values.

Large proportions of the studies that have investigated the utility and psychometric properties of the Rorschach have focused on Exner's scoring system in particular. Utilizing Exner'scoring system, some investigators have compared the responses of a normative sample of adults on the Rorschach to samples of individuals who where depressed, schizophrenic, or had character problems. It has been reported that the scoring system might be a valid probe for schizophrenia, but it did not demonstrate very strong clinical utility for individuals with either depression or character problems. Likewise, investigators have found that, when using Exner's system, the Rorschach appeared to detect the presence of thought disorder among a sample of adolescent individuals who exhibited a broad range of psychopathology. Another study that investigated the use of the Rorschach with a sample of children ages 5 to 16 years found that the measure was useful in detecting cognitive disruption such as degree of complexity, richness of ideas, precision of thinking, integration, conformity to socially acceptable ways of thinking, and decreases in unrealistic, egocentric ideas. Likewise, this same study also claimed that the Rorschach was able to ascertain certain affective characteristics such as differences in the uncontrolled expression of affect and an increase in withdrawal or inwardness.

Based on the results of these studies, it appears that the Rorschach Inkblot, when scored utilizing Exner's scoring system, is quite useful in characterizing psychotic symptomatology both in adults and children. Therefore, a clinician may choose to incorporate this measure into his or her assessment protocol to gain a broader picture of the nature of the patient's symptoms.

Thematic Apperception Test

The Thematic Apperception Test (TAT) is an instrument that has been used frequently over the past few decades. Essentially, this instrument is used to indicate how a youth interprets certain test stimuli. For this instrument, ambiguous pictures are presented to the individual, and the young person is asked to interpret or tell a story about each picture. Often, the test is used to probe a youth's psychological needs or intrapsychic issues. A young person's responses on the TAT may also provide the examiner with information about how the youth deals with other people on an interpersonal level.

The TAT is comprised of 30 pictures that portray individuals in several types of situations. In addition to the 30 cards, there is also one blank card. The cards are ambiguous in that they do not illustrate precisely what the people in the pictures are thinking or doing. Hence, the ambiguity allows for a variety of potential interpretations by the person to whom the instrument is being administered. The clinician usually does not select all 31 cards to give to the patient. Rather, he or she may select a portion of them (between 6 and 12). It has been recommended that two sets of 10 cards be presented in two separate sessions. However, it is entirely up to the clinician to decide how many cards will be used. Once the clinician has chosen which cards to administer, he or she may transcribe the patient's responses in several different ways. The examiner may choose to tape-record, videotape, or write down the patient's responses. In addition, the patient may be asked to write out his or her interpretation of each card.

The TAT has been used successfully with adolescents. However, according to the TAT manual, when administered to young children, the information obtained from the TAT may not be as rich as when it is administered to teenagers. Despite this fact, the instrument may be used in children as young as 4 years of age. However, only three of the cards appear to be suitable for use with young children and a picture of a child is included on only four of the cards. Therefore, an alternative projective test such as the CAT may be more suitable to use with younger children.

Psychometric Properties. The psychometric properties of projective tests are normally not strong when compared to other psychometric measures. This is due primarily to the fact that there are several ways that a clinician may chose to interpret a patient's response to a particular item. The TAT manual provides guidelines regarding interpretation, but clinicians often do not interpret the measure in a systematic fashion. Rather, a clinician may decipher the responses based on previous experiences with other patients or in a manner that appears to make intuitive sense. Therefore, due to the variety of ways that the responses can be interpreted, it is difficult to establish reliability and validity for a test such as the TAT. There have been some attempts to establish the concurrent validity of the TAT by comparing scores on the TAT with therapist evaluations.

Despite the fact that reliability and validity for the TAT have not been established, the instrument can provide beneficial information if utilized by a professional who has been properly trained on how to use the instrument. Considering that the TAT is an instrument with a history of revealing useful information in a variety of settings, one may want to make it a part of a youth's assessment.

Children's Apperception Test

The Children's Apperception Test (CAT) is a projective test that is used primarily for children from 3 to 10 years of age. Although the CAT was derived from the TAT, the instrument has features that are not characteristic of those of the TAT. The cards of the CAT are black and white pictures that contain animals with human-like qualities. Animals were placed on the cards instead of humans because children tend to find animals to be less threatening, which makes it easier for children to address difficult feelings and thoughts associated with the cards. Another feature that differentiates the CAT from the TAT is that the cards are less ambiguous than the cards of the TAT. In addition, the manual recommends that all 10 of the cards be administered using a specific sequence.

Psychometric Properties. Similar to the TAT, sufficient reliability and validity have not been established for the CAT. Again, this may be attributed primarily to the fact that there are various ways that a clinician may choose to interpret a child's responses to each item. Likewise, several different scoring systems and guidelines have been created for the CAT. Often the clinician may choose to interpret the responses based on his or her previous experiences with the instrument. In addition, the clinician may use his or her own intuition regarding the nature of the child's responses. Needless to say, it is important to emphasize that this instrument is often used to provide a unique contribution to the assessment protocol, but should not be used as a diagnostic tool. Therefore, the clinician is advised to utilize the instrument as a way to supplement the data obtained from more reliable and valid instruments.

Clinicians have utilized both the CAT and the Draw-A-Person test to assess the quality of delusional thoughts in a preschool-aged child with psychotic symptomatology. However, considering the CAT's psychometric properties, it is crucial that the clinician is trained on how to use the instrument properly and that the scores are treated merely as a way to facilitate diagnosis.

Draw-A-Person

The Draw-A-Person technique is another form of projective testing that has been used frequently in a variety of clinical settings. A very comprehensive description of the technique has been described. Essentially, the clinician administers the test using a blank piece of paper and a pencil, and asks the patient to draw a person. It is believed that the manner in which an individual draws a person illustrates a great deal about the individual's ideas regarding the self and body in relation to the environment. If a person focuses on or exaggerates a certain part of the body, this may have some interpretive significance.

A more version of the technique is called The Draw-A-Person: A Quantitative Scoring System (DAP). The DAP has been normed using a sample of children between the ages of 5 to 17 years. It may be utilized with children who may have verbal or communication difficulties. Basically, the technique uses three different stimuli—a man, a woman, and oneself. Approximately 64 scoring items are used to interpret the three drawings. Some of the criteria used for scoring include how the individual draws the body parts and whether or not he or she draws them proportionately and in their proper locations. The administration time for the DAP is brief, often taking no more than 5 minutes. The DAP manual provides the clinician with a standard scoring system. Essentially, the range of raw scores is from 0 to 64. The scores are derived from combining the child's performance on all three drawings into a total raw score.

Psychometric Properties. Considering that the DAP utilizes a more standard scoring system in comparison to other projective tests, the technique has been shown to have fairly good reliability and validity. It has also been reported that the DAP has strong internal consistency reliability. The alpha coefficients for the man, woman, and self drawings range from .56 to .78 (mean = .70) when scored separately. Likewise, one study that administered the technique to a sample of 112 first through seventh graders yielded temporal stability coefficients ranging from .60 to .89 (mean = .74). In addition, the DAP has shown to demonstrate interrater reliability coefficients ranging from .93 to .95.

In addition to adequate reliability, the DAP has also demonstrated fairly strong validity. It has been shown that the DAP had high concurrent validity with the Goodenough-Harris Draw-a-Man technique. The validity coefficients ranged from .70 to .90.

As with the other projective tests, the DAP can be a very valuable source of information when used in conjunction with other more reliable and valid assessment instruments. When screening for psychotic features, the nature of a child's drawings may reveal how a child perceives his or her environment. Specifically, the drawings may provide the clinician with more insight regarding any maladaptive thoughts or cognitions that exist. It must be emphasized, however, that the clinician should be properly trained on how to administer and score the instrument prior to making any inferences regarding the child's psychological state.

MEASURING ANTIPSYCHOTIC-RELATED SIDE EFFECTS

The antipsychotics are generally the mainstays of treatment for youths with schizophrenia and its related disorders. Unfortunately, the antipsychotic medications are often associated with neurological side effects. These side effects include abnormal involuntary movements, Parkinsonian-like symptoms, and akathisia. For this reason, it may be helpful for the clinician to assess for the presence of these medication-related neurological side effects during the course of antipsychotic pharmacotherapy. Several commonly used instruments are employed to assess for the presence or absence of these adverse events.

Abnormal Involuntary Movement Scale

Abnormal involuntary movements can occur during the course of antipsychotic pharmacotherapy. These include tardive dyskinesia, tardive dystonia, and withdrawal dyskinesia. Because the symptoms of tardive movement disorders can be distressing, disfiguring and irreversible, it is important to monitor for this possibility during antipsychotic pharmacotherapy.

Probably the most commonly-employed rating scale used to measure involuntary movements is the Abnormal Involuntary Movement Scale (AIMS). This instrument has been used in numerous studies with children and adolescents. The AIMS is a 12-item scale and the score is based on the results of physical examination of the patient. Seven items reflect facial, oral, extremity and trunk movements. Clinical judgments about the severity and incapacitation due to these movements account for three items. The 10 questions are scored from 0 to 4. The mental status of the patient makes up two items which are rated as 0 (*absent*) or 1 (*present*). An overall score of 0 indicates the absence of abnormal involuntary movements and higher scores reflect greater degrees of dyskinesia.

Tardive dyskinesia and tardive dystonia are two of the most significant adverse events that can occur as a result of the use of psychotropic medications in children and adolescents. The AIMS provides a well-established means by which a clinician can systematically assess for these phenomena in a longitudinal fashion.

Neurological Rating Scale

Symptoms of Parkinsonism and other neurological side effects may also occur as untoward events associated with antipsychotic pharmacotherapy. These symptoms, although not necessarily as catastrophic as tardive movement disorders, can effect tolerability and, therefore, medication compliance in patients with chronic psychotic disorders. It is typically Parkinsonian symptoms that lead patients who are being treated with antipsychotics to look "drugged" or look "like a zombie." One of the most commonly used scales to assess Parkinsonian symptoms in young people is the Neurological Rating Scale (NRS).

The NRS is a 10-item measure. Each item is scored 0 to 4. Higher scores are indicative of greater neurological symptoms. The NRS is rated based on the results of a systematic physical examination that assesses movements of the trunk, extremities, face, and head. This scale has been used in several studies that have examined Parkinsonian symptoms in children and adolescents treated with antipsychotics.

Parkinsonian symptoms are side effects that often develop early in the course of antipsychotic pharmacotherapy. Because symptoms of Parkinsonism can affect a child's or adolescent's outward appearance, this extrapyramidal side effect can adversely alter the course of pharmacotherapy. Patients, especially appearance-conscious teenagers, who know they look medicated, may wish not to comply with antipsychotic medications as prescribed. Parents who feel their child looks like a "zombie" may be reticent to maintain antipsychotic pharmacotherapy. The NRS is an easy-to-use tool to help monitor the severity of Parkinsonian and other neurological symptoms during antipsychotic treatment.

Barnes Akathisia Scale

Akathisia is a side effect of antipsychotic medication that seems to occur more commonly in young patients treated with older or "typical" antipsychotics. Akathisia is characterized by patients developing an inner sense of restlessness that is subjectively experienced as distressing. Because akathisia can be distressing to young people treated with antipsychotic medications, the development of treatment-induced akathisia can have a significantly adverse impact on medication compliance. The Barnes Akathisia Scale (BAS) is a brief questionnaire with good interrater reliability that measures the severity of medication-induced akathisia. Although developed for use in adults, the BAS may be employed when working with young people who are treated with antipsychotics.

The BAS has four items. The first item involves an objective assessment of the patient's restlessness obtained from direct observation. Two questions pertain to the subjective experience of akathisia. One question measures distress due to the restlessness. These three questions are scored on a 0 to 3 scale. The final item is a global assessment of the severity of akathisia and a score of 0 to 5 is assigned. Higher scores reflect greater degrees of akathisia.

Noncompliance with antipsychotics may be a significant impediment to the long-term treatment of psychotic disorders. In addition, it appears that the unease associated with akathisia can significantly contribute to poor medication compliance. For these reasons, assessment of akathisia during the course of antipsychotic pharmacotherapy may be an important aspect of medication management. The BAS can provide the clinician with a brief, easy-to-use means by which to objectively track this distressing medication-induced adverse event.

SUMMARY

The proper assessment of psychotic symptomatology, other symptom domains, levels of disability, and medication-induced side effects is crucial for successful diagnosis and treatment of young people with psychotic disorders. A variety of instruments exist that can be very helpful to this end. When assessing a youth in whom a psychotic disorder is suspected, it is important that a clinician chose several different types of instruments to assess several of the aforementioned domains. Once a diagnosis is made and a treatment plan is implemented, it is also important that the clinician administer follow-up assessments utilizing the same or similar instruments. These should be done to ensure that the progress of the child or adolescent is properly monitored.

10

FUTURE DIRECTIONS FOR RESEARCH

As can be seen from the previous sections of this book, quite a lot is known about the psychotic disorders in children and adolescents. It is also clear that there is much yet to be learned about these conditions in young people. However, it is possible that improved insights into the longitudinal history, neurobiology, and treatment of these illnesses will become available in the near future. Although for many years relatively little research was performed that focused on the pediatric psychoses. Now this area of investigation is being actively considered by several research groups. For this reason, it is not unrealistic to be optimistic that new research will eventually provide clinicians with the ability to give improved care to their patients.

For example, only within the past few years has it become generally appreciated that psychotic illnesses do in fact occur in young people. Relatively recently conducted phenomenological research has shown that the symptoms of psychosis that occur in adults also occur in young people with psychotic disorders. For this reason, it is now appreciated that the diagnostic symptom criteria that are used in adults with psychosis can also be employed in children and adolescents.

In addition, appreciation has increased regarding the many syndromal conditions and nonsyndromal circumstances that need to be considered as part of a differential diagnosis when a young person presents with psychotic symptoms. Moreover, due to the potentially debilitating nature of the psychotic disorders, it has become clearer to mental health professionals that the possibility of a psychotic disorder being present should be considered if a youth is experiencing significant psychosocial dysfunction.

When compared to what is known about adults with psychotic disorders, the available scientific evidence about the natural history, phenomenology, neurobiology, and treatment of young people who suffer from these conditions is indeed quite sparse. There are several reasons that this is so. As mentioned before, the fact that the psychotic disorders can be diagnosed reliably and consistently in children and adolescents has only recently become clear to practitioners and investigators. In addition, research centers that have performed pivotal studies in adults with psychotic disorders often have limited access to young patients with similar illnesses. These research programs are often located in state hospitals for adults, clinical programs for adults at academic medical centers, or in Veteran's Administration hospitals.

However, there are several key reasons that research should be performed in children and adolescents with psychotic disorders and not just adults who suffer from these conditions. First, an earlier age at onset of schizophrenia is generally associated with a poorer outcome than an adult age at onset of psychosis. For this reason, effective interventions are needed in this younger population to change the poor prognosis that accompanies the early onset form of this condition. In addition, because early-onset forms of the psychotic disorders may be more malignant expressions of the adult-onset forms of these illnesses, studying young patients who suffer from these conditions may provide researchers important insights into the phenomenology and pathophysiology of the psychotic disorders.

Another reason that research should focus on young patients with psychotic illnesses is that the available scientific information as it pertains to adults might not be applicable to young people. Although many similarities have been shown to exist between adult patients and younger ones, significant differences in longitudinal course, clinical presentation, and treatment response have also been identified between these two patient groups. This is another reason that further research should be performed in young people with psychotic disorders.

It is important to appreciate that one of the most substantial factors that impedes the ability of investigators to study the psychotic disorders in young people is that relatively small numbers of patients are brought to the scientific centers that are conducting research in these conditions. For research programs to provide meaningful insights into the pediatric-onset forms of these conditions, an adequate number of patients need to be enrolled in scientific studies. If only small sample sizes are analyzed, then only the most pronounced findings will be able to be detected. More subtle effects of these conditions will be missed due to inadequate statistical power. One way in which concerns about obtaining appropriate sample sizes can be addressed is by having multisite studies. By having collaborative protocols conducted across several different research centers, larger numbers of patients could then be enrolled in a variety of different studies.

Other than multisite protocols, longitudinal studies into the psychotic disorders may eventually provide useful insights into the natural history of these conditions. Particularly important may be examinations into how these syndromes affect the development of young people during their childhood and adolescence. Also of importance will be to compare the adult outcomes of patients who develop these conditions at various stages in the life cycle. If specific areas of dysfunction associated with early-onset forms of these illnesses can be identified, then it may be possible to develop interventions tailored to reduce the morbidity associated with the childhood- and adolescent-onsets of these disorders.

In addition, many of the psychotic illnesses are associated with prodromal phases in which subtle manifestations of these conditions may be expressed. Longitudinal assessments of youths at high-risk for developing psychotic disorders might provide insights into the phenomenology and developmental unfolding of these illnesses. With a better understanding of the phenomenology and natural history of the prodromal period, it is possible that interventions could be developed for implementation during the prodromal phase of the illness with the hope that these treatments would both reduce symptomatology and prevent the full expression of the conditions.

Because the differential diagnosis of psychotic disorders is extensive, and because many youths with psychotic disorders are not readily identified, it would be useful to develop means by which practitioners could more accurately and reliably assess youths in whom a psychotic disorder may be present. Currently, only a few measures exist for the assessment of psychotic disorders in this age group. Most of these tools are not readily implemented in clinical practice. In addition, other instruments that are easily employed in the assessment of children and adolescents, although often extremely informative and widely used, do not specifically target psychotic symptomatology.

These yet-to-be-developed assessments will need to have both reliability and validity and also will need to be practical for use in clinical settings. Optimally, these instruments would consider differences in cognitive capabilities during the first two decades of life and how these differences might affect the expression of psychotic symptomatology. In addition, academic demands, intrafamilial expectations, and peer pressures differ across childhood and adolescence. It would be ideal if these measures also considered the effects that psychotic disorders have on these domains that clearly affect a young person's quality of life.

Just as the development of specific assessment measures for pediatric psychosis may provide insights into the psychotic spectrum disorders, the availability of easy-to-use assessment measures that could help the busy clinician reliably delineate psychotic from nonpsychotic hallucinations and delusions could be quite useful. Because many youths with hallucinations do not suffer from a psychotic disorder, there is also a need to better understand and describe the presence of psychotic-like symptomatology in the absence of a psychotic disorder. Based on the current research on this topic, the expression of these symptoms can be affected by a youth's home environment, developmental stage, the presence of a general medical condition, or the occurrence of traumatic events. At present, it is unclear why certain individuals may manifest these psychotic symptoms without actually developing a psychotic disorder. Research into this area might provide a more comprehensive understanding of how and why psychotic-like symptoms develop in some children and adolescents and how these symptoms differ from those seen in youths with psychotic disorders.

In addition, it is clear that there are many youths who suffer from psychotic symptomatology, but do not meet full symptom criteria for a well-defined psychotic syndrome. At present, these patients generally meet diagnostic criteria for psychotic disorder not otherwise specified. The development of other assessment measures may allow the field to develop a clearer phenomenological picture of this cohort of youths who clearly have psychotic-like disorders, but do not have full expressions of a prototypic psychotic illness.

Although our insights into the neurobiology of psychotic illnesses in adults have expanded rapidly during the last decade, neuropsychiatric research in young people who suffer from these conditions has lagged behind by a considerable amount. Areas for further investigation include genetics, structural and functional neuroimaging, neurophysiology, and neuropsychology. Due to an appreciation that further scientific investigations in this population may provide vital insights into these disorders, these kinds of studies are now being performed in young people with psychotic illnesses.

Another area for future investigation will clearly be that of treatment. With the release of the atypical antipsychotics, safe, better-tolerated medications than were available in the past are now first-line treatment to millions of adult patients with psychotic disorders. Because young people may not respond to medications as do adults, it will be important to study new medications, as they become available, in both children and adolescents. Acute and maintenance studies will be needed to assess the safety, tolerability, and efficacy of these agents in young people. In addition to medications, the benefits associated with nonpharmacological interventions and family involvement in adults with psychosis have been clearly identified. Although the treatment research in the pediatric psychosis is relatively sparse, more and more investigators are beginning to conduct treatment studies in this population.

A lot still needs to be learned about the psychotic disorders in young people. Despite this fact, the promise of a brighter future for these patients is better now than ever before. As it has become more and more clear that children and adolescents are afflicted by psychotic disorders and suffer from these illnesses' effects, an ever-increasing amount of research has been directed toward this patient population. With the expanded knowledge base that will be obtained from scientific inquiry in the years to come, improved treatments and outcomes can be expected for those vulnerable children and adolescents who suffer from psychotic disorders.

BIBLIOGRAPHY

Aarkrog, T. (1981). The borderline concept in childhood, adolescence and adulthood. Borderline adolescents in psychiatric treatment and 5 years later. *Acta Psychiatrica Scandinavica, 293* (Suppl.), 1–300.

Abe, K., & Ohta, M. (1998). Recurrent brief episodes with psychotic features in adolescence: Periodic psychosis of puberty revisited. *Psychiatry and Clinical Neurosciences, 52* (Suppl.), S313–S316.

Achenbach, T. M. (1991). *Manual for the Child Behavior Checklist/4–18 and 1991 Profile.* Burlington, VT: University of Vermont Department of Psychiatry.

Achte, K., Jarho, L., Kyykka, T., & Vesterinen, E. (1991). Paranoid disorders following war brain damage. Preliminary report. *Psychopathology, 24,* 309–315.

Ackerknecht, E. H. (1959). *A short history of psychiatry.* (S. Wolff, Trans.) New York: Hafner.

Agrawal, P., Bhatia, M. S., & Malik, S. C. (1997). Postpartum psychosis: A clinical study. *International Journal of Social Psychiatry, 43,* 217–222.

Alaghband-Rad, J., McKenna, K., Gordon, C. T., Albus, K. E., Hamburger, S. D., Rumsey, J. M., Frazier, J. A., Lenane, M. C., & Rapoport, J. L. (1995). Childhood-onset schizophrenia: The severity of premorbid course. *Journal of the American Academy of Child and Adolescent Psychiatry, 34,* 1273–1283.

Alexander, F. G., & Selesnick, S. T. (1966). *The history of psychiatry: An evaluation of psychiatric thought and practice from prehistoric times to the present.* New York: Harper & Row.

Allen, J. G., & Coyne, L. (1995). Dissociation and vulnerability to psychotic experience. The Dissociative Experiences Scale and the MMPI-2. *Journal of Nervous and Mental Disease, 183,* 615–622.

Allen, J. G., Coyne, L., & Console, D. A. (1997). Dissociative detachment relates to psychotic symptoms and personality decompensation. *Comprehensive Psychiatry, 38,* 327–334.

Altman, H., Collins, M., & Mundy, P. (1997). Subclinical hallucinations and delusions in nonpsychotic adolescents. *Journal of Child Psychology and Psychiatry, 38,* 413–420.

Amador, X. F. (1998). Psychopathologic domains and insight in schizophrenia. *Psychiatric Clinics of North America, 21,* 27–42.

Ambrosini, P. J., Wagner, K. D., Biederman, J., Glick, I., Tan, C., Elia, J., Hebeler, J. R., Rabinovich, H., Lock, J., & Geller, D. (1999). Multicenter open-label sertraline study in adolescent outpatients with major depression. *Journal of the American Academy of Child and Adolescent Psychiatry, 38,* 566–572.

American Academy of Child and Adolescent Psychiatry. (1998). Practice parameters for the assessment and treatment of children and adolescents with depressive disorders. *Journal of the American Academy of Child and Adolescent Psychiatry, 37* (Suppl. 10), 63S–83S.

American Psychiatric Association. (1980). *Diagnostic and statistical manual of mental disorders* (3rd ed.). Washington, DC: Author.

American Psychiatric Association. (1987). *Diagnostic and statistical manual of mental disorders* (3rd ed., rev.). Washington, DC: Author.

American Psychiatric Association. (1989). *Treatment of psychiatric disorders* (Vol. 2). Washington, DC: Author.

American Psychiatric Association. (1994). *Diagnostic and statistical manual of mental disorders* (4th ed.). Washington, DC: Author.

American Psychiatric Association. (1999). Practice guideline for the treatment of patients with delirium. *American Journal of Psychiatry, 156* (Suppl. May), 1–20.

Andreasen, N. C. (1979). Thought, language, and communication disorders: I. Clinical assessment, definition of terms, and evaluation of their reliability. *Archives of General Psychiatry, 36*, 1315–1321.

Andreasen, N. C. (1979). Thought, language, and communication disorders: II. Diagnostic significance. *Archives of General Psychiatry, 36*, 1325–1331.

Andreasen, N. C. (1984). *Scale for the Assessment of Negative Symptoms (SANS)*. Iowa City: University of Iowa.

Angst, J., Felder, W., & Lohmeyer, B. (1979). Schizoaffective disorders. Results of a genetic investigation. I. *Journal of Affective Disorders, 1*, 139–153.

Apter, A., Orvaschel, H., Laseg, M., Moses, T., & Tyano, S. (1989). Psychometric properties of the K-SADS-P in an Israeli adolescent inpatient population. *Journal of the American Academy of Child and Adolescent Psychiatry, 28*, 61–65.

Archer, R. P., Maruish, M., Imhof, E. A., & Piotrowski, C. (1991). Psychological test usage with adolescent clients: 1990 survey findings. *Professional Psychology: Research and Practice, 22*, 247–252.

Armenteros, J. L., Whitaker, A. H., Welikson, M., Stedge, D. J., & Gorman, J. (1997). Risperidone in adolescents with schizophrenia: An open pilot study. *Journal of the American Academy of Child and Adolescent Psychiatry, 36*, 694–700.

Armstrong, J., Silberg, J. L., & Parente, F. J. (1986). Patterns of thought disorder on psychological testing. Implications for adolescent psychopathology. *Journal of Nervous and Mental Disease, 174*, 448–456.

Asarnow, J. R., & Ben-Meir, S. (1988). Children with schizophrenia spectrum and depressive disorders: A comparative study of premorbid adjustment, onset pattern and severity of impairment. *Journal of Child Psychology and Psychiatry, 29*, 477–488.

Asarnow, J. R., Goldstein, M. J., & Ben-Meir, S. (1988). Parental communication deviance in childhood onset schizophrenia spectrum disorders and depressive disorders. *Journal of Child Psychology and Psychiatry, 29*, 825–838.

Asarnow, J. R., Tompson, M. C., & Goldstein, M. J. (1994). Childhood-onset schizophrenia: A follow-up study. *Schizophrenia Bulletin, 20*, 599–617.

Asarnow, R. F., Asamen, J., Granholm, E., Sherman, T., Watkins, J. M., & Williams, M. E. (1994). Cognitive/neuropsychological studies of children with a schizophrenic disorder. *Schizophrenia Bulletin, 20*, 647–669.

Barnes, T. R. E. (1989). A rating scale for drug-induced akathisia. *British Journal of Psychiatry, 154*, 672–676.

Barnes, T. R. E., & McPhillips, M. A. (1995). How to distinguish between the neuroleptic-induced deficit syndrome, depression and disease-related negative symptoms in schizophrenia. *International Clinical Psychopharmacology, 10* (Suppl. 3), 115–121.

Bartholomew, R. E. (1994). Disease, disorder, or deception? Latah as habit in a Malay extended family. *Journal of Nervous and Mental Disease, 182,* 331–338.

Battaglia, M., Bernardeschi, L., Franchini, L., Bellodi, L., & Smeraldi, E. (1995). A family study of schizotypal disorder. *Schizophrenia Bulletin, 21,* 33–45.

Bauman, A., & Phongsavan, P. (1999). Epidemiology of substance use in adolescence: Prevalence, trends and policy implications. *Drug and Alcohol Dependence, 55,* 187–207.

Beitchman, J. H. (1985). Childhood schizophrenia: A review and comparison with adult-onset schizophrenia. *Psychiatric Clinics of North America, 8,* 793–814.

Bell, M., Milstein, R., Beam-Goulet, J., Lysaker, P., & Cicchetti, D. (1992). The Positive and Negative Syndrome Scale and the Brief Psychiatric Rating Scale: Reliability, comparability, and predictive validity. *Journal of Nervous and Mental Disease, 180,* 723–728.

Bellack, L. (1992). *The TAT, the CAT and the SAT in clinical use* (5th ed.). Orlando, FL: Grune & Stratton.

Bellack, L., & Bellack, S. S. (1991). *Children's Apperception Test Manual (CAT)* (8th rev. ed.). Larchmont, NY: C.P.S.

Beratis, S., Gabriel, J., & Hoidas, S. (1994). Age at onset in subtypes of schizophrenic disorders. *Schizophrenia Bulletin, 20,* 287–296.

Bernstein, D. P., Cohen, P., Velez, N. C., Schwab-Stone, M., Siever, L. J., & Shinsato, L. (1993). Prevalence and stability of the *DSM-III-R* personality disorders in a community-based survey of adolescents. *American Journal of Psychiatry, 150,* 1237–1243.

Bernstein, J. G. (1995). Antipsychotic drugs. In J. G. Bernstein (Ed.), *Handbook of drug therapy in psychiatry* (3rd ed., pp. 70–82). St. Louis, MO: Mosby.

Bertelsen, A., & Gottesman, I. I. (1995). Schizoaffective psychoses: Genetical clues to classification. *American Journal of Medical Genetics, 60,* 7–11.

Berzirganian, S., Cohen, P., & Brook, J. S. (1993). The impact of mother-child interaction on the development of borderline personality disorder. *American Journal of Psychiatry, 150,* 1836–1842.

Biederman, J., Russell, R., Soriano, J., Wozniak, J., & Faraone, S. V. (1998). Clinical features of children with both ADHD and mania: Does ascertainment source make a difference? *Journal of Affective Disorders, 51,* 101–112.

Bird, H. R., Andrews, H., Schwab-Stone, M., Goodman, S., Dulcan, M., Richters, J., Rubio-Stipec, M., Moore, R., Chiang, P., Hoven, C., Canino, G., Fisher, P., & Gould, M. (1996). Global measures of impairment for epidemiologic and clinical use with children and adolescents. *International Journal of Methods in Psychiatric Research, 6,* 295–307.

Bird, H. R., Canino, G. J., Rubio-Stipec, M., & Ribera, J. C. (1987). Further measures of the psychometric properties of the Children's Global Assessment Scale. *Archives of General Psychiatry, 44,* 821–824.

Birmaher, B., Ryan, N. D., Williamson, D. E., Brent, D. A., Kaufman, J., Dahl, R. E., Perel, J., & Nelson, B. (1996). Childhood and adolescent depression: A review of the past 10 years. Part I. *Journal of the American Academy of Child and Adolescent Psychiatry, 35,* 1427–1439.

Black, D. (1978). Annotation: The bereaved child. *Journal of Child Psychology and Psychiatry and Allied Disciplines, 19,* 287–292.

Black, D., & Urbanowicz, M. A. (1987). Family intervention with bereaved children. *Journal of Child Psychology and Psychiatry and Allied Disciplines, 28,* 467–476.

Bleiberg, E. (1994). Borderline disorders in children and adolescents: The concept, the diagnosis, and the controversies. *Bulletin of the Menninger Clinic, 58*, 169–196.

Bleuler, E. (1950). *Dementia praecox of the group of schizophrenias*. New York: International Universities Press.

Bloom, A. S., Russell, L. J., Weisskopf, B., & Blackerby, J. L. (1988). Methylphenidate-induced delusional disorder in a child with attention deficit disorder with hyperactivity. *Journal of the American Academy of Child and Adolescent Psychiatry, 27*, 88–89.

Brent, D. A., Holder, D., Kolko, D., Birmaher, B., Baugher, M., Roth, C., Iyengar, S., & Johnson, B. A. (1997). A clinical psychotherapy trial for adolescent depression comparing cognitive, family, and supportive therapy. *Archives of General Psychiatry, 54*, 877–885.

Brewerton, T. D. (1997). The phenomenology of psychosis associated with complex partial seizure disorder. *Annals of Clinical Psychiatry, 9*, 31–51.

Brockington, I. F., Martin, C., Brown, G. W., Goldberg, D., & Margison, F. (1990). Stress and puerperal psychosis. *British Journal of Psychiatry, 157*, 331–334.

Broome, K. M., Knight, D. K., Knight, K., Hiller, M. L., & Simpson, D. D. (1997). Peer, family, and motivational influences on drug treatment process and recidivism for probationers. *Journal of Clinical Psychology, 53*, 387–397.

Buckley, P. F. (1998). The clinical stigmata of aberrant neurodevelopment in schizophrenia. *Journal of Nervous and Mental Disease, 186*, 79–86.

Buckley, P. F., Sajatovich, M., & Meltzer, H. Y. (1994). Treatment of delusional disorders with clozapine. *American Journal of Psychiatry, 151*, 1394–1395.

Buitelaar, J. K., & Van der Gaag, R. J. (1998). Diagnostic rules for children with PDD-NOS and multiple complex developmental disorder. *Journal of Child Psychology and Psychiatry and Allied Disciplines, 39*, 911–919.

Burd, L., & Kerbeshian, J. (1987). A North Dakota prevalence study of schizophrenia in childhood. *Journal of the American Academy of Child and Adolescent Psychiatry, 26*, 347–350.

Butler, R. W., Mueser, K. T., Sprock, J., & Braff, D. L. (1996). Positive symptoms of psychosis in posttraumatic stress disorder. *Biological Psychiatry, 39*, 839–844.

Camlin, K. L., Berry, S. A., Whyte, E. M., Jesberger, J. A., & Schulz, S. C. (1999). Olanzapine safety and efficacy in patients with borderline personality disorder and co-morbid dysthymia. *Schizophrenia Research, 36*, 273.

Campbell, M., Armenteros, J. L., Spencer, E. K., Kowalik, S. C., & Erlenmeyer-Kimling, L. (1997). Schizophrenia and psychotic disorders. In J. M. Wiener (Ed.), *Textbook of child and adolescent psychiatry* (2nd ed., pp. 303–332). Washington, DC: American Psychiatric Press.

Campbell, M., & Palij, M. (1985). Measurement of side effects including tardive dyskinesia. *Psychopharmacology Bulletin, 21*, 1063–1066.

Cannon, T. D., Kaprio, J., Lonnqvist, J., Huttunen, M., & Koskenvuo, M. (1998). The genetic epidemiology of schizophrenia in a Finnish twin cohort. A population-based modeling study. *Archives of General Psychiatry, 55*, 67–74.

Cantwell, R., Brewin, J., Glazebrook, C., Dalkin, T., Fox, R., Medley, I., & Harrison, G. (1999). Prevalence of substance misuse in first-episode psychosis. *British Journal of Psychiatry, 174*, 150–153.

Caplan, R. (1994). Communication deficits in childhood schizophrenia spectrum disorders. *Schizophrenia Bulletin, 20*, 671–683.

Caplan, R. (1994). Thought disorder in childhood. *Journal of the American Academy of Child and Adolescent Psychiatry, 33*, 605–615.

Caplan, R., & Guthrie, D. (1992). Communication deficits in childhood schizotypal personality disorder. *Journal of the American Academy of Child and Adolescent Psychiatry, 31,* 961–967.

Caplan, R., Guthrie, D., & Komo, S. (1996). Conversational repair in schizophrenic and normal children. *Journal of the American Academy of Child and Adolescent Psychiatry, 35,* 950–958.

Caplan, R., Perdue, S., Tanguay, P. E., & Fish, B. (1990). Formal thought disorder in childhood onset schizophrenia and schizotypal personality disorder. *Journal of Child Psychology and Psychiatry, 31,* 1103–1114.

Carlson, G. A. (1983). Bipolar affective disorders in childhood and adolescence. In D. P. Cantwell & G. A. Carlson (Eds.), *Affective disorders in childhood and adolescence: An Update.* New York: Spectrum.

Carlson, G. A. (1998). Mania and ADHD: Comorbidity or confusion. *Journal of Affective Disorders, 51,* 177–187.

Casacchia, M., de Cataldo, S., Roncone, R., & Marcelli, G. (1996). Schizophreniform disorder: A 1-year follow-up study. *Psychopathology, 29,* 104–108.

Cerel, J., Fristad, M. A., Weller, E. B., & Weller, R. A. (1999). Suicide-bereaved children and adolescents: A controlled longitudinal examination. *Journal of the American Academy of Child and Adolescent Psychiatry, 38,* 672–679.

Chambers, W. J., Puig-Antich, J., Hirsch, M., Paez, P., Ambrosini, P. J., Tabrizi, M. A., & Davies, M. (1985). The assessment of affective disorders in children and adolescents by semistructured interview: Test-retest reliability of the Schedule for Affective Disorders and Schizophrenia for School-Age Children, Present Episode Version. *Archives of General Psychiatry, 42,* 696–702.

Chambers, W. J., Puig-Antich, J., Tabrizi, M. A., & Davies, M. (1982). Psychotic symptoms in prepubertal major depressive disorder. *Archives of General Psychiatry, 39,* 921–927.

Chandler, L. A., Shermis, M. D., & Lempert, M. E. (1989). The need-threat analysis: A scoring system for the Children's Apperception Test. *Psychology in the Schools, 26,* 47–54.

Clark, D. B., & Neighbors, B. (1996). Adolescent substance abuse and internalizing disorders. *Child and Adolescent Psychiatry Clinics of North America, 5,* 45–57.

Clarke, G. N., Rohde, P., Lewinsohn, P. M., Hops, H., & Seeley, J. R. (1999). Cognitive-behavioral treatment of adolescent depression: Efficacy of acute group treatment and booster sessions. *Journal of the American Academy of Child and Adolescent Psychiatry, 38,* 272–279.

Coccaro, E. F. (1998). Clinical outcome of psychopharmacologic treatment of borderline and schizotypal personality disordered subjects. *Journal of Clinical Psychiatry, 59* (Suppl. 1), 30–35.

Cohen, B. M., Allen, M. G., Pollin, V., & Hrubec, Z. (1972). Relationship of schizoaffective psychosis to manic depressive psychosis and schizophrenia. Findings in 15,909 veteran pairs. *Archives of General Psychiatry, 26,* 539–546.

Coker, S. B. (1991). The diagnosis of childhood neurodegenerative disorders presenting as dementia in adults. *Neurology, 41,* 794–798.

Cornelius, J. R., Salloum, I. M., Ehler, J. G., Jarrett, P. J., Cornelius, M. D., Perel, J. M., Thase, M. E., & Black, A. (1997). Fluoxetine in depressed alcoholics: A double-blind, placebo-controlled trial. *Archives of General Psychiatry, 54,* 700–705.

Coryell, W., & Tsuang, M. T. (1982). DSM-III schizophreniform disorder: Comparisons with schizophrenia and affective disorder. *Archives of General Psychiatry, 39,* 66–69.

Crow, T. J. (1995). Brain changes and negative symptoms in schizophrenia. *Psychopathology, 28,* 18–21.

Cuesta, M. J., & Peralta, V. (1993). Does formal thought disorder differ among patients with schizophrenic, schizophreniform, and manic schizoaffective disorders? *Schizophrenia Research, 10,* 151–158.

Cummings, J. L. (1985). Organic delusions: Phenomenology, anatomical correlations, and review. *British Journal of Psychiatry, 146,* 184–197.

Daly, J. M., & Wilens, T. (1998). The use of tricyclic antidepressants in children and adolescents. *Pediatric Clinics of North America, 45,* 1123–1135.

Davidson, J. (1992). Drug therapy of post-traumatic stress disorder. *British Journal of Psychiatry, 160,* 309–314.

Davidson, J. R. T., Weisler, R. H., Malik, M. L., & Connor, K. M. (1998). Treatment of post-traumatic stress disorder with nefazodone. *International Clinical Psychopharmacology, 13,* 111–113.

Del Beccaro, M. A., Burke, P., & McCauley, E. (1988). Hallucinations in children: A follow-up study. *Journal of the American Academy of Child and Adolescent Psychiatry, 27,* 462–465.

DiMario, F. J., Jr., & Packer, R. J. (1990). Acute mental status changes in children with systemic cancer. *Pediatrics, 85,* 353–360.

Dingemans, P. M., Linszen, D. H., Lenior, M. E., & Smeets, R. M. (1995). Component structure of the expanded Brief Psychiatric Rating Scale (BPRS-E). *Psychopharmacology, 122,* 263–267.

Doran, A. R., Breier, A., & Roy, A. (1986). Differential diagnosis and diagnostic systems in schizophrenia. *Psychiatric Clinics of North America, 9,* 17–33.

Dornette, W. H. L. (Ed.) (1982). *Illustrated Stedman's medical dictionary* (5th ed.). Cincinnati, OH: Anderson.

Drake, R., Haddock, G., Hopkins, R., & Lewis, S. (1998). The measurement of outcome in schizophrenia. In T. Wykes, N. Tarrier, & S. Lewis (Eds.), *Outcome and innovation in psychological treatment of schizophrenia* (pp. 43–57). Chichester, UK: Wiley.

Edwards, C. P., & Kumru, A. (1999). Culturally-sensitive assessment. *Child and Adolescent Psychiatric Clinics of North America, 8,* 409–424.

Egdell, H. G., & Kolvin, I. (1972). Childhood hallucinations. *Journal of Child Psychology and Psychiatry, 13,* 279–287.

El Sendiony, M. F. (1974). The problem of cultural specificity of mental illness: The Egyptian mental disease and the Zar ceremony. *Australian and New Zealand Journal of Psychiatry, 8,* 103–107.

Elizur, E., & Kaffman, M. (1983). Factors influencing the severity of childhood bereavement reactions. *American Journal of Orthopsychiatry, 53,* 668–676.

Emslie, G. J., Rush, A. J., Weinberg, W. A., Kowatch, R. A., Hughes, C. W., Carmody, T., & Rintelmann, J. (1997). A double-blind, randomized, placebo-controlled trial of fluoxetine in children and adolescents with depression. *Archives of General Psychiatry, 54,* 1031–1037.

Emslie, G. J., Walkup, J. T., Pliszka, S. R., & Ernst, M. (1999). Nontricyclic antidepressants: Current trends in children and adolescents. *Journal of the American Academy of Child and Adolescent Psychiatry, 38,* 517–528.

Endicott, J., Spitzer, R., Fleiss, J., & Cohen, J. (1976). The Global Assessment Scale: A procedure for measuring overall severity of psychiatric disturbance. *Archives of General Psychiatry, 33,* 766–771.

Everson, M. D. (1997). Understanding bizarre, improbable, and fantastic elements in children's accounts of abuse. *Child Maltreatment, 2*, 134–149.

Exner, J. E. (1986). *The Rorschach: A comprehensive system* (Vol. 1, 2nd ed.). New York: John Wiley.

Famularo, R., Kinscherff, R., & Fenton, T. (1988). Propranolol treatment for childhood post-traumatic stress disorder, acute type: A pilot study. *American Journal of Diseases of Children, 142*, 1244–1247.

Famularo, R., Kinscherff, R., & Fenton, T. (1992). Psychiatric diagnoses of maltreated children: Preliminary findings. *Journal of the American Academy of Child and Adolescent Psychiatry, 37*, 863–867.

Faraone, S. V., & Tsuang, M. T. (1988). Familial links between schizophrenia and other disorders: Application of the multifactorial polygenic model. *Psychiatry, 51*, 37–47.

Fields, J. H., Grochowski, S., Lindenmayer, J. P., Kay, S. R., Grosz, D., Hyman, R. B., & Alexander, G. (1994). Assessing positive and negative symptoms in children and adolescents. *American Journal of Psychiatry, 151*, 249–253.

Findling, R. L. (1996). Open-label treatment of comorbid depression and attentional disorders with co-administration of serotonin reuptake inhibitors and psychostimulants in children, adolescents, and adults: A case series. *Journal of Child and Adolescent Psychopharmacology, 6*, 165–175.

Findling, R. L., Friedman, L., Kenny, J. T., Swales, J. T., Cola, D. M., & Schulz, S. C. (1995). Adolescent schizophrenia: A methodologic review of the current neuroimaging and neuropsychologic literature. *Journal of Autism and Developmental Disorders, 25*, 627–639.

Findling, R. L., Jayathilake, K., & Meltzer, H. Y. (1996). Pre-morbid asociality and neuroleptic-resistant and neuroleptic-responsive schizophrenia. *Psychological Medicine, 26*, 1033–1041.

Findling, R. L., Reed, M. D., & Blumer, J. L. (1999). The pharmacological treatment of depression in children and adolescents. *Paediatric Drugs, 1*, 161–182.

Findling, R. L., Reed, M. D., Myers, C., O'Riordan, M. A., Fiala, S., Branicky, L., Waldorf, B., & Blumer, J. L. (1999). Paroxetine pharmacokinetics in depressed children and adolescents. *Journal of the American Academy of Child and Adolescent Psychiatry, 38*, 952–959.

Findling, R. L., Schulz, S. C., Reed, M. D., & Blumer, J. L. (1998). The antipsychotics: A pediatric perspective. *Pediatric Clinics of North America, 45*, 1205–1232.

Flaum, M., & Schultz, S. K. (1996). When does amphetamine-induced psychosis become schizophrenia? *American Journal of Psychiatry, 153*, 812–815.

Fowler, R. C., McCabe, M. S., Cadoret, R. J., & Winokur, G. (1972). The validity of good prognosis schizophrenia. *Archives of General Psychiatry, 26*, 182–185.

Freedman, R., Adler, L. E., & Leonard, S. (1999). Alternative phenotypes for the complex genetics of schizophrenia. *Biological Psychiatry, 45*, 551–558.

Fricchione, G. L., Carbone, L., & Bennett, W. I. (1995). Psychotic disorders caused by a general medical condition, with delusions. Secondary "organic" delusional syndromes. *Psychiatric Clinics of North America, 18*, 363–378.

Friedman, L., Findling, R. L., Kenny, J. T., Swales, T., Stuve, T., Jesberger, J. A., Lewin, J. S., & Schulz, S. C. (1999). A magnetic resonance imaging study of adolescent patients with either schizophrenia or bipolar disorder as compared to healthy controls. *Biological Psychiatry, 46*, 78–88.

Fristad, M. A., Gavazzi, S. M., Centolella, D. M., & Soldano, K. W. (1996). Psychoeducation: A promising intervention strategy for families of children and adolescents with mood disorders. *Contemporary Family Therapy, 18*, 371–383.

Furman, E. (1983). Studies in childhood bereavement. *Canadian Journal of Psychiatry, 28*, 241–247.

Galdson, I. (1967). *Historic derivations of modern psychiatry.* New York: McGraw-Hill.

Garralda, M. E. (1984). Hallucinations in children with conduct and emotional disorders: I. The clinical phenomena. *Psychological Medicine, 14*, 589–596.

Garralda, M. E. (1984). Hallucinations in children with conduct and emotional disorders: II. The follow-up study. *Psychological Medicine, 14*, 597–694.

Geis, H. K., Whittlesey, S. W., McDonald, N. B., Smith, K. L., & Pfefferbaum, B. (1998). Bereavement and loss in childhood. *Child and Adolescent Psychiatric Clinics of North America, 7*, 73–85.

Gelder, M., Gath, D., & Mayou, R. (1989). *Oxford textbook of psychiatry* (2nd ed.). New York: Oxford University Press.

Geller, B., Cooper, T. B., Sun, K., Zimerman, B., Frazier, J., Williams, M., & Heath, J. (1998). Double-blind and placebo-controlled study of lithium for adolescents with bipolar disorders with secondary substance dependency. *Journal of the American Academy of Child and Adolescent Psychiatry, 37*, 171–178.

Geller, B., Fox, L. W., & Clark, K. A. (1994). Rate and predictors of prepubertal bipolarity during follow-up of 6- to 12-year-old depressed children. *Journal of the American Academy of Child and Adolescent Psychiatry, 33*, 461–468.

Geller, B., & Luby, J. (1997). Child and adolescent bipolar disorder: A review of the past 10 years. *Journal of the American Academy of Child and Adolescent Psychiatry, 36*, 1168–1176.

Gershon, E. S., Badner, J. A., Goldin, L. R., Sanders, A. R., Cravchik, A., & Detera-Wadleigh, S. D. (1998). Closing in on genes for manic-depressive illness and schizophrenia. *Neuropsychopharmacology, 18*, 233–242.

Ghaemi, S. N., & Goodwin, F. K. (1999). Use of atypical antipsychotic agents in bipolar and schizoaffective disorders: Review of the empirical literature. *Journal of Clinical Psychopharmacology, 19*, 354–361.

Gittelman, R. (1980). The role of psychological tests for differential diagnosis in child psychiatry. *Journal of the American Academy of Child Psychiatry, 19*, 413–438.

Goff, D. C., & Wine, L. (1997). Glutamate and schizophrenia: Clinical and research implications. *Schizophrenia Research, 27*, 157–168.

Golden, K. M. (1977). Voodoo in Africa and the United States. *American Journal of Psychiatry, 134*, 1425–1427.

Goldman, S. J., D'Angelo, E. J., & DeMaso, D. R. (1993). Psychopathology in families of children and adolescents with borderline personality disorder. *American Journal of Psychiatry, 150*, 1832–1835.

Goldman, S. J., D'Angelo, E. J., DeMaso, D. R., & Mezzacappa, E. (1992). Physical and sexual abuse histories among children with borderline personality disorder. *American Journal of Psychiatry, 149*, 1723–1726.

Goodwin, D. W., Schulsinger, F., Hermansen, L., Guze, S. B., & Winokur, G. (1973). Alcoholism and the hyperactive child syndrome. *Journal of Nervous Mental Disorders, 160*, 349–353.

Gottling, S. (1985). *Comparison of the reliability of the Goodenough-Harris Draw-a-Man Test with the Naglieri Draw-A-Person Test: A quantitative scoring system.* Unpublished master's thesis, The Ohio State University, Columbus.

Graham, T. F. (1967). *Medieval minds: Mental health in the middle ages.* London: Allen & Unwin.

Grcevich, S. J., Findling, R. L., Rowane, W. A., Friedman, L., & Schulz, S. C. (1996). Risperidone in the treatment of children and adolescents with schizophrenia: A retrospective study. *Journal of Child and Adolescent Psychopharmacology, 6,* 251–257.

Green, B., Shirk, S., Hanze, D., & Wanstrath, J. (1994). The Children's Global Assessment Scale in clinical practice: An empirical evaluation. *Journal of the American Academy of Child and Adolescent Psychiatry, 33,* 1158–1164.

Green, M. F., & Nuechterlein, K. H. (1999). Should schizophrenia be treated as a neurocognitive disorder? *Schizophrenia Bulletin, 25,* 309–318.

Grossman, L. S., Harrow, M., Fudala, J. L., & Meltzer, H. Y. (1984). The longitudinal course of schizoaffective disorders. A prospective follow-up study. *Journal of Nervous and Mental Disease, 172,* 140–149.

Grossman, L. S., Harrow, M., Goldberg, J. F., & Fichtner, C. G. (1991). Outcome of schizoaffective disorder at two long-term follow-ups: Comparisons with outcome of schizophrenia and affective disorders. *American Journal of Psychiatry, 148,* 1359–1365.

Gualtieri, C. T., Quade, D., Hicks, R. E., Mayo, J. P., & Schroeder, S. R. (1984). Tardive dyskinesia and other clinical consequences of neuroleptic treatment in children and adolescents. *American Journal of Psychiatry, 141,* 20–23.

Guarnaccia, P. J., Canino, G., Rubio-Stipec, M., & Bravo, M. (1993). The prevalence of ataque de nervios in the Puerto Rico disaster study. The role of culture in psychiatric epidemiology. *Journal of Nervous and Mental Disease, 181,* 157–165.

Guzder, J., Paris, J., Zelkowitz, P., & Marchessault, K. (1996). Risk factors for borderline pathology in children. *Journal of the American Academy of Child and Adolescent Psychiatry, 35,* 26–33.

Hafner, H., Riecher-Rossler, A., Maurer, K., Fatkenheuer, B., & Loffler, W. (1992). First onset and early symptomatology of schizophrenia: A chapter of epidemiological and neurobiological research into age and sex differences. *European Archives of Psychiatry and Clinical Neurosciences, 242,* 109–118.

Hagino, O. R., Weller, E. B., Weller, R. A., Washing, D., Fristad, M. A., & Kontras, S. B. (1995). Untoward effects of lithium treatment in children aged four through six years. *Journal of the American Academy of Child and Adolescent Psychiatry, 34,* 1584–1590.

Hanna, G. L. (1992). Assessment of mood disorders. *Child and Adolescent Clinics of North America, 1,* 73–88.

Harmon, R. J., & Riggs, P. D. (1996). Clonidine for posttraumatic stress disorder in preschool children. *Journal of the American Academy of Child and Adolescent Psychiatry, 35,* 1247–1249.

Hart, J., & McClure, G. M. (1989). Capgras' syndrome and folie à deux involving mother and child. *British Journal of Psychiatry, 154,* 552–554.

Harvey, P. D., Earle-Boyer, E. A., Weilgus, M. S., & Levinson, J. C. (1986). Encoding, memory, and thought disorder in schizophrenia and mania. *Schizophrenia Bulletin, 12,* 252–261.

Haworth, M. R. (1965). Children's Apperception Test. In A. I. Rabin (Ed.), *Projective techniques for adolescents and children* (pp. 37–42). New York: Springer.

Hedlund, J. L., & Vieweg, B. W. (1980). The Brief Psychiatric Rating Scale. *Acta Psychiatrica Scandanavica, 86*, 1–6.

Helzer, J. E., & Winokur, G. (1974). A family interview study of male manic depressives. *Archives of General Psychiatry, 31*, 73–77.

Hemphill, R. E. (1952). Incidence and nature of puerperal psychiatric illness. *British Medical Journal, 2*, 1232–1235.

Hirono, N., Mori, E., Ishii, K., Kitagaki, H., Sasaki, M., Ikejiri, Y., Imamura, T., Shimomura, T., Ikeda, M., & Yamashita, H. (1998). Alteration of regional cerebral glucose utilization with delusions in Alzheimer's disease. *Journal of Neuropsychiatry and Clinical Neurosciences, 10*, 433–439.

Hirschowitz, J., Casper, R., Garver, D. L., & Chang, S. (1980). Lithium response in good prognosis schizophrenia. *American Journal of Psychiatry, 137*, 916–920.

Hobson, J. A., & McCarley, R. W. (1977). The brain as a dream state generator: An activation-synthesis hypothesis of the dream process. *American Journal of Psychiatry, 134*, 1335–1348.

Holzman, P. S., Shenton, M. E., & Solovay, M. R. (1986). Quality of thought disorder in differential diagnosis. *Schizophrenia Bulletin, 12*, 360–371.

Horrigan, J. P. (1996). Guanfacine for PTSD nightmares [letter]. *Journal of the American Academy of Child and Adolescent Psychiatry, 35*, 975–976.

Howard, R. (1993). Transcultural issues in puerperal mental illness. *International Review of Psychiatry, 5*, 253–260.

Hurley, A. D. (1996). Psychiatric disorders in children and adolescents with mental retardation and developmental disabilities. *Current Opinion in Pediatrics, 8*, 361–365.

Imade, A. G., & Ebie, J. C. (1991). A retrospective study of symptom patterns of cannabis-induced psychosis. *Acta Psychiatrica Scandinavica, 83*, 134–136.

Jablensky, A. (1997). The 100-year epidemiology of schizophrenia. *Schizophrenia Research, 28*, 111–125.

Jacobsen, L. K., & Rapoport, J. L. (1998). Research update: Childhood-onset schizophrenia: Implications of clinical and neurobiological research. *Journal of Child Psychology and Psychiatry, 39*, 101–113.

Jensen, P., Roper, M., Fisher, P., Piacentini, J., Canino, G., Richters, J., Rubio-Stipec, M., Dulcan, M., Goodman, S., Davies, M., Rae, D., Shaffer, D., Bird, H., Lahey, B., & Schwab-Stone, M. (1995). Test-retest reliability of the Diagnostic Interview Schedule for Children (DISC 2.1): Parent, child, and combined algorithms. *Archives of General Psychiatry, 52*, 61–71.

Johnston, L. D., & O'Malley, P. M. (1986). Why do the nation's students use drugs and alcohol? Self-reported reasons from nine national surveys. *Journal of Drug Issues, 16*, 29–66.

Jones, P., & Cannon, M. (1998). The new epidemiology of schizophrenia. *Psychiatric Clinics of North America, 21*, 1–25.

Jørgensen, P., Bennedsen, B., Christensen, J., & Hyllested, A. (1996). Acute and transient psychotic disorder: Comorbidity with personality disorder. *Acta Psychiatrica Scandinavica, 94*, 460–464.

Kafantaris, V. (1995). Treatment of bipolar disorder in children and adolescents. *Journal of the American Academy of Child and Adolescent Psychiatry, 34*, 732–741.

Kaminer, Y., Burleson, J. A., Blitz, C., Sussman, J., & Rounsaville, B. J. (1998). Psychotherapies for adolescent substance abusers: A pilot study. *Journal of Nervous and Mental Disease, 186*, 684–690.

Kamphaus, R. W., & Pleiss, K. L. (1991). Draw-A-Person techniques: Tests in search of a construct. *Journal of School Psychology, 29*, 395–401.

Kaplan, H. I., & Sadock, B. J. (1998). *Synopsis of psychiatry: Behavioral sciences/clinical psychiatry* (8th ed.). Baltimore: Williams & Wilkins.

Kapur, S., & Remington, G. (1996). Serotonin-dopamine interaction and its relevance to schizophrenia. *American Journal of Psychiatry, 153*, 466–476.

Kasanin, J. (1994). The acute schizoaffective psychoses. *American Journal of Psychiatry, 151* (Suppl.), 144–154.

Kashani, J. H., McGee, R. O., Clarkson, S. E., Anderson, J. C., Walton, L. A., Williams, S., Silva, P. A., Robins, A. J., Cytryn, L., & McKnew, D. H. (1984). Depression in a sample of 9-year-old children: Prevalence and associated characteristics. *Archives of General Psychiatry, 40*, 1217–1223.

Kashani, J. H., & McNaul, J. P. (1997). Mood disorders in adolescents. In J. M. Wiener (Ed.), *Textbook of child and adolescent psychiatry* (2nd ed., pp. 343–385). Washington, DC: American Psychiatric Press.

Kashani, J. H., & Nair, J. (1996). Affective/mood disorders. In J. M. Wiener (Ed.), *Diagnosis and psychopharmacology of childhood and adolescent disorders* (2nd ed.). New York: John Wiley.

Kashani, J. H., & Ray, J. S. (1987). Major depression with delusional features in a preschool-age child. *Journal of the American Academy of Child and Adolescent Psychiatry, 26*, 110–112.

Kashani, J. H., & Simonds, J. F. (1979). Incidence of depression in children. *American Journal of Psychiatry, 136*, 1203–1205.

Kashiwase, H., & Kato, M. (1997). Folie à deux in Japan- analysis of 97 cases in the Japanese literature. *Acta Psychiatrica Scandinavica, 96*, 231–234.

Katz, L., Fleisher, W., Kjernisted, K., & Milanese, P. (1996). A review of the psychobiology and pharmacotherapy of posttraumatic stress disorder. *Canadian Journal of Psychiatry, 41*, 233–238.

Kaufman, J., Birmaher, B., Brent, D., Rao, U., Flynn, C., Moreci, P., Williamson, D., & Ryan, N. (1997). Schedule for Affective Disorders and Schizophrenia for School-age Children-Present and Lifetime version (K-SADS-PL): Initial reliability and validity data. *Journal of the American Academy of Child and Adolescent Psychiatry, 36*, 980–988.

Kaufman, J., Birmaher, B., Clayton, S., Retano, A., & Wongchaowart, B. (1997). Case study: Trauma-related hallucinations. *Journal of the American Academy of Child and Adolescent Psychiatry, 36*, 1602–1605.

Kay, S. R., Fiszbein, A., & Opler, L. A. (1987). The Positive and Negative Syndrome Scale (PANSS) for schizophrenia. *Schizophrenia Bulletin, 13*, 261–276.

Kay, S. R., & Sevy, S. (1990). Pyramidical model of schizophrenia. *Schizophrenia Bulletin, 16*, 537–545.

Keefe, R. S. E., Silva, S. G., Perkins, D. O., Lieberman, J. A. (1999). The effects of atypical antipsychotic drugs on neurocognitive impairment in schizophrenia: A review and meta-analysis. *Schizophrenia Bulletin, 25*, 201–222.

Keepers, G. A., Clappison, V. J., & Casey, D. E. (1983). Initial anticholinergic prophylaxis for neuroleptic-induced extrapyramidal syndromes. *Archives of General Psychiatry, 40*, 1113–1117.

Kendell, R. E., Chalmers, J. C., & Platz, C. (1987). Epidemiology of puerperal psychosis. *British Journal of Psychiatry, 150*, 662–673.

Kendler, K. S. (1982). Demography of paranoid psychosis (delusional disorder): A review and comparison with schizophrenia and affective illness. *Archives of General Psychiatry, 39*, 890–902.

Kendler, K. S., Gruenberg, A. M., & Strauss, J. S. (1981). An independent analysis of the Copenhagen sample of the Danish adoption study. II. The relationship between schizotypal personality disorder and schizophrenia. *Archives of General Psychiatry, 38*, 982–984.

Kendler, K. S., McGuire, M., Gruenberg, A. M., O'Hare, A., Spellman, M., & Walsh, D. (1993). The Roscommon Family Study: III. Schizophrenia-related personality disorders in relatives. *Archives of General Psychiatry, 50*, 781–788.

Kendler, K. S., McGuire, M., Gruenberg, A. M., & Walsh, D. (1995). Examining the validity of DSM-III-R schizoaffective disorder and its putative subtypes in the Roscommon Family Study. *American Journal of Psychiatry, 152*, 755–764.

Kendler, K. S., & Walsh, D. (1995). Schizophreniform disorder, delusional disorder and psychotic disorder not otherwise specified: Clinical features, outcome and familial psychopathology. *Acta Psychiatrica Scandinavica, 91*, 370–378.

Kenny, J. T., Friedman, L., Findling, R. L., Swales, T. P., Strauss, M. E., Jesberger, J. A., & Schulz, S. C. (1997). Cognitive impairment in adolescents with schizophrenia. *American Journal of Psychiatry, 154*, 1613–1615.

Kernberg, P. F. (1983). Borderline conditions: Childhood and adolescent aspects. In K. S. Robinson (Ed.), *The Borderline Child* (pp. 101–109). New York: McGraw-Hill.

Kestenbaum, C. J. (1994). Psychotic and prepsychotic disorders. In J. M. Oldham & M. B. Riba (Eds.), *American Psychiatric Press Review of Psychiatry* (Vol. 13, pp. 571–588). Washington, DC: American Psychiatric Press.

Ketter, T. A., Andreason, P. J., George, M. S., Lee, C., Gill, D. S., Parekh, P. I., Willis, M. W., Herscovitch, P., & Post, R. M. (1996). Anterior paralimbic mediation of procaine-induced emotional and psychosensory experiences. *Archives of General Psychiatry, 53*, 59–69.

Kety, S. S., Rosenthal, D., Wender, P. H., Schulsinger, F., & Jacobsen, B. (1978). The biological and adoptive families of adopted individuals who became schizophrenic: Prevalence of mental illness and other characteristics. In L. C. Wynne, R. L. Cromwell, & S. Matthysse (Eds.), *The nature of schizophrenia* (pp. 25–37). New York: John Wiley.

Kety, S. S., Wender, P. H., Jacobsen, B., Ingraham, L. J., Jansson, L., Faber, B., & Kinney, D. K. (1994). Mental illness in the biological and adoptive relatives of schizophrenic adoptees: Replication of the Copenhagen study in the rest of Denmark. *Archives of General Psychiatry, 51*, 442–455.

Kimura, S., Yuri, K., & Ichikawa, M. (1978). On so-called atypical psychosis in early and mid-adolescence. *Folia Psychiatrica et Neurologica Japonica, 32*, 525–537.

King, R. A., & Lewis, M. (1994). The difficult child. *Child and Adolescent Psychiatric Clinics of North America, 3*, 531–541.

King, S., & Dixon, M. J. (1999). Expressed emotion and relapse in young schizophrenia outpatients. *Schizophrenia Bulletin, 25*, 377–386.

Kinney, D. K., Holzman, P. S., Jacobsen, B., Jansson, L., Faber, B., Hildebrand, W., Kasell, E., & Zimbalist, M. E. (1997). Thought disorder in schizophrenic and control adoptees and their relatives. *Archives of General Psychiatry, 54*, 475–479.

Kliman, G. (1968). *Psychological emergencies in childhood*. New York: Grune & Stratton.

Klin, A., Mayes, L. C., Volkmar, F. R., & Cohen, D. J. (1995). Multiplex developmental disorder. *Journal of Developmental and Behavioral Pediatrics, 16* (Suppl.), S7–S11.

Kolvin, I. (1971). Studies in the childhood psychoses. I. Diagnostic criteria and classification. *British Journal of Psychiatry, 118*, 381–384.

Konner, M. (1989). Anthropology and psychiatry. In H. I. Kaplan & B. J. Sadock (Eds.), *Comprehensive textbook of psychiatry/V* (pp. 283–297). Baltimore: Williams & Wilkins.

Kotrla, K. J., Chacko, R. C., Harper, R. G., & Doody, R. (1995). Clinical variables associated with psychosis in Alzheimer's disease. *American Journal of Psychiatry, 152*, 1377–1379.

Kotsopoulos, S., Kanigsberg, J., Cote, A., & Fiedorowicz, C. (1987). Hallucinatory experiences in nonpsychotic children. *Journal of the American Academy of Child and Adolescent Psychiatry, 26*, 375–380.

Kovacs, M. (1996). Presentation and course of major depressive disorder during childhood and later years of the life span. *Journal of the American Academy of Child and Adolescent Psychiatry, 35*, 705–715.

Kovacs, M., & Pollack, M. (1995). Bipolar disorder and comorbid conduct disorder in childhood and adolescence. *Journal of the American Academy of Child and Adolescent Psychiatry, 34*, 715–723.

Kowatch, R. A., & Bucci, J. P. (1998). Mood stabilizers and anticonvulsants. *Pediatric Clinics of North America, 45*, 1173–1186.

Kraepelin, E. (1990). In J. M. Quen (Ed.), *Psychiatry: A textbook for students and physicians*. Canton, MA: Watson Publishing International.

Kranzler, E. M., Shaffer, D., Wasserman, G., & Davies, M. (1990). Early childhood bereavement. *Journal of the American Academy of Child and Adolescent Psychiatry, 29* (4), 513–520.

Kumar, R. (1994). Postnatal illness: A transcultural perspective. *Social Psychiatry and Psychiatric Epidemiology, 29*, 250–264.

Kumra, S. (1998). Children and adolescents with psychotic disorders. In B. T. Walsh (Ed.), *Child psychopharmacology* (pp. 65–89). Washington, DC: American Psychiatric Press.

Kumra, S., Frazier, J., Jacobsen, L., McKenna, K., Gordon, C. T., Lenane, M. C., Hamburger, S. D., Smith, A. K., & Albus, K. E. (1996). Childhood-onset schizophrenia: A double-blind clozapine-haloperidol comparison. *Archives of General Psychiatry, 53*, 1090–1097.

Kumra, S., Jacobsen, L. K., Lenane, M., Karp, B. I., Frazier, J. A., Smith, A. K., Bedwell, J., Lee, P., Malanga, C. J., Hamburger, S., & Rapoport, J. L. (1998). Childhood-onset schizophrenia: An open-label study of olanzapine in adolescents. *Journal of the American Academy of Child and Adolescent Psychiatry, 37*, 377–385.

Kumra, S., Jacobsen, L. K., Lenane, M., Zahn, T. P., Wiggs, E., Alaghband-Rad, J., Castellanos, F. X., Frazier, J. A., McKenna, K., Gordon, C. T., Smith, A., Hamburger, S., & Rapoport, J. L. (1998). "Multidimensionally impaired disorder": Is it a variant of very early-onset schizophrenia? *Journal of the American Academy of Child and Adolescent Psychiatry, 37*, 91–99.

Kutcher, S., Kachur, E., Marton, P., Szalai, J., & Jaunkalns, R. (1992). Substance abuse among adolescents with chronic mental illnesses: A pilot study of descriptive and differentiating features. *Canadian Journal of Psychiatry, 37*, 428–431.

Kutcher, S. P. (1997). Individual baseline psychiatric assessment for psychopharmacologic treatment. In J. Fletcher (Ed.), *Child and Adolescent Psychopharmacology* (pp. 15–35). Philadelphia: W. B. Saunders.

Lay, B., Schmidt, M. H., & Blanz, B. (1997). Course of adolescent psychotic disorder with schizoaffective episodes. *European Child and Adolescent Psychiatry, 6*, 32–41.

Lehna, C. R. (1995). Children's descriptions of their feelings and what they found helpful during bereavement. *American Journal of Hospice and Palliative Care, 12*, 24–30.

Levinson, D. F., Umapathy, C., & Musthaq, M. (1999). Treatment of schizoaffective disorder and schizophrenia with mood symptoms. *American Journal of Psychiatry, 156*, 1138–1148.

Lewinsohn, P. M., Clarke, G. N., Seeley, J. R., & Rohde, P. (1994). Major depression in community adolescents: Age at onset, episode duration, and time to recurrence. *Journal of the American Academy of Child and Adolescent Psychiatry, 33*, 809–818.

Lewinsohn, P. M., Klein, D. N., & Seeley, J. R. (1995). Bipolar disorders in a community sample of older adolescents: Prevalence, phenomenology, comorbidity, and course. *Journal of the American Academy of Child and Adolescent Psychiatry, 34*, 454–463.

Lewinsohn, P. M., Rohde, P., Klein, D. N., & Seeley, J. R. (1999). Natural course of adolescent major depressive disorder: I. Continuity into adulthood. *Journal of the American Academy of Child and Adolescent Psychiatry, 38*, 56–63.

Lewis, D. O., & Yeager, C. A. (1994). Abuse dissociative phenomena, and childhood multiple personality disorder. *Child and Adolescent Clinics of North America, 3*, 729–743.

Lewis, M. (1996). Borderline features in childhood disorders. In F. R. Volkmar (Ed.), *Psychoses and pervasive developmental disorders in childhood and adolescence* (pp. 89–105). Washington, DC: American Psychiatric Press.

Lieberman, J. A., Mailman, R. B., Duncan, G., Sikich, L., Chakos, M., Nichols, D. E., & Kraus, J. E. (1998). Serotonergic basis of antipsychotic drug effects in schizophrenia. *Biological Psychiatry, 44*, 1099–1117.

Lifrak, P. D., Alterman, A. I., O'Brien, C. P., & Volpicelli, J. R. (1997). Naltrexone for alcoholic adolescents. *American Journal of Psychiatry, 154*, 439–440.

Lincoln, A. J., Bloom, D., Katz, M., & Boksenbaum, N. (1998). Neuropsychological and neurophysiological indices of auditory processing impairment in children with multiple complex developmental disorder. *Journal of the American Academy of Child and Adolescent Psychiatry, 37*, 100–112.

Lo, Y., Tsai, S. -J., Chang, C. -H., Hwang, J. -P., & Sim, C. -B. (1997). Organic delusional disorder in psychiatric in-patients: Comparison with delusional disorder. *Acta Psychiatrica Scandinavica, 95*, 161–163.

Lofgren, D. P., Bemporad, J., King, J., Lindem, K., & O'Driscoll, G. (1991). A prospective follow-up study of so-called borderline children. *American Journal of Psychiatry, 148*, 1541–1547.

Looff, D., Grimley, P., Kuller, F., Martin, A., & Shonfield, L. (1995). Carbamazepine for PTSD [letter]. *Journal of the American Academy of Child and Adolescent Psychiatry, 34*, 703–704.

Loranger, A. W. (1984). Sex difference in age at onset of schizophrenia. *Archives of General Psychiatry, 41*, 157–161.

Lukianowicz, N. (1969). Hallucinations in non-psychotic children. *Psychiatrica Clinica, 2*, 321–337.

Lukoff, D., Nuechterlein, K. H., & Ventura, J. (1986). Manual for the expanded BPRS. *Schizophrenia Bulletin, 12*, 594–602.

Mahowald, M. W., & Thorpy, M. J. (1995). Nonarousal parasomnias in the child. In R. Ferber & M. Kryger (Eds.), *Principles and practice of sleep medicine in the child* (pp. 115–134). Philadelphia: W. B. Saunders.

Maier, W., Lichtermann, D., Minges, J., Heun, R., Hallmayer, J., & Benkert, O. (1992). Schizoaffective disorder with mood-incongruent psychotic features: Keep separate or combine? Evidence from a family study. *American Journal of Psychiatry, 149,* 1666–1673.

Manschreck, T. C. (1995). Delusional disorder and shared psychotic disorder. In H. I. Kaplan & B. J. Sadock (Eds.), *Comprehensive textbook of psychiatric disorders* (6th ed., pp. 1031–1049). Baltimore: Williams & Wilkins.

Manschreck, T. C. (1996). Delusional disorder: The recognition and management of paranoia. *Journal of Clinical Psychiatry, 57* (Suppl. 3), 32–38.

Marder, S. R., & Meibach, R. C. (1994). Risperidone in the treatment of schizophrenia. *American Journal of Psychiatry, 151,* 825–835.

Max, J. E., Smith, W. L., Jr., Sato, Y., Mattheis, P. J., Castillo, C. S., Lindgren, S. D., Robin, D. A., & Stierwalt, J. A. G. (1997). Traumatic brain injury in children and adolescents: Psychiatric disorders in the first three months. *Journal of the American Academy of Child and Adolescent Psychiatry, 36,* 94–102.

McAdams, L. A., Harris, J. M., Bailey, A., Fell, R., & Jeste, D. V. (1996). Validating specific psychopathology scales in older outpatients with schizophrenia. *Journal of Nervous and Mental Disease, 184,* 246–251.

McClellan, J. M., & Werry, J. S. (1992). Schizophrenia. *Psychiatric Clinics of North America, 15,* 131–148.

McClellan, J., & Werry, J. (1994). Practice parameters for the assessment and treatment of children and adolescents with schizophrenia. *Journal of the American Academy of Child and Adolescent Psychiatry, 33,* 616–635.

McConville, B., Arvanitis, L., Thyrum, P., & Smith, K. (1999). Pharmacokinetics, tolerability, and clinical effectiveness of quetiapine in adolescents with selected psychotic disorders [abstract]. *European Neuropsychopharmacology, 9* (Suppl. 5), S267.

McCracken, J. T. (1987). Lead intoxication psychosis in an adolescent. *Journal of the American Academy of Child and Adolescent Psychiatry, 26,* 274–276.

McDermott, B. E., Sautter, F. J., & Garver, D. L. (1991). Heterogeneity of schizophrenia: Relationship to latency of neuroleptic response. *Psychiatry Research, 37,* 97–103.

McDonald, L. V., & Lake, C. R. (1995). Psychosis in an adolescent patient with Wilson's disease: Effects of chelation therapy. *Psychosomatic Medicine, 57,* 202–204.

McElroy, S. L., Strakowski, S. M., West, S. A., Keck, P. E., Jr., & McConville, B. J. (1997). Phenomenology of adolescent and adult mania in hospitalized patients with bipolar disorder. *American Journal of Psychiatry, 154,* 44–49.

McGuire, P. K., Quested, D. J., Spence, S. A., Murray, R. M., Frith, C. D., & Liddle, P. F. (1998). Pathophysiology of "positive" thought disorder in schizophrenia. *British Journal of Psychiatry, 173,* 231–235.

McKenna, K., Gordon, C. T., Lenane, M., Kaysen, D., Fahey, K., & Rapoport, J. L. (1994). Looking for childhood-onset schizophrenia: The first 71 cases screened. *Journal of the American Academy of Child and Adolescent Psychiatry, 33,* 636–644.

McNeil, T. F., Harty, B., Blennow, G., & Cantor-Graae, E. (1993). Neuromotor deviation in offspring of psychotic mothers: A selective developmental deficiency in two groups of children at heightened psychiatric risk? *Journal of Psychiatric Research, 27,* 39–54.

Meakin, C. J., Brockington, I. F., Lynch, S., & Jones, S. R. (1995). Dopamine supersensitivity and hormonal status in puerperal psychosis. *British Journal of Psychiatry, 166,* 73–79.

Meijer, M., Goedhart, A. W., & Treffers, P. D. (1998). The persistence of borderline personality disorder in adolescence. *Journal of Personality Disorders, 12,* 13–22.

Mela, M., Obenbe, A., & Farmer, A. E. (1997). Folie a quatre in a large Nigerian sub-ship. *Schizophrenia Research, 23*, 91–93.

Meltzer, H. Y., Rabinowitz, J., Lee, M. A., Cola, P. A., Ranjan, R., Findling, R. L., & Thompson, P. A. (1997). Age at onset and gender of schizophrenic patients in relation to neuroleptic resistance. *American Journal of Psychiatry, 154*, 475–482.

Mezzich, J. E., & Keh-Ming, L. (1995). Acute and transient psychotic disorders and culture-bound syndromes. In H. I. Kaplan & B. J. Sadock (Eds.), *Comprehensive textbook of psychiatric disorders* (6th ed., pp. 1049–1058). Baltimore: Williams & Wilkins.

Michals, M. L., Crismon, M. L., Roberts, S., & Childs, A. (1993). Clozapine response and adverse effects in nine brain-injured patients. *Journal of Clinical Psychopharmacology, 13*, 198–203.

Miklowitz, D. J. (1994). Family risk indicators in schizophrenia. *Schizophrenia Bulletin, 20*, 137–149.

Milin, R. P. (1996). Comorbidity of substance abuse and psychotic disorders: Focus on adolescents and young adults. *Child and Adolescent Psychiatric Clinics of North America, 5*, 111–121.

Mufson, L., & Fairbanks, J. (1996). Interpersonal psychotherapy for depressed adolescents: A one-year naturalistic follow-up study. *Journal of the American Academy of Child and Adolescent Psychiatry, 35*, 1145–1155.

Munro, A., & Mok, H. (1995). An overview of treatment of paranoia/delusional disorder. *Canadian Journal of Psychiatry, 40*, 616–622.

Murphy, H. B. M. (1982). The acute reactive psychosis. In *Comparative psychiatry* (pp. 91–114). New York: Springer.

Murray, H. A. (1943). *Thematic Apperception Test: Manual.* Cambridge, MA: Harvard University Press.

Myers, W. C., Donahue, J. E., & Goldstein, M. R. (1994). Disulfiram for alcohol use disorders in adolescents. *Journal of the American Academy of Child and Adolescent Psychiatry, 33*, 484–489.

Naglieri, J. A. (1988). *Draw A Person: A quantitative scoring system.* San Antonio, TX: Psychological Corporation.

Naglieri, J. A., & Pruett, P. N. (1990). Nonverbal intelligence measures: A selected view of instruments and their use. In C. R. Reynolds & R. W. Kamphaus (Eds.), *Handbook of psychological and educational assessment of children* (pp. 348–370). New York: Guilford Press.

National Institute of Mental Health. (1985). Abnormal Involuntary Movement Scale (AIMS). *Psychopharmacology Bulletin, 21*, 1077–1080.

Neppe, V. M., & Tucker, G. J. (1989). Atypical, unusual, and cultural psychoses. In H. I. Kaplan & B. J. Sadock (Eds.), *Comprehensive textbook of psychiatry* (5th ed., pp. 842–852). Baltimore: Williams & Wilkins.

Nicolson, R., Giedd, J. N., Lenane, M., Hamburger, S., Singaracharlu, S., Bedwell, J., Fernandez, T., Thaker, G. K., Malaspina, D., & Rapoport, J. L. (1999). Clinical and neurobiological correlates of cytogenetic abnormalities in childhood-onset schizophrenia. *American Journal of Psychiatry, 156*, 1575–1579.

Nurcombe, B., Mitchell, W., Begtrip, R., Tramontaria, M., LaBasbera, J., & Pruitt, J. (1996). Dissociative hallucinations and allied conditions. In F. Volkmar (Ed.), *Psychoses and pervasive developmental disorders in childhood and adolescence* (pp. 107–128). Washington, DC: American Psychiatric Press.

O'Donovan, M. C., & Owen, M. J. (1999). Candidate-gene association studies of schizophrenia. *American Journal of Human Genetics, 65*, 587–592.

Olfson, M., Marcus, S. C., Pincus, H. A., Zito, J. M., Thompson, J. W., & Zarin, D. A. (1998). Antidepressant prescribing practices of outpatient psychiatrists. *Archives of General Psychiatry, 55*, 310–316.

Olin, S. S., & Mednick, S. A. (1996). Risk factors of psychosis: Identifying vulnerable populations premorbidly. *Schizophrenia Bulletin, 22*, 223–240.

Olin, S. S., Raine, A., Cannon, T. D., Parnas, J., Schulsinger, F., & Mednick, S. A. (1997). Childhood behavior precursors of schizotypal personality disorder. *Schizophrenia Bulletin, 23*, 93–103.

Oosthuizen, P., Russouw, H., & Roberts, M. (1995). Is puerperal psychosis bipolar mood disorder? A phenomenological comparison. *Comprehensive Psychiatry, 36*, 77–81.

Opjordsmoen, S., & Retterstöl, N. (1993). Outcome in delusional disorder in different periods of time. *Psychopathology, 26*, 90–94.

Oquendo, M., Horwath, E., & Martinez, A. (1992). Ataques de nervios: Proposed diagnostic criteria for a culture specific syndrome. *Culture, Medicine and Psychiatry, 16*, 367–376.

Overall, J. E. (1972). The Brief Psychiatric Rating Scale in psychopharmacology. *Research Psychometric Laboratory Reports, 29*, University of Texas, Galveston.

Overall, J. E. (1976). The Brief Psychiatric Rating Scale. In W. Guy (Ed.), *ECDEU assessment manual* (pp. 159–169). Rockville, MD: NIMH.

Paris, J. (1994). *Borderline personality disorder: A multidimensional approach*. Washington, DC: American Psychiatric Press.

Parker, K. C. H., Hanson, R. K., & Hunsley, J. (1988). MMPI, Rorschach, and WAIS: A meta-analytic comparison of reliability, stability, and validity. *Psychological Bulletin, 103*, 367–373.

Parnas, J., Schulsinger, F., Schulsinger, H., Mednick, S. A., & Teasdale, T. W. (1982). Behavioral precursors of schizophrenia spectrum: A prospective study. *Archives of General Psychiatry, 39*, 658–664.

Parraga, H. C., Simonds, J. F., & Butterfield, P. T. (1982). Iatrogenic behavioral and psychiatric symptoms in children with partial complex seizures. *Journal of Developmental & Behavioral Pediatrics, 3*, 25–28.

Parry, B. L. (1995). Postpartum psychiatric syndromes. In H. I. Kaplan & B. J. Sadock (Eds.), *Comprehensive textbook of psychiatric disorders* (6th ed., pp. 1059–1066). Baltimore: Williams & Wilkins.

Patton, L. H. (1995). Adolescent substance abuse: Risk factors and protective factors. *Pediatric Clinics of North America, 42*, 283–293.

Peralta, V., & Cuesta, M. J. (1994). Psychometric properties of the Positive and Negative Syndrome Scale (PANSS) in schizophrenia. *Psychiatry Research, 53*, 31–40.

Peralta, V., Cuesta, M. J., & DeLeon, J. (1995). Positive and negative symptoms/syndromes in schizophrenia: Reliability and validity of different diagnostic systems. *Psychological Medicine, 25*, 43–50.

Percy, A. K. (1987). The inherited neurodegenerative disorders of childhood: Clinical assessment. *Journal of Child Neurology, 2*, 82–97.

Phares, E. J. (1992). *Clinical psychology: Concepts, methods, and profession* (4th ed.). Pacific Grove, CA: Brooks/Cole.

Pihl, R. O., & Peterson, J. B. (1993). Alcohol/drug use and aggressive behavior. In S. Hodgins (Ed.), *Mental disorder and crime* (pp. 263–283). Newbury Park, CA: Sage.

Pine, D. S., Cohen, P., & Brook, J. (1996). The association between major depression and headache: Results of a longitudinal epidemiologic study in youth. *Journal of Child and Adolescent Psychopharmacology, 6*, 153–164.

Polonio, P., & Figueirido, M. (1955). On the structure of mental disorders associated with childbearing. *Monatsschrift Psychiatric Neurology, 130*, 304–318.

Ponce, D. E. (1997). Adolescent psychopathology. In W. Tseng & J. Streltzer (Eds.), *Culture and psychopathology* (pp. 206–222). New York: Brunner/Mazel.

Pool, D., Bloom, W., Milk, D. H., Roniger, J. J., Jr., & Gallant, D. M. (1976). A controlled evaluation of loxitane in seventy-five adolescent schizophrenic patients. *Current Therapeutic Research, Clinical & Experimental, 19*, 99–104.

Poole, R., & Brabbins, C. (1997). Substance misuse and psychosis. *British Journal of Hospital Medicine, 58*, 447–450.

Post, R. M. (1995). Mood disorders and somatic treatment. In H. I. Kaplan & B. J. Sadock (Eds.), *Comprehensive textbook of psychiatric disorders* (6th ed., pp. 1152–1177). Baltimore: Williams & Wilkins.

Post, R. M., Findling, R. L., & Kahn, R. S. (1991). Interfaces between seizures and affective disorders: The uses of visually mapping the evolution and longitudinal course of an illness. *Mount Sinai Journal of Medicine, 58*, 310–323.

Post, R. M., Weiss, S. R. B., Leverich, G. S., George, M. S., Frye, M., & Ketter, T. A. (1996). Developmental psychobiology of cyclic affective illness: Implications for early therapeutic intervention. *Development and Psychopathology, 8*, 273–305.

Prince, R. (1985). The concept of culture-bound syndromes: Anorexia nervosa and brain-fag. *Social Sciences and Medicine, 21*, 197–203.

Prugh, D. G., Wagonfeld, S., Metcalf, D., & Jordan, K. (1980). A clinical study of delirium in children and adolescents. *Psychosomatic Medicine, 42* (Suppl. 2), 177–195.

Pulver, A. E., Brown, C. H., Wolyniec, P. S., McGrath, J. A., & Tam, D. (1991). Psychiatric morbidity in the relatives of patients with *DSM-III* schizophreniform disorder: Comparisons with the relatives of schizophrenic and bipolar disorder patients. *Journal of Psychiatric Research, 25*, 19–29.

Rabinowitz, J., Bromet, E. J., Lavelle, J., Carlson, G., Kovasznay, B., & Schwartz, J. E. (1998). Prevalence and severity of substance use disorders and onset of psychosis in first-admission psychotic patients. *Psychological Medicine, 28*, 1411–1419.

Rall, T. W., & Schleifer, L. S. (1980). Drugs effective in the therapy of the epilepsies. In L. S. Goodman & A. Gilman (Eds.), *The pharmacological basis of therapeutics* (6th ed.). New York: Macmillan.

Realmuto, G. M., Erickson, W. D., Yellin, A. M., Hopwood, J. H., & Greenberg, L. M. (1984). Clinical comparison of thiothixene and thioridazine in schizophrenic adolescents. *American Journal of Psychiatry, 141*, 440–442.

Rechtschaffen, A., & Roth, B. (1969). A polygraphic study of night sleep in patients with hypersomnia. *Electroencephalography and Clinical Neurophysiology, 26*, 230.

Reese, C., & Wilborn, B. (1983). Correlates of drug abuse in adolescents: A comparison of families of drug abusers with families of non-drug abusers. *Journal of Youth and Adolescence, 12*, 55–63.

Remschmidt, H., Schulz, E., & Martin, M. (1994). An open trial of clozapine in thirty-six adolescents with schizophrenia. *Journal of Child and Adolescent Psychopharmacology, 4*, 31–41.

Remschmidt, H. E., Schulz, E., Matthias, M., Warnke, A., & Trott, G. E. (1994). Childhood-onset schizophrenia: History of the concept and recent studies. *Schizophrenia Bulletin, 20*, 727–745.

Rey, J. M., & Walter, G. (1997). Half a century of ECT use in young people. *American Journal of Psychiatry, 154*, 595–602.

Richardson, M. A., Haugland, G., & Craig, T. J. (1991). Neuroleptic use, Parkinsonian symptoms, tardive dyskinesia, and associated factors in child and adolescent psychiatric patients. *American Journal of Psychiatry, 148*, 1322–1328.

Ring, N., Tantam, D., Montague, L., Newby, D., & Morris, J. (1991). Gender differences in the incidence of definite schizophrenia and atypical psychosis-focus on negative symptoms of schizophrenia. *Acta Psychiatrica Scandanavica, 84*, 489–496.

Robinson, D. G., Woerner, M. G., Alvir, J. M. J., Geisler, S., Koreen, A., Sheitman, B., Chakos, M., Mayerhoff, D., Bilder, R., Goldman, R., & Lieberman, J. A. (1999). Predictors of treatment response from a first episode of schizophrenia or schizoaffective disorder. *American Journal of Psychiatry, 156*, 544–549.

Rogeness, G. A., Hernandez, J. M., Macedo, C. A., Amrung, S. A., & Hoppe, S. K. (1986). Near-zero plasma dopamine-B-hydroxylase and conduct disorder in emotionally disturbed boys. *Journal of the American Academy of Child Psychiatry, 25*, 521–527.

Rogeness, G. A., Hernandez, J. M., Macedo, C. A., Mitchell, E. L., Amrung, S. A., & Harris, W. R. (1984). Clinical characteristics of emotionally disturbed boys with very low activities of dopamine-B-hydroxylase. *Journal of the American Academy of Child Psychiatry, 23*, 203–208.

Rojas-Fernandez, C. H., & MacKnight, C. (1999). Dementia with Lewy bodies: Review and pharmacotherapeutic implications. *Pharmacotherapy, 19*, 795–803.

Rosenthal, R. N., & Miner, C. R. (1997). Differential diagnosis of substance-induced psychosis and schizophrenia in patients with substance use disorders. *Schizophrenia Bulletin, 23*, 187–193.

Rosse, R. B., Collins, J. P., Jr., Fay-McCarthy, M., Alim, T. N., Wyatt, R. J., & Deutsch, S. I. (1994). Phenomenologic comparison of the idiopathic psychosis of schizophrenia and drug-induced cocaine and phencyclidine psychoses: A retrospective study. *Clinical Neuropharmacology, 17*, 359–369.

Rossi, A., Serio, A., Stratta, P., Petruzzi, C., Schiazza, G., Mancini, F., & Casacchia, M. (1994). Planum temporale asymmetry and thought disorder in schizophrenia. *Schizophrenia Research, 12*, 1–7.

Rothstein, A. (1981). Hallucinatory phenomena in childhood. A critique of the literature. *Journal of the American Academy of Child and Adolescent Psychiatry, 20*, 623–635.

Ruppin, E., Reggia, J. A., & Horn, D. (1996). Pathogenesis of schizophrenic delusions and hallucinations: A neural model. *Schizophrenia Bulletin, 22*, 105–123.

Russell, A. T. (1994). The clinical presentation of childhood-onset schizophrenia. *Schizophrenia Bulletin, 20*, 631–646.

Rutter, M. (1966). *Children of sick parents*. Oxford, UK: Oxford University Press.

Rutter, M. (1971). Parent-child separation: Psychological effects on children. *Journal of Child Psychology and Psychiatry, 12*, 233–260.

Sachdev, P. S. (1985). Koro epidemic in north-east India. *Australian and New Zealand Journal of Psychiatry, 19*, 433–438.

Sacks, M. H. (1988). Folie à deux. *Comprehensive Psychiatry, 29*, 270–277.

Sandel, M. E., Olive, D. A., & Rader, M. A. (1993). Chlorpromazine-induced psychosis after brain injury. *Brain Injury, 7*, 77–83.

Sandler, I. N., West, S. G., Baca, L., Pillow, D. R., Gersten, J. C., Rogosch, F., Virdin, L., Beals, J., Reynolds, K. D., Kallgren, C., Tein, J., Kriege, G., Cole, E., & Ramirez, R.

(1992). Linking empirically based theory and evaluation: The family bereavement program. *American Journal of Community Psychology, 20*, 491–521.

Saraway, S. M., & Pardes, H. (1967). Auditory elementary hallucinations in alcohol withdrawal psychosis. *Archives of General Psychiatry, 16*, 652–658.

Satel, S. L. (1990). Mental status changes in children receiving glucocorticoids: Review of the literature. *Clinical Pediatrics, 29*, 382–388.

Satel, S. L., Southwick, S. M., & Gawin, F. H. (1991). Clinical features of cocaine-induced paranoia. *American Journal of Psychiatry, 148*, 495–498.

Schopf, J., & Rust, B. (1994). Follow-up and family study of postpartum psychosis part II: Early versus late onset postpartum psychoses. *European Archives of Psychiatry and Clinical Neuroscience, 244*, 135–137.

Schopf, J., & Rust, B. (1994). Follow-up and family study of postpartum psychosis part III: Characteristics of psychoses occurring exclusively in relation to childbirth. *European Archives of Psychiatry and Clinical Neuroscience, 244*, 138–140.

Schreier, H. A. (1998). Auditory hallucinations in nonpsychotic children with affective syndromes and migraines: Report of 13 cases. *Journal of Child Neurology, 13*, 377–382.

Schreier, H. A. (1998). Hallucinations in non-psychotic children: More common than we think? *Journal of the American Academy of Child and Adolescent Psychiatry, 38*, 623–625.

Schreier, H. A., & Libow, J. A. (1986). Acute phobic hallucinations in very young children. *Journal of the American Academy of Child Psychiatry, 25*, 574–578.

Schulz, S. C., Findling, R. L., Wise, A., Friedman, L., & Kenny, J. (1998). Child and adolescent schizophrenia. *Psychiatric Clinics of North America, 21*, 43–56.

Schulz, S. C., Koller, M. M., Kishore, P. R., Hamer, R. M., Gehl, J. J., & Friedel, R. O. (1983). Ventricular enlargement in teenage patients with schizophrenia spectrum disorder. *American Journal of Psychiatry, 140*, 1592–1595.

Shaffer, D., Gould, M. S., Brasic, J., Ambrosini, P., Fisher, P., Bird, H., & Aluwahlia, S. (1983). A children's global assessment scale (CGAS). *Archives of General Psychiatry, 40*, 1228–1231.

Shanee, N., Apter, A., & Weizman, A. (1997). Psychometric properties of the K-SADS-PL in an Israeli adolescent clinical population. *Israel Journal of Psychiatry and Related Sciences, 34*, 179–186.

Sharp, L. A. (1994). Exorcists, psychiatrists, and the problems of possession in northwest Madagascar. *Social Science and Medicine, 38*, 525–542.

Shirar, L. (1996). *Dissociative children: Bridging the inner and outer worlds.* New York: Norton.

Shiwach, R. S., & Sheikha, A. S. (1998). Delusional disorder in a boy with phenylketonuria and amine metabolites in the cerebrospinal fluid after treatment with neuroleptics. *Journal of Adolescent Health, 22*, 244–246.

Silva, H., Jerez, S., Ramirez, A., Renteria, P., Aravena, N., Salazar, D., & Labarca, R. (1998). Effects of pimozide on the psychopathology of delusional disorder. *Progress in Neuro-Psychopharmacology & Biological Psychiatry, 22*, 331–340.

Silveira, J. M., & Seeman, M. V. (1995). Shared psychotic disorder: A critical review of the literature. *Canadian Journal of Psychiatry, 40*, 389–395.

Simon, B. (1978). *Mind and madness in ancient Greece: The classical roots of modern psychiatry.* Ithaca, NY: Cornell University Press.

Simonds, J. F., & Glenn, T. (1976). Folie à deux in a child. *Journal of Autism and Childhood Schizophrenia, 6*, 61–73.

Simpson, D. M. (1999). Human immunodeficiency virus-associated dementia: Review of pathogenesis, prophylaxis, and treatment studies of zidovudine therapy. *Clinical Infectious Diseases, 29,* 19–34.

Simpson, G. M., & Angus, J. W. S. (1970). A rating scale for extrapyramidal side effects. *Acta Psychiatrica Scandinavica, 212* (Suppl.), 11–19.

Singer, K., Ney, P. G., & Lieh-Mak, F. (1978). A cultural perspective on child psychiatric disorders. *Comprehensive Psychiatry, 19,* 533–540.

Siris, S. G., & Lavin, M. R. (1995). Schizoaffective disorder, schizophreniform disorder, and brief psychotic disorder. In H. I. Kaplan & B. J. Sadock (Eds.), *Comprehensive textbook of psychiatric disorders* (6th ed., pp. 1019–1031). Baltimore: Williams & Wilkins.

Small, G. W. (1998). Differential diagnosis and early detection of dementia. *American Journal of Geriatric Psychiatry, 6* (Suppl. 1), S26–S33.

Small, J. G., Hirsch, S. R., Arvanitis, L. A., Miller, B. G., Link, C. G. G., and the Seroquel Study Group. (1997). Quetiapine in patients with schizophrenia: A high- and low-dose double-blind comparison with placebo. *Archives of General Psychiatry, 54,* 549–557.

Solomon, J. G., Fernando, T. G., & Solomon, S. M. (1978). Mother-son folie a deux: A case report. *Journal of Clinical Psychiatry, 39,* 819–820.

Sondheimer, A. (1988). Clomipramine treatment of delusional disorder-somatic type. *Journal of the American Academy of Child and Adolescent Psychiatry, 27,* 188–192.

Songer, D. A., & Roman, B. (1996). Treatment of somatic delusional disorder with atypical antipsychotic agents. *American Journal of Psychiatry, 153,* 578–579.

Soutullo, C. A., Cottingham, E. M., & Keck, P. E., Jr. (1999). Psychosis associated with pseudoephedrine and dextromethorphan. *Journal of the American Academy of Child and Adolescent Psychiatry, 38,* 1471–1472.

Spence, S. A., Brooks, D. J., Hirsch, S. R., Liddle, P. F., Meehan, J., & Grasby, P. M. (1997). A PET study of voluntary movement in schizophrenic patients experiencing passivity phenomena (delusions of alien control). *Brain, 120* (Pt. 11), 1997–2011.

Spencer, E. K., & Campbell, M. (1994). Children with schizophrenia: Diagnosis, phenomenology, and pharmacotherapy. *Schizophrenia Bulletin, 20,* 713–725.

Spencer, E. K., Kafantaris, V., Padron-Gayol, M. V., Rosenberg, C. R., & Campbell, M. (1992). Haloperidol in schizophrenic children: Early findings from a study in progress. *Psychopharmacology Bulletin, 20,* 685–695.

Spensley, J. (1972). *Folie à deux* with methylphenidate psychosis. *Journal of Nervous and Mental Disease, 155,* 288–290.

Squires-Wheeler, E., Skodol, A. E., Friedman, D., & Erlenmeyer-Kimling, L. (1988). The specificity of *DSM-III* schizotypal personality traits. *Psychological Medicine, 18,* 757–765.

Steinberg, D. (1985). Psychotic and other severe disorders in adolescence. In M. Rutter & L. Hersov (Eds.), *Child and adolescent psychiatry: Modern approaches* (pp. 567–583). Oxford, UK: Blackwell Scientific.

Steinhausen, H. (1987). Global assessment of child psychopathology. *Journal of the American Academy of Child and Adolescent Psychiatry, 26,* 203–206.

Stern, G., & Kruckman, L. (1983). Multidisciplinary perspectives on postpartum depression: An anthropological critique. *Social Science & Medicine, 17,* 1027–1041.

Strakowski, S. M. (1994). Diagnostic validity of schizophreniform disorder. *American Journal of Psychiatry, 151,* 815–824.

Strakowski, S. M., Keck, P. E., Jr., Sax, K. W., McElroy, S. L., & Hawkins, J. M. (1999). Twelve-month outcome of patients with *DSM-III-R* schizoaffective disorder:

Comparisons to matched patients with bipolar disorder. *Schizophrenia Research, 35*, 167–174.

Summit, R. R. (1983). The child abuse accommodation syndrome. *Child Abuse and Neglect, 7*, 177–183.

Susser, E., Varma, V. J., Malhotra, S., Conover, S., & Amador, X. F. (1995). Delineation of acute and transient psychotic disorders in a developing country setting. *British Journal of Psychiatry, 167*, 216–219.

Suzuki, H., Tsukamoto, C., Nakano, Y., Aoki, S., & Kuroda, S. (1998). Delusions and hallucinations in patients with borderline personality disorder. *Psychiatry and Clinical Neurosciences, 52*, 605–610.

Swaiman, K. F. (1994). *Pediatric neurology: Principles and practice.* St. Louis, MO: Mosby.

Swales, T. P., Findling, R. L., Friedman, L., Kenny, J. T., Cola, D., & Schulz, S. C. (1995). Quality of life in adolescents with schizophrenia. *Schizophrenia Research, 15*, 221.

Szechtman, H., Woody, E., Bowers, K. S., & Nahmias, C. (1998). Where the imaginal appears real: A positron emission tomography study of auditory hallucinations. *Proceedings of the National Academy of Sciences of the United States of America, 95*, 1956–1960.

Szeszko, P. R., Bilder, R. M., Dunlop, J. A., Walder, D. J., & Lieberman, J. A. (1999). Longitudinal assessment of methylphenidate effects on oral word-production and symptoms in first-episode schizophrenia at acute and stabilized phases. *Biological Psychiatry, 45*, 680–686.

Szigethy, E., Brent, S., & Findling, R. L. (1998). Quetiapine for refractory schizophrenia. *Journal of the American Academy of Child and Adolescent Psychiatry, 37*, 1127–1128.

Szigethy, E., Wiznitzer, M., Branikcky, L. A., Maxwell, K., & Findling, R. L. (1999). Risperidone-induced hepatotoxicity in children and adolescents? A chart review study. *Journal of Child and Adolescent Psychopharmacology, 9*, 93–98.

Szymanski, S. R., Cannon, T. D., Gallacher, F., Erwin, R. J., & Gur, R. E. (1996). Course of treatment response in first-episode and chronic schizophrenia. *American Journal of Psychiatry, 153*, 519–525.

Takeshita, J. (1997). Psychosis. In W. Tseng & J. Streltzer (Eds.), *Culture and psychopathology*, (pp. 124–138). New York: Brunner/Mazel.

Taylor, M. A., & Abrams, R. (1975). Manic-depressive illness and good prognosis schizophrenia. *American Journal of Psychiatry, 132*, 741–742.

Terr, L. C. (1981). Psychic trauma in children: Observations following the Chowchilla school-bus kidnapping. *American Journal of Psychiatry, 138*, 14–19.

Terr, L. C. (1983). Chowchilla revisited: The effects of psychic trauma four years after a school-bus kidnapping. *American Journal of Psychiatry, 140*, 1543–1550.

Terr, L. C. (1989). Treating psychic trauma in children: A preliminary discussion. *Journal of Traumatic Stress, 2*, 3–20.

Terr, L. C. (1991). Childhood traumas: An outline and overview. *American Journal of Psychiatry, 148*, 10–20.

Thomsen, P. H. (1996). Borderline conditions in childhood. A register-based follow-up study over a 22-year period. *Psychopathology, 29*, 357–362.

Tolbert, H. A. (1996). Psychoses in children and adolescents: A review. *Journal of Clinical Psychiatry, 57* (Suppl. 3), 4–8.

Tollefson, G. D., Beasley, C. M., Tran, P. V., Street, J. S., Krueger, J. A., Tamura, R. N., Graffeo, K. A., & Thieme, M. E. (1997). Olanzapine versus haloperidol in the treatment of schizophrenia and schizoaffective and schizophreniform disorders: Results of an international collaborative trial. *American Journal of Psychiatry, 154*, 457–465.

Tompson, M. C., Asarnow, J. R., Hamilton, E. B., Newell, L. E., & Goldstein, M. J. (1997). Children with schizophrenia-spectrum disorders: Thought disorder and communication problems in a family interactional context. *Journal of Child Psychology and Psychiatry and Allied Disciplines, 38*, 421–429.

Towbin, K. E., Dykens, E. M., Pearson, G. S., & Cohen, D. J. (1993). Conceptualizing "borderline syndrome of childhood" and "childhood schizophrenia" as a developmental disorder. *Journal of the American Academy of Child and Adolescent Psychiatry, 32*, 775–782.

Tran, P. V., Hamilton, S. H., Kuntz, A. J., Potvin, J. H., Andersen, S. W., Beasley, C., Jr., & Tollefson, G. D. (1997). Double-blind comparison of olanzapine versus risperidone in the treatment of schizophrenia and other psychotic disorders. *Journal of Clinical Psychopharmacology, 17*, 407–418.

True, W. R., Rice, J., Eisen, S. A., Heath, A. C., Goldberg, J., Lyons, M. J., & Nowak, J. (1993). A twin study of genetic and environmental contributions to liability for post-traumatic stress symptoms. *Archives of General Psychiatry, 50*, 257–264.

Tsuang, D., & Coryell, W. (1993). An 8-year follow-up of patients with *DSM-III-R* psychotic depression, schizoaffective disorder, and schizophrenia. *American Journal of Psychiatry, 150*, 1182–1188.

Tumuluru, R. V., Yaylayan, S., Weller, E. B., & Weller, R. A. (1996). Affective psychoses, I: Major depression with psychosis. In F. R. Volkmar (Ed.), *Psychoses and pervasive developmental disorders in childhood and adolescence* (pp. 49–69). Washington, DC: American Psychiatric Press.

Turetz, M., Mozes, T., Toren, P., Chernauzan, N., Yoran-Hegesh, R., Mester, R., Wittenberg, N., Tyano, S., & Wiezman, A. (1997). An open trial clozapine in neuroleptic-resistant childhood-onset schizophrenia. *British Journal of Psychiatry, 170*, 507–510.

Uhde, T. W., Redmond, E., Jr., & Kleber, H. D. (1982). Psychosis in the opioid addicted patient: Assessment and treatment. *Journal of Clinical Psychiatry, 43*, 240–247.

Van der Gaag, R. J., Buitelaar, J., Van den Ban, E., Bezemer, M., Njio, L., & Van Engeland, H. (1995). A controlled multivariate chart review of multiple complex developmental disorder. *Journal of the American Academy of Child and Adolescent Psychiatry, 34*, 1096–1106.

Van der Kolk, B. A., & van der Hart, O. (1989). Pierre Janet and the breakdown of adaptation in psychological trauma. *American Journal of Psychiatry, 146*, 1530–1540.

Vela, R. M., & Petti, T. A. (1988). *Borderline disorder of childhood: Theory and practice.* Paper presented at the 141st Annual Meeting of the American Psychiatric Association, Montreal, Quebec, Canada.

Verhulst, F., & Van Der Ende, J. (1992). Six-year stability of parent-reported problem behavior in an epidemiological sample. *Journal of Abnormal Child Psychology, 20*, 595–610.

Videbech, P., & Gouliaev, G. (1995). First admission with puerperal psychosis: 7–14 years of follow-up. *Acta Psychiatrica Scandinavica, 91*, 167–173.

Vincent, K. R., & Harman, M. J. (1991). The Exner Rorschach: An analysis of its clinical validity. *Journal of Clinical Psychology, 47*, 596–599.

Vita, A., Dieci, M., Giobbio, G. M., Caputo, A., Ghiringhelli, L., Comazzi, M., Garbarini, M., Mendini, A. P., Marganti, C., Tenconi, F., Cesana, B., & Invernizzi, G. (1995). Language and thought disorder in schizophrenia: Brain morphological correlates. *Schizophrenia Research, 15*, 243–251.

Volkmar, F. R. (1996). Childhood and adolescent psychosis: A review of the past 10 years. *Journal of the American Academy of Child and Adolescent Psychiatry, 35*, 843–851.

Volkmar, F. R., & Cohen, D. J. (1991). Comorbid association of autism and schizophrenia. *American Journal of Psychiatry, 148*, 1705–1707.

Von Knorring, L., & Lindstrom, E. (1992). The Swedish version of the Positive and Negative Syndrome Scale (PANSS) for schizophrenia. *Acta Psychiatrica Scandanavica, 86*, 463–468.

Wada, T., Kawakatsu, S., Nadaoka, T., Okuyama, N., & Otani, K. (1999). Clomipramine treatment of delusional disorder, somatic type. *International Clinical Psychopharmacology, 14*, 181–183.

Waddington, J. L., Lane, A., Scully, P. J., Larkin, C., & O'Callaghan, E. (1998). Neurodevelopmental and neuroprogressive process in schizophrenia: Antithetical or complementary, over a lifetime trajectory of disease? *Psychiatric Clinics of North America, 21*, 123–149.

Walk, R. D. (1980). Perception. In M. Rutter (Ed.), *Scientific foundations of developmental psychiatry* (pp. 177–184). London: Heinemann.

Walther, V. N. (1997). Postpartum depression: A review for perinatal social workers. *Social Work in Health Care, 24*, 99–111.

Weiden, P., Rapkin, B., Mott, T., Zygmunt, A., Goldman, D., Horvitz-Lennon, M., & Frances, A. (1994). Rating of Medication Influences (ROMI) scale in schizophrenia. *Schizophrenia Bulletin, 20*, 297–310.

Weinberg, N. Z., Rahdert, E., Colliver, J. D., & Glantz, M. D. (1998). Adolescent substance abuse: A review of the past 10 years. *Journal of the American Academy of Child and Adolescent Psychiatry, 37*, 252–261.

Weiss, M., Zelkowitz, P., Feldman, R. B., Vogel, J., Heyman, M., & Paris, J. (1996). Psychopathology in offspring of mothers with borderline personality disorder: A pilot study. *Canadian Journal of Psychiatry, 41*, 285–290.

Weissman, M. M., Leckman, J. F., Merikangas, K. R., Gammon, G. D., & Prusoff, B. A. (1984). Depression and anxiety disorders in parents and children. *Archives of General Psychiatry, 41*, 845–852.

Weller, E. B., & Weller, R. A. (1991). Mood disorders. In M. Lewis (Ed.), *Comprehensive textbook of child and adolescent psychiatry* (pp. 646–664). Baltimore: Williams & Wilkins.

Weller, R. A., Weller, E. B., Fristad, M. A., & Bowes, J. M. (1991). Depression in recently bereaved prepubertal children. *American Journal of Psychiatry, 148*, 1536–1540.

Wenar, C., & Curtis, K. M. (1991). The validity of the Rorschach for assessing cognitive and affective changes. *Journal of Personality Assessment, 57*, 291–308.

Wergeland, H. (1979). A follow-up study of 29 borderline psychotic children 5 to 20 years after discharge. *Acta Psychiatrica Scandinavica, 60*, 465–476.

Wherry, J., Dawes, M., Rost, K., Smith, G. R., Jolly, J., Vaught, L., & Hudson, R. (1992). Concurrent validity of the Child Behavior Checklist as completed by staff in residential treatment settings. *Residential Treatment for Children and Youth, 10*, 35–45.

Werry, J., McClellan, J. M., Andrews, L. K., & Ham, M. (1994). Clinical features and outcome of child and adolescent schizophrenia. *Schizophrenia Bulletin, 20*, 619–630.

Werry, J. S. (1992). Child psychiatric disorders: Are they classifiable? *British Journal of Psychiatry, 161*, 472–480.

Werry, J. S., McClellan, J. M., & Chard, L. (1991). Childhood and adolescent schizophrenic, bipolar, and schizoaffective disorders: A clinical outcome study. *Journal of the American Academy of Child and Adolescent Psychiatry, 30*, 457–465.

Williamson, D. E., Ryan, N. D., Birmaher, B., Dahl, R. E., Kaufman, J., Rao, U., & Puig-Antich, J. (1995). A case-controlled family history study of depression in adolescents. *Journal of the American Academy of Child and Adolescent Psychiatry, 34,* 1596–1607.

Willner, P. (1997). The dopamine hypothesis of schizophrenia: Current status, future prospects. *International Clinical Psychopharmacology, 12,* 297–308.

Wilson, T. G., O'Leary, D. K., & Nathan, P. E. (1992). *Abnormal psychology.* Englewood Cliffs, NJ: Prentice Hall.

Winokur, G. (1979). Alcoholism and depression in the same family. In D. W. Goodwin & C. K. Erickson (Eds.), *Alcoholism and affective disorders: Clinical, genetic, and biochemical studies.* Jamaica, NY: SP Medical & Scientific Books.

Wolf, D. V., & Wagner, K. D. (1993). Tardive dyskinesia, tardive dystonia, and tardive Tourette's syndrome in children and adolescents. *Journal of Child and Adolescent Psychopharmacology, 3,* 175–198.

Wolff, S. (1991). "Schizoid" personality in childhood and adult life. I: The vagaries of diagnostic labeling. *British Journal of Psychiatry, 159,* 615–620, 634–635.

Wood, A., Harrington, R., & Moore, A. (1996). Controlled trial of a brief cognitive-behavioural intervention in adolescent patients with depressive disorders. *Journal of Child Psychology and Psychiatry, 37,* 737–746.

Yamada, N., Nakajima, S., & Noguchi, T. (1998). Age at onset of delusional disorder is dependent on the delusional theme. *Acta Psychiatrica Scandinavica, 97,* 122–124.

Yates, T. T., & Bannard, J. R. (1988). The "haunted" child: Grief, hallucinations, and family dynamics. *Journal of the American Academy of Child and Adolescent Psychiatry, 27,* 573–581.

Yaylayan, S., Tumuluru, R. V., Weller, E. B., & Weller, R. A. (1996). Affective psychoses, II: Bipolar disorder with psychosis. In F. R. Volkmar (Ed.), *Psychoses and pervasive developmental disorders in childhood and adolescence* (pp. 71–87). Washington, DC: American Psychiatric Press.

Yung, A. R., & McGorry, P. D. (1996). The prodromal phase of first-episode psychosis: Past and current conceptualizations. *Schizophrenia Bulletin, 22,* 353–370.

Yung, A. R., McGorry, P. D., McFarlane, C. A., Jackson, H. J., Patton, G. C., & Rakkar, A. (1996). Monitoring and care of young people at incipient risk of psychosis. *Schizophrenia Bulletin, 22,* 283–303.

Zanarini, M. C., & Frankenburg, F. R. (1997). Pathways to the development of borderline personality disorder. *Journal of Personality Disorders, 11,* 93–104.

Zhang-Wong, J., Beiser, M., Bean, G., & Iacono, W. G. (1995). Five-year course of schizophreniform disorder. *Psychiatry Research, 59,* 109–117.

INDEX

ABOUT THE AUTHORS

Robert L. Findling, MD, is Director of Child and Adolescent Psychiatry at University Hospitals of Cleveland and Associate Professor of Psychiatry and Pediatrics at Case Western Reserve University School of Medicine. Dr. Findling's clinical and research efforts have focused on the early-onset psychoses and pediatric psychopharmacology.

S. Charles Schulz, MD, is Professor and Chairman of the Department of Psychiatry at the University of Minnesota. He is an internationally respected investigator whose work has focused on schizophrenia, border-line personality disorder, and the psychopharmacology of antipsychotics.

Javad H. Kashani, MD, is Director of Child and Adolescent Psychiatric Services at University Hospitals Health System Laurelwood Hospital and Counseling Centers and Professor of Psychiatry at Case Western Reserve University School of Medicine.

Elena Harlan, BA, is a graduate student of clinical psychology at the University of Missouri-Columbia.